# *Sunset* Travel Guide to
# Northern California

**By the Editors of Sunset Books
and Sunset Magazine**

Lane Publishing Co. • Menlo Park, California

Hours, admission fees, prices, telephone numbers, and highway designations in this book are accurate as of November, 1975.

Maps have been provided in each chapter for the special purpose of highlighting significant regions, routes, or attractions in the area. Check automobile clubs, oil companies, and chambers of commerce or visitors bureaus in major cities as possible sources for detailed road maps of Northern California.

## Edited by Barbara J. Braasch

**Design and artwork: Ted Martine**

Cover: View of San Francisco from Marin Headlands. Photographed by Glenn M. Christiansen.

Editor, Sunset Books: David E. Clark

Third Printing April 1977

Copyright © 1970, 1975, Lane Publishing Co., Menlo Park, CA 94025. Fourth Edition. World rights reserved. No part of this publication may be reproduced by any mechanical, photographic, or electronic process or in the form of a phonographic recording, nor may it be stored in a retrieval system, transmitted, or otherwise copied for public or private use without prior written permission from the publisher. Library of Congress No. 75-6219. ISBN Title No.0-376-06554-0. Lithographed in the United States.

# Contents

## Special Features

# Introduction to Northern California

"Kaleidoscopic" is the best word to describe Northern California. Vacationers can choose from a wide range of activities: fishing, hiking, and camping in the high mountains or recapturing the past at a ghost town in the Sierra foothills; beach-combing along the coast or strolling through stately redwood groves; savoring San Francisco's big-city pleasures.

This *Travel Guide to Northern California* contains information on exploring both the well-established, well-known attractions and the lesser-known but equally appealing spots.

San Francisco—famous for its bay, bridges, hills, views, waterfront, and fine food—is Northern California's biggest tourist attraction. Along with the surrounding Bay Area, this is also Northern California's largest cultural, business, and industrial center.

The state capital, Sacramento, is the main city in the agriculturally important Central Valley. Sacramento is currently undergoing a rigorous redevelopment program, scheduled for completion by the end of the 1970s. This will create cultural and trade centers and re-create an Old Sacramento. To the east of the valley rises the mighty Sierra Nevada, whose western foothills hold remnants of days when gold ruled the lives of Californians.

Other popular destinations in Northern California are Sonoma, with its Spanish landmarks; the Napa Valley, with its vineyards and wineries; Monterey, with its historical buildings and waterfront; Carmel, with its quaint shops; and Mendocino, with its dramatic coast and arts and crafts atmosphere. Those who prefer to get away head for the Northern Wonderland, above Redding, where lonesome roads lead to small villages in which time seems to have stood still. The most visited spots for outdoor recreation are Lake Tahoe, Yosemite National Park, Lake Shasta, and the Redwood National Park.

*Double lines on Northern California map indicate main arteries running through major parts of state. For more complete road guide, see area maps throughout book.*

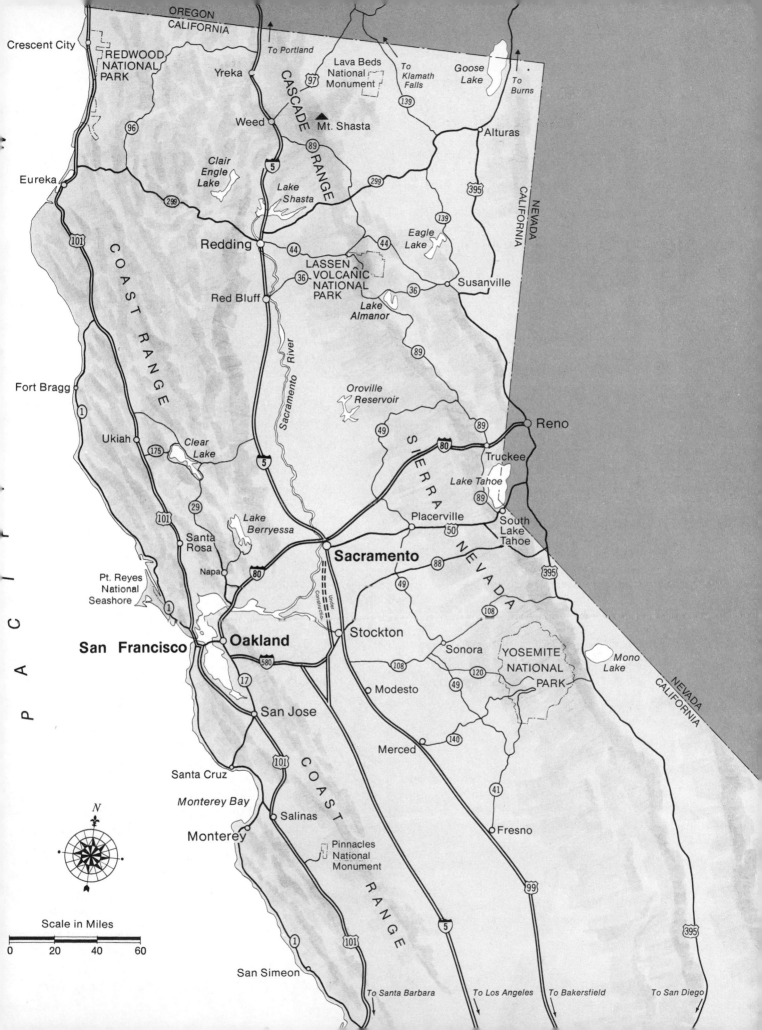

# Differences between Northern and Southern California

The area covered in this book differs from the southern part of the state in climate, history, topography, and temperament. For this reason, separate books are devoted to exploring Northern California and Southern California.

The boundary line that we have used to divide the state begins at the ocean near San Simeon, continues across the Coast Range and the southern tip of the Central Valley, and then turns northward across the Sierra Nevada south of Yosemite National Park. The area south of this arbitrary dividing line is described in the *Sunset* book *Travel Guide to Southern California*.

## Climate and terrain

Northern California has three distinct climate zones. Coastal temperatures are mild the year around; rarely will there be extremes in temperature. Fog frequently blankets the coast during the summer, especially in the morning and evening, and in the winter it rains.

As you move inland, the seasons become more pronounced. Summers become hotter (with relatively little humidity), winters colder (with an occasional snow). The Sierra Nevada has the most dramatic seasonal changes. Summer days are warm, ideal for outdoor recreation; autumn brings a crispness to the air and dramatic fall colors; heavy snowfalls during the winter make the mountains a mecca for skiers.

## Driving in Northern California

Major highways carry a heavy flow of traffic, especially near large cities and especially during the morning and evening commute hours. California's roads are exceptionally well maintained—most thoroughfares are divided, four-lane express highways. Road tolls are unknown here. The speed limit is a maximum 55 miles per hour or as posted.

For scenic beauty, the best north-south route through Northern California is State Highway 1. It's a winding coastal route, overlooking the ocean most of the way; plan to drive it leisurely. If you're in a hurry, take the inland routes. U.S. Highway 101, Interstate Highway 5, and State 99 are the faster routes. The most heavily traveled east-west routes are Interstates 580 (U.S. 50) and 80, which connect San Francisco and Lake Tahoe.

When traveling in the mountains during the winter, always carry tire chains.

# Where to Get Information

San Francisco's Convention & Visitors Bureau, 1390 Market St., San Francisco, CA 94102 (telephone (415) 626-5500), should be a city visitor's first stop. Here you will receive maps of the city, lists of hotels and motels, restaurant guides, and data on main visitor attractions. In San Francisco, dial 391-2000 for a 2-minute summary of daily events.

**Sampling the grape,** *popular pastime in Northern California, includes tips on tasting at most wineries.*

**Houseboating or speedboating** *at Lake Shasta — take your choice. Mt. Shasta's snowy peak bulks to north.*

**Awe-inspiring redwoods** *soar to remarkable heights in Jedediah Smith Redwoods State Park grove.*

The Redwood Empire Association publishes a free Visitors' Guide for San Francisco, Marin, Sonoma, Napa, Lake, Mendocino, Humboldt, and Del Norte counties. For the booklet, write the Redwood Empire Association, 476 Post St., San Francisco, CA 94102.

The Wine Institute, 717 Market St., San Francisco, CA 94103, lists the Northern California wineries, describes tasting rooms and picnic facilities, and lists the hours they are open.

For travel information on the Monterey Peninsula, stop by the Chamber of Commerce and Visitors and Convention Bureau at 380 Alvarado Street, Monterey. Or write in advance to P.O. Box 1770, Monterey, CA 93940.

## Accommodations

Other major cities and resort areas usually have plenty of hotel and motel space. If you want to stay at a particular place or if you are traveling during the summer or on a weekend, it's best to make advance reservations.

If you're uncertain of where to stay, write to local chambers of commerce. They usually have listings of available accommodations.

## Camping

If you plan to camp in a state park, there is a 7 to 15-day camping limit at some parks during the heavy-use period (usually June 1 to the end of September). Extended limits apply to most state parks the rest of the year. Camping fees are based on the type of campsite: from $1.50 for primitive campsites to $4 for trailer hookup sites. For a pamphlet listing California's state parks, write to the Department of Parks and Recreation, P.O. Box 2390, Sacramento, CA 95811.

Though reservations are not required for camping in state parks, they are advised during the summer or on weekends. Requests for reservations should be sent to the Parks and Recreation Department in Sacramento at least 2 weeks in advance.

Reservations may also be made at any of the 150 Ticketron offices located around the state. To locate the nearest Ticketron office, in San Francisco call (415) 788-2828 and in Sacramento call (916) 445-8828. Information number for Ticketron in Los Angeles is (213) 670-1242; in San Diego call (714) 565-9947.

No reservations are accepted on Sunday. You will pay the campsite fee and a small reservation fee when you make your reservation.

To camp in a national park or forest, you'll usually pay a modest fee per day. Most campsites are available on a first come, first served basis. For a Recreation Guide to national forest campgrounds, write to the U.S. Forest Service, 630 Sansome St., San Francisco, CA 94111. For information on national park campgrounds, write the National Park Service, 450 Golden Gate Ave., San Francisco, CA 94102.

Northern California also has numerous county and private campgrounds. For a listing of private as well as public campgrounds, see the *Sunset* special interest magazine *Western Campsites*.

## Hunting and fishing

Rules change yearly governing the hunting season and the animals you may hunt. The Department of Fish and Game, 1416 9th St., Sacramento, CA 95814, publishes a pamphlet every May that lists the current hunting regulations.

A pamphlet distributed in the spring by the department outlines both fresh-water and salt-water fishing regulations. Both of these publications, as well as hunting and fishing licenses, can be obtained at sporting goods stores.

## Winter sports

In the Sierra Nevada—the main winter sports area in Northern California—most major ski resorts cluster around Lake Tahoe. Other skiing centers are in the Donner Summit area, along U.S. 50 and Interstate 80, and at Yosemite National Park.

Mt. Shasta, north of Redding, offers a long skiing season; you can also ski at Lassen Volcanic National Park.

# San Francisco

 What makes San Francisco so compelling? This is a question often asked by people who have never visited "The City," and it's hard for even a native to answer. Much of its charm lies in its location, its climate, its topography—and its people.

Surrounded on three sides by water, San Francisco still harbors the flavor of its early-day remoteness. And because of its setting, the weather is tempered to perpetual spring.

It's a city of hills. Someone once said that if you get tired of climbing up them, you can always lean against them. But it's on top of these hills that you get the well-touted views—watching the fog roll in from the ocean across the Golden Gate Bridge, gazing east along the meandering span of the San Francisco-Oakland Bay Bridge, or peering north across the bay, past the islands anchored in the channel, to the bluffs of Marin County.

San Francisco was a city from the first cry of "Gold!" Few miners found anything here worth shouting about, but the Gold Rush transformed the town into a booming metropolis where literally anything went, providing you could pay for it. The wide assortment of nationalities who settled here gave the city its aura of cosmopolitan sophistication—an urban world center quite out of proportion to its actual size.

San Francisco is a compact city. Part of its charm lies in the ease with which a visitor can move from attraction to attraction. You can park your car if you wish and get around on foot, by cable car, streetcar, bus, and BART (the sparkling transbay subway). If you're a first-time visitor, we suggest following the 49-Mile Drive (see page 13), a marked route leading throughout the city on a trip of discovery.

**Eye-riveting hilltop views** *of city and bay are San Francisco's stock in trade. Here, bus climbs Steiner Street hill. Below sprawls the Marina District; across the water — the tree-dotted East Bay.*

# The City in the North

San Francisco is a big city without being big. Even with a total geographical area of only 47 square miles and a population of less than 800,000, it has the qualities common to all of the world's great cities—a rich historical background, a diversity of activities, cultural depth, hustle and bustle, pervasive charm based on an unmistakable character —and more.

"The City" (as it is called by natives; *never* call it "Frisco") is noted for its many and various-size hills and spectacular sweeping views. Its skyline is jagged with new skyscrapers dwarfing once-tall buildings; a closer look shows crowded row houses and apartments marching endlessly up and down the hills, roof-to-roof.

One of the world's most visited cities, San Francisco welcomes its guests. Whether the visit is your first or your fifth, you will enjoy seeing old landmarks as well as browsing around the new ones.

Maps in this section include the downtown area, a scenic drive, and Golden Gate Park.

## A city of bridges and water

Part of San Francisco's charm stems from its setting. Whether you drive on the bridges or merely glimpse the spans across the water from one of many observation spots, you'll notice the dramatic relationship between San Francisco and the water that surrounds it on three sides.

**The bridges** connect the city to the rest of the world, to the east and to the north.

Most glamorous of San Francisco's bridges is the Golden Gate, recently designated the country's most popular manmade attraction. One of the best things about this suspended structure is that you can walk and bike across it. As a pedestrian or bicyclist, you can enjoy gull's eye views (220 feet down) denied the automobile traveler. Park your car at the toll plaza and walk out to the middle and back for some magnificent views of the San Francisco skyline. The Marin County lookout at the north end of the bridge gives an exceptional wide-angle view of the city. You pay to cross the Golden Gate Bridge only when coming south into San Francisco; northbound you don't stop.

San Francisco's main bridge connection to the east is across the San Francisco-Oakland Bay Bridge. From San Francisco, two spans are joined at a central anchorage. The roadway follows a tunnel through Yerba Buena Island, coming out on a 1,400-foot cantilever span followed by a series of truss bridges. The bridge is in two levels (eastbound traffic uses lower deck; westbound, upper deck) and altogether extends 8¼ miles.

Two bridges connect the peninsula and the East Bay (San Mateo Bridge, from San Mateo to Hayward; and Dumbarton Bridge, from Menlo Park to Fremont); another crosses north of San Francisco between Richmond and San Rafael. Recent change to one-way toll collections (westbound) helps the flow of traffic.

**The water** around San Francisco keeps the city air-conditioned all year. The average high is 65°, the low 45°. Fog is frequent in early morning and evening, especially during the summer. Usually the rains begin in November and last into April. September is normally San Francisco's warmest month.

The city's continual mild temperatures call for lightweight wools at any time of the year. Usually a coat is needed in the evening. Natives tend to shy away from casual clothes, preferring to dress conservatively and elegantly, especially downtown; many women still wear hats.

## A brief history

Though founded in 1776 by the Spanish as a mission post, San Francisco hardly existed until the discovery of gold in 1849. The peninsula village was transformed from a drowsy Spanish pueblo to an instant city as "49ers" came rushing to California from every point of the compass. Few found any gold, but the boom transformed the town into a metropolis almost overnight. These immigrants—a unique blend of races, customs, and nationalities— set the pattern for the city's future personality. An adage of the era was, "The weak never made it to California and the timid never tried."

Growth accelerated with the discovery of Nevada's Comstock silver lode and the completion of the first transcontinental railroad to San Francisco in 1869.

In the earthquake of April 18, 1906, and the 3-day fire that followed, 28,000 buildings were destroyed and some 500 people died. But San Franciscans rebuilt, showing off their "new" city at the Panama-Pacific International Exposition in 1915. Later, Treasure Island, dredged up in the mid-bay, became a stage for the Golden Gate International Exposition in 1939 and 1940.

Today, the city is still changing: old factories become unique shopping areas; fountains splash where warehouses once stood; and part of the formerly raucous Barbary Coast (Jackson Street) is now a tamed, handsome showcase of interior design.

## Cosmopolitan San Francisco

If San Francisco has a look of its own, it's probably because nearly one out of seven of its inhabitants

**Bikers along shore** *at Ft. Point watch sleek liner glide toward Pacific Ocean underneath Golden Gate Bridge.*

**Hillside deck** *near Twin Peaks overlooks typically staggered roofs, distant skyscrapers.*

was born outside the U.S. or has foreign-born parents. Its culture has been enriched by the traditions and life styles of countless ethnic groups. Three distinct "cities" exist within San Francisco: Chinatown, the largest settlement of its kind outside of Asia; "Little Italy," magnet for some 150,000 San Franciscans of Italian extraction; and Japantown, landmarked by the $15 million Japan Center. You'll find some 22 foreign language publications throughout the city, and its lauded cuisine offers choices of food from all parts of the globe.

## How to See San Francisco

The first stop for any newcomer to San Francisco should be the San Francisco Convention & Visitors Bureau, 1390 Market St., San Francisco, CA 94102. Here you'll find information on transportation, lodging, and what's happening where. By dialing 391-2000 you'll get an around-the-clock daily run-down of special events, cultural happenings, sports news, and sightseeing trips. From outside the Bay Area, phone area code 415 first, to take advantage of San Francisco's tele-itinerary.

## Driving in the city

San Francisco's steep hills are part of the city's charm, but they may be disconcerting to the out-of-town visitor. If you're a stranger to hills or just don't like city driving, you will probably enjoy your sightseeing more if you park your car. The downtown area is best explored on foot, and public transportation will take you to other points of interest (see page 12).

If you do drive the hills, have confidence in your car and take it slowly downhill. Remember to shift into low before starting up or down a hill. San Francisco law requires you to curb your front wheels every time you park on a hill. Failure to do so will result in a ticket and a fine. The city also has a strict "tow-away" law. Signs in certain areas tell you very clearly that, if you park between specified hours (usually 7 to 9 A.M. and 4 to 6 P.M.) Monday through Friday, your car will be towed away.

Many of San Francisco's streets are one-way, and they don't always fit into a predictable sequence. Watch carefully for the one-way signs. Intersections don't always have stop signs or lights, so look before starting across. Watch for darting pedestrians and don't drive on a cable car track.

# Ever ride a national landmark?

A cable car ride is a must for every visitor. An excellent means of transportation in the most heavily congested part of the city, the cable cars also provide thrills and good views.

You'll find three cable car lines—two that run on Powell Street and one on California Street. Cars from the line on Powell leave the turntable at Powell and Market (Hallidie Plaza) and are spectacular hill climbers. They take you steeply up Powell, then down and around several sharp turns to arrive in 15 or 20 minutes at their respective turntables at the north waterfront. Cars marked "Powell and Market/Bay and Taylor" clang through the edge of Chinatown, along a section of North Beach, and come to the end of their line at Bay and Taylor at Fisherman's Wharf. The cars marked "Powell and Market/Hyde and Beach" bypass most of Chinatown and North Beach. But they take you down Hyde for a magnificent view of the bay and a hang-on-tight ride to your destination below Hyde and Beach at Aquatic Park.

The red-painted cars of the California Street line leave from California and Market and take you through the financial district and Chinatown, up steep Nob Hill, and finally down a more gentle grade to the end of the line at Van Ness Avenue.

San Francisco's "municipal rollercoaster" costs only 25 cents to ride, and a bus or streetcar transfer is given upon request.

There's no easy way to get on or off a cable car. Usually there are more people waiting to ride than there is room. When the car stops, step right up to find a place. If you're on the outside, hang on tight. Don't ring the bell when you want off—just tell the conductor.

For a close look at how a cable car works, visit the Cable Car Barn at Mason and Washington (you pass it on the Bay/Taylor line) which houses the power system. Built around 1878, the barn was restored and refurbished to include a gallery and museum.

Open from 10 A.M. to 6 P.M. daily, it houses the city's first cable car and some historic San Francisco photographs, as well as giant 14-foot wheels you can watch as they wind the cable that provides power for the system.

## Other ways to get around

Whether you ride above ground or below, take a cab or join a tour, San Francisco is one of the easiest big cities in which to get around.

**Buses and streetcars** run frequently on an efficient schedule from morning through early evening. You will find a route map and a description of routes at the front of the Yellow Pages of the San Francisco telephone directory.

The city's municipal railway system (buses, cable cars, streetcars) operates an information service. If you call 673-MUNI, information center personnel will tell you which line to take to reach your destination. Take note: Express buses, making limited stops, may not stop at your destination. Local buses and streetcars charge 25 cents a ride. Since drivers do not carry change, you must have the exact fare ready.

On weekdays from 10 A.M. to 3 P.M., "shoppers' shuttle buses" run at 5-minute intervals through the downtown shopping district. These buses fly yellow flags and charge only 10 cents a ride.

**Taxicabs** are more numerous than in most other western cities, and as distances are short between most of San Francisco's main points of interest, taxis are popular.

**BART** (Bay Area Rapid Transit), a futuristic, direct, and comfortable subway system, recently began operation in the East Bay and in San Francisco, connecting the two areas by a tube under the bay. In downtown San Francisco, you'll find three stations (see map page 15). Phone BART's Information Center (778-BART) toll-free from San Francisco.

**Distant slice** *of Bay Bridge forms backdrop for cable car along steep California Street hill.*

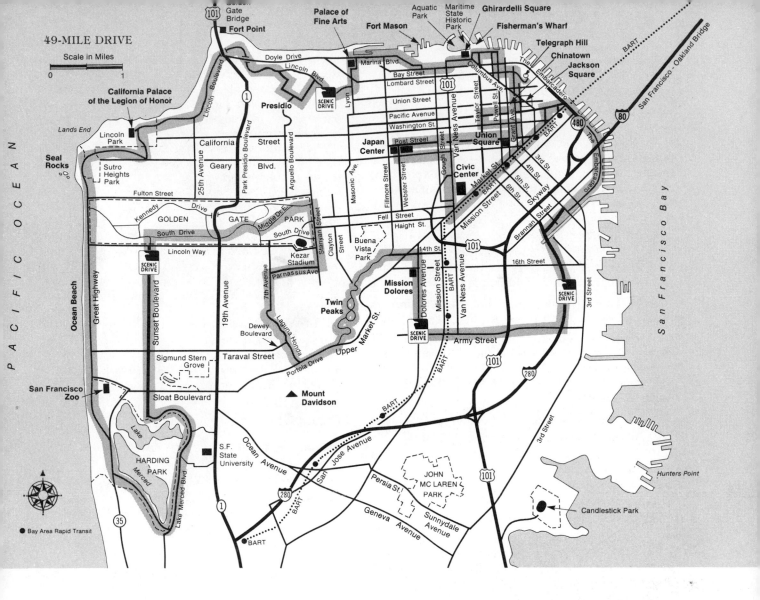

**Guided sightseeing tours** are popular—particularly with first-time visitors. Gray Line offers several different ones. You can make arrangements to be picked up at major hotels, or you can board a shuttle bus at Union Square, opposite the St. Francis Hotel, which will take you to the depot. Buses leave from First and Mission streets at the East Bay Bus Terminal.

A number of sightseeing companies offer limousine tours for small groups. Native Sons Tours (operated solely by people who grew up in San Francisco) offers a unique experience of viewing the city with "insiders."

Make arrangements for any tour through your hotel or check the Yellow Pages of the telephone directory.

## Begin with the 49-Mile Drive

This scenic drive is a good way to grasp the city as a whole; later you can return to explore on foot the places that interest you most. Well marked by blue, white, and orange seagull signs, the 49-Mile Drive is easy to follow, though it does take you through the most congested streets of the downtown area. You should allow about a half-day to fully enjoy the sights along the route.

You can start anywhere, but here are some highlights, beginning at the Civic Center (see page 14) on Van Ness Avenue and McAllister Street:

**Van Ness Avenue.** This is automobile row. Look for elegant showrooms.

**Union Square.** Bordered by Geary, Post, Powell, and Stockton streets, this is the heart of the shopping district downtown. (See page 14.)

**Chinatown.** Grant Avenue leads through this exotic, bustling community. (See page 18.)

**North Beach.** Here, where Columbus Avenue crosses Grant (and north to the Wharf), is San Francisco's Italian community, its Bohemia—a region of numerous good restaurants and a lively center of night life. (See page 19.)

**Telegraph Hill.** Coit Tower crowns this site of spectacular bay and bridge views. (See page 28.)

**Marina.** Beautiful residences look out to the Yacht Harbor across the Green—favorite place for flying kites, walking dogs, sunbathing. (See page 23.)

**Palace of Fine Arts.** A "temporary" structure for the 1915 Panama-Pacific International Exposition, it is now restored and houses a museum of science. (See page 23.)

**Presidio.** Active military post established by the Spanish in 1776. Adobe Officer's Club is one of the city's two oldest buildings. Historic Trail Guide, available at the Military Police office, offers hikers a look at terrain, views, and points of interest.

**Lincoln Park.** Home of the imposing California Palace of the Legion of Honor. (See page 27.)

**Great Highway.** The successor to the original Cliff House Restaurant stands at the north end, with Seal Rocks behind it. Up the hill is Sutro Heights Park, once the grand estate of Adolph Sutro, Comstock Lode millionaire.

**San Francisco Zoo.** One of the country's best zoos; visit Storyland and Children's Zoo. (See page 28.)

**Golden Gate Park.** Probably the finest city park in the country; includes museums and Japanese Tea Garden. (See page 24.)

**Mission Dolores.** Sixth mission in the California chain, it was established in 1776. (See page 31.)

**Ferry Building.** Living reminder of days when the only traffic on the bay was the ferry. The World Trade Center and geology exhibit are here. Vaillancourt Fountain is across the street.

*Ornate City Hall dominates Civic Center park. Opera House, Civic Auditorium, Art Museum are near.*

# City Areas You Should Know

Once you take an overall look at San Francisco by following the 49-Mile Drive, you will want a closer view of some of the city's areas. Because of its compact size, the major points of interest are easy to reach. Bring comfortable shoes and plan to do some walking; it's the best way to make your own discoveries.

## Civic Center—heart of the city

A monumental cluster of federal, state, and city structures, San Francisco's Civic Center is one of the most spacious in the United States. City Hall, a model of French Renaissance grandeur, is crowned by a lofty dome rising 300 feet above the ground. Its rotunda, staircase, and colonnade are worth a look. The War Memorial Opera House, site of the signing of the United Nations Charter in 1945, is home for the San Francisco Opera, San Francisco Symphony, and San Francisco Ballet. Its companion building, the War Memorial Veteran's Building, houses the San Francisco Museum of Art on its top floors. The Civic Auditorium, seating more than 8,000, is the scene of conventions, as well as sports and cultural events; two adjoining halls each provide seating for more than 1,000 people. Brooks Exhibit Hall, underneath the Civic Center Plaza, was added in 1958. The Main Public Library, another handsome neo-Renaissance building, is open weekdays from 9 A.M. to 9 P.M., Saturday until 6. Nearby are the Federal Building, the Federal Office Building, and the State Office Building.

## Union Square—for shoppers

For browsing and shopping in the downtown area, Union Square makes an ideal starting point. You can park your car in the cavernous garage beneath the square—it goes down four floors and provides places for over 1,000 automobiles.

Stop first at the square itself. On a nice day, its benches will be lined with people relaxing in the sun or feeding the hundreds of pigeons that swirl about and congregate around the feet of anyone who offers a handout. On the sidewalk, craftsmen will be offering their wares.

Union Square is a center of activity, hosting fashion shows, rallies, and concerts. In spring, Rhododendron Days are celebrated—huge tubs of colorful plants are placed throughout the square. A summer activity is the Cable Car Bell Ringing Contest.

In the center of the square stands a 97-foot granite monument commemorating Admiral Dewey's victory at Manila Bay during the Spanish-American War.

The fashionable St. Francis Hotel is on the west side of the square, across Powell. Many visiting dignitaries stop here—if you see a foreign flag displayed above the entrance, you can assume it is honoring a very important special guest from that particular country. You'll enjoy browsing through some of the hotel shops.

Post, Stockton, and Geary streets also border the square. The Children's Fountain in the plaza of the Hyatt on Union Square deserves a stop. Its bas-relief, whimsical look at the city's history was designed by Ruth Asawa, who also designed the fountain in Ghirardelli Square.

Around Union Square and spreading south toward Market and east toward Kearny, are some of San Francisco's smartest shops.

You can't miss the colorful sidewalk flower stands, a kind of street-side almanac: sprigs of daphne and violets in spring, tiny Pinocchio roses in summer, chrysanthemums in fall, and holly in winter.

On the east side of the square across Stockton is Maiden Lane, a two-block, tree-lined alley transformed from its bawdy past to a street of intriguing shops. Of particular interest is a building designed by Frank Lloyd Wright, with an unusual yellow brick front and an interior circular ramp; it houses a boutique.

In early April, Maiden Lane ushers in spring with the annual Daffodil Festival. The lane is then closed to traffic, and local dignitaries, bands, troubadours, and lots of blossoms are on hand.

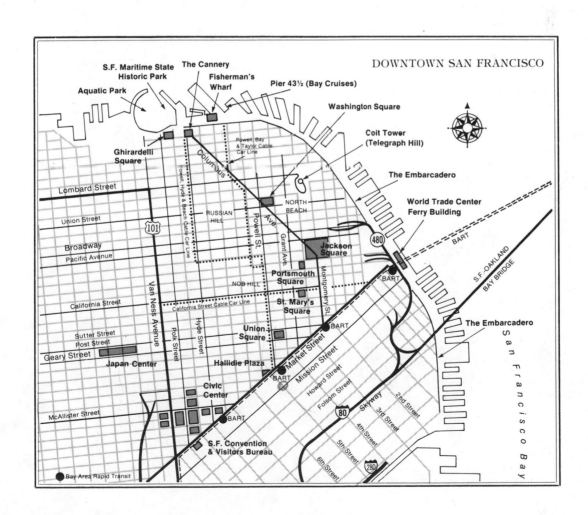

More smart shops and large department stores are located along Grant, Geary, Post, and Stockton. Especially interesting is the floral shop of Podesta Baldocchi. The floral decorations in its windows and inside the shop are indeed remarkable; visitors are welcome.

A major attraction in the Union Square area is Gump's on Post near Stockton. It is noted especially for its Jade Room, which contains an amazing collection of jade in all known shades. Other rooms contain rare imports and unusual locally made items.

## The financial district

North of Market Street, impressive office buildings shade the narrow slot that is Montgomery Street, heart of San Francisco's business and financial district. Here, and spreading into the nearby streets, are the banking, brokerage, and insurance firms that are a part of the Wall Street of the West. Here also are the general offices of many of the West's largest business organizations.

The heart of the financial district is the Pacific Coast Stock Exchange (Pine and Sansome streets), where business begins early in the morning so as to coincide with the hours of the New York Stock Exchange. From the visitors' gallery, you can see the trading floor—in the center is a telegraph operator's booth, and a machine endlessly spews out a serpentine of ticker tape. If you turn on one of the listening boxes in the gallery, you'll hear a brief explanation of how business is transacted and coordinated between two floors (San Francisco and Los Angeles) 400 miles apart. You can visit the Exchange from 7 A.M. to 2:30 P.M. Monday through Friday. Guided tours are given to groups of visitors.

One block west of the stock exchange is the headquarters for the world's largest bank, Bank of America. The 779-foot-high, 52-story bank, with its bronze-tinted, bay-windowed facade, covers most of the California, Pine, Kearny, and Montgomery block. A magnificent view can be had from the public restaurant—the Carnelian Room—on the 52nd floor.

At Montgomery, Washington, and Clay, the 853-

*Circular* Children's Fountain **(below),** *designed by sculptor Ruth Asawa, decorates approach to Hyatt Hotel near Union Square. Close-up* **(right)** *shows caricature of serpentine Lombard Street.*

**Colorful flower stand** *at Union Square corner tempts passing San Francisco businessmen.*

foot-high Transamerica Pyramid is also a recent addition to the changing skyline.

Another skyscraper, the Wells Fargo Building at 44 Montgomery, rises 43 stories—561 feet. On the 16th floor of this unusual glass and steel structure is Montgomery Lane, where diverse shops open onto a mall-like area with benches, canopies, and a brick walkway. Just below the main lobby level is a restaurant displaying early California artifacts from the Wells Fargo History Room. The History Room, at 420 Montgomery, highlights photographs, documents, and mementos from Gold Rush days to the 1906 earthquake. The collection includes a circa-1860 stagecoach that ran south of San Francisco over the Santa Cruz Mountains. Visitors are welcome on banking days from 10 A.M. to 3 P.M.

The Bank of California's Collection of Money of the American West, finest of its kind in the country, features pioneer gold quartz, gold and silver ingots, privately minted gold coins, and currency from the West. Open during banking hours (10 A.M. to 3 P.M.), it's located on the lower level at 400 California Street.

## The Golden Gateway

The product of a $150 million waterfront renewal program, this 51-acre complex (bounded by Clay, Battery, and Jackson streets) has generated new urban vitality with its maze of office buildings, apartment houses, town houses, shops, parks, and fountains. Coit Tower overlooks sunny, two-block-square Maritime Plaza, an elevated park with pedestrian bridges that serve as arteries to all sections of the center. At the middle is the dark-glassed, dramatic Alcoa Building, framed with an exposed diagonal grid.

To the south is the Embarcadero Center, a new financial district focal point. Current buildings include the 45-story Security Pacific Bank Building, the 35-story Levi Strauss Building (historical room on plaza level), and the architecturally innovative Hyatt Regency Hotel with a revolving restaurant at the top offering a 360° view of the bay. All structures spring from a three-level pedestal laced with plazas, promenades, and shopping arcades and linked by pedestrian bridges to the Golden Gateway Center.

## Jackson Square

Although most of Jackson Square's showrooms are closed to the general public (except for once a year, usually in October), anyone with an enthusiasm for elegant old buildings or anyone who simply enjoys window shopping will find a stroll through Jackson Square rewarding.

This unique merchandising center supplies all of the Bay Area decorators, architects, and retailers

**Elegant, wafer-thin** *45-story building rises in Embarcadero Center beyond elevated wharfside freeway.*

**Artistic masterpiece** *or junk pile? Walk-through Vaillancourt Fountain stirs controversy.*

with interior furnishings and accessories. The wholesale houses occupy handsomely restored buildings in the area surrounding Jackson Street —roughly bounded by Pacific Avenue and Montgomery, Washington, and Battery streets.

Once San Francisco's rowdy Barbary Coast, this part of the city became a dismal warehouse area when the city rebuilt in other directions following the 1906 fire. The old buildings were eventually boarded up and deserted and remained so until, in 1951, an enterprising group pioneered the development of the exclusive and unusual decorative center that is today's Jackson Square. Chic specialty shops and fine restaurants add to its charm.

Restored buildings include such old structures as the A. P. Hotaling Co. liquor warehouse, now the Kneedler-Fauchere Building, housing four wholesale fabric showrooms. Around the corner the McGuire Company has restored the old Hotaling livery stable. Oldest of the area's buildings is 472 Jackson Street; it was the Lucas, Turner & Co. Bank, established in 1853 by General William T. Sherman.

## Chinatown

The largest Oriental community outside the Orient, San Francisco's Chinatown covers about 24 blocks and is roughly bordered by Kearny, Mason, and Bush streets and Broadway. It's best to arrive in Chinatown on foot or by public transportation, for the area is heavily congested with traffic.

**That's roast duck,** *a Chinese delicacy, attracting passersby in this Chinatown window along Grant Street.*

**Grant Avenue** is the main street. For eight blocks, between Bush and Columbus, visitors are ensured a delightfully unusual walk. You can get there from either the financial district, Union Square, or Nob Hill. Remember that if you are atop a hill, your walk will be down several steep blocks. The California Street cable car will put you in the heart of Chinatown.

One of the most colorful approaches to Chinatown is a walk down Sacramento to Grant. You will see peaked pagoda-style rooftops and bright-colored balconies in the foreground and the bay and bridge beyond. Along Grant Avenue is the tourists' Chinatown—curio shops, import shops, restaurants.

To get a glimpse of the "inside," prowl up and down some of the cross streets and side alleys that parallel Grant. Scattered among gift shops and restaurants are stores and markets with exotic smells and sounds. The chatter here is still mostly Cantonese.

Between California and Pine is St. Mary's Square, a quiet little park with Beniamino Bufano's striking marble and stainless steel statue of China's one-time president, Sun Yat-sen. Dr. Sun stands with a block-long row of poplars at his back. Beneath the park is an underground garage; entrances are on Kearny, Pine, and California.

Old St. Mary's Church, a San Francisco landmark since 1854, stands at Grant and California. The Gothic structure was built of granite from China and brick brought around Cape Horn from New England.

**Portsmouth Square,** just east of Grant Avenue, at Kearny and Clay, is where San Francisco began. Here Captain John B. Montgomery raised the American flag in 1846, proclaiming the Mexican village to be a possession of the United States. Portsmouth Square (named for Montgomery's ship, the *USS Portsmouth)* today is a landscaped park atop a parking garage. Among the pines is the first memorial to author and poet Robert Louis Stevenson, who, during his visits to San Francisco, spent considerable time at the plaza.

From Portsmouth Square you can cross a footbridge east over Kearny Street to the dramatic A-frame Chinese Cultural and Trade Center, and the Holiday Inn. This 27-story structure includes an exhibition hall for Chinese art, an auditorium, a Chinese library, meeting halls, and a hotel.

The Chinese Telephone Exchange at 743 Washington, now the Bank of Canton, is a Chinatown landmark. The building once held the main switchboard for the "China" exchange, when Chinese operators memorized as many as 2,400 names and numbers of Chinatown subscribers. You can see photographs of these formidable ladies at the Chinese Historical Museum on Adler Place, an alley one-half block south of Broadway off Grant Avenue.

**Futuristic hotel** *also houses Chinese Cultural Center. You approach across walkway over Kearny Street.*

**Stag heads preside** *over busy luncheon scene in German restaurant. Sauerbraten is a Friday favorite.*

On display are memorabilia covering a century of Chinese life in America. The free museum is open Tuesday through Sunday from 1 to 5 P.M.

## North Beach

Not really a beach at all, the area traces its name to the 1850s, when a finger of the bay extended inland and the neighborhood was a sunny shore between Telegraph and Russian hills.

Here, in the center of the Italian community, are Italian bakeries, pastry shops, delicatessens, and kitchen specialty stores. In the pastry shops you'll find rum babas, marzipan, and cylindrical *cannolis* filled with sweetened ricotta cheese and glacéed fruits.

The bakeries, or bread shops, offer long loaves of sweet and sourdough French breads and *panettone*, a round, sweet, Italian bread filled with raisins and candied fruits.

The kitchen specialty shops sell noodle machines, cheese graters, *caffe espresso* machines, ravioli rolling sticks, baking irons for *pizzele* and *cialdi* cookies, copper *polenta* pots, and round-bottomed pans.

Excellent meals are served in the restaurants of North Beach. Besides the well-known establishments, look for modest, unassuming little ones serving savory specialties.

For many years a flourishing colony of painters, writers, and craftsmen has had its headquarters in the North Beach area. Once a year, usually in June, these artists display their crafts in a street bazaar that draws thousands of art lovers to look or to buy. To inspect this interesting area, walk north on Grant Avenue beyond Columbus. You'll pass small galleries, studios, and shops—some brightly painted outposts of the city's bohemian life. Inside are ceramics, paintings, jewelry, poster art, cloth dolls, and sandals.

Interspersed along Grant and adjacent streets are meat markets, espresso cafes, and bakeries.

Parking in the district is at a premium at all times, but the Taylor and Bay cable car runs along Mason between Vallejo and Union. From there it's only a 3-block walk east to shops on Grant Avenue.

**The Broadway district,** in the heart of North Beach, is a perfect place to indulge in some of San Francisco's wildest nightlife. Fanning out from the intersection of Broadway and Columbus, North Beach is a bright mosaic of cabarets, sidewalk cafes, offbeat bistros, and *cappuccino* houses, with entertainment ranging from impromptu opera to jazz or exotic dancing.

**Washington Square,** at Columbus and Union, is a perfect spot for a picnic lunch in the sun with the local *paisanos*. The Church of Saints Peter and Paul is across Filbert Street from the square. Its two tall towers, illuminated at night, are visible from many sections of the city. The two statues in the square honor San Francisco's firemen and Benjamin Franklin—a typically unusual San Francisco combination.

## The north waterfront

San Francisco's north waterfront, run-down and neglected a decade ago, is now pulling and pleasing tremendous crowds. Today, this 22-block district fronts on small parks and contains unusual museums, art galleries, old ships on public display, many restaurants, excellent shops, small theaters, good parking, and some good walking.

Here are the turn-around points for two of the city's cable car lines and the pier for the bay tour boats.

In the north waterfront district, you'll see items ranging from painted seashells and postcards sold near Fisherman's Wharf to bronze turnbuckles at a ship chandler's, from zebra skins in an import shop to a choice of 200 cheeses on sale at The Cannery.

Biggest and most famous retailer is Cost Plus Imports, a rambling bazaar of housewares, antiques, foods, jewelry, and garden supplies. At the east end of the district is the Northpoint Shopping Center. Its street floor has a candymaker, a market, an ice cream parlor, and several restaurants. Up the escalator is Akron, a home-and-housewares market.

At the west end of the district are Ghirardelli Square and The Cannery. A majority of all north waterfront shops are open every day of the week.

**Fisherman's Wharf** (Jones and Jefferson streets) is a world-famous combination of tourist attractions, sidewalk seafood stalls, steaming cauldrons, and seafood restaurants.

# Gourmet Tips for City Dining

San Francisco menus are as international as the U.N. itself. With restaurants ranging from modest to expensive, the city has more than 2,600 places to dine. The quality and variety of their cuisine—from Basque, Moroccan, or Hungarian delicacies to gold field creations—have made eating San Francisco's number one attraction.

San Franciscans take food seriously. Many arguments rage over the relative merits of a favorite restaurant. Proper atmosphere is almost as important to enjoyable dining as good food, and San Francisco's restaurants have risen to the challenge. You'll find elegant restaurants in grand hotels, cozy corners in family-run eateries, and salty atmosphere at Fisherman's Wharf, where crab cocktails are served along the sidewalk.

The sea provides many traditional San Francisco delicacies—Dungeness crab, abalone, and Hang Town Fry (an oyster and egg dish favored by the 49ers). Other local favorites are the crusty sourdough French bread (don't expect to be served fresh bread on Monday or Thursday; they don't bake on Sunday or Wednesday), green goddess salad, artichoke specialties, cheeses from neighboring counties, and California wines, among the best in the world.

Because of the prominent international influence, you can expect to find Spanish and Mexican cuisines (they *are* different) competing for diners' attention with Chinese, French, and German food. You'll also discover Russian, Italian, Korean, Filipino, Japanese, Greek, and Scandinavian menus.

Chinese cooking is in a class of its own; selection is the problem. Most is Cantonese, predominantly steamed and braised foods, lightly seasoned. You'll notice the crisp vegetables. Sauces are light and thin in consistency. Mandarin and Szechwan dishes are more highly spiced (sometimes volcanically) and usually stir-fried. Wine is often incorporated in the cooking.

The larger your group, the greater selection of dishes. You'll probably be served chopsticks in addition to silverware; don't hesitate to try them. Your waiter will explain how to operate them to advantage. You'll be expected to drink tea.

Don't go to a Japanese restaurant with a hole in your sock, for you'll probably be asked to remove your shoes. You may find yourself sitting on the floor; your food might be cooked at the table. Although your waitress will greet you with a charming smile, she probably speaks only basic English.

Plunge right in and try *sushi* (a combination of rice with an endless variety of fillings). *Sukiyaki* is best known, but try *sashimi, tempura,* or *teriyaki. Sake* (the Japanese wine) is served warm.

Italian food is a never-ending series of courses. Go easy on each dish because, after antipasto, soup, salad, and pasta, you may find it difficult to eat your entree.

French cooking needs little introduction. It's done more imaginatively in San Francisco than almost any other place in the United States. Some of the most elegant restaurants feature French cuisine; the sauce is the secret. Ask your waiter for house specialties.

Basque food centers around lamb. You'll probably eat boarding house-style with community dishes. A bottle of wine is served for every four people and a bowl of fruit is your dessert.

Armenian, Jewish, Swiss, and Indian fare are only a sampling of the around-the-world discoveries in the city. You might want to end a meal with an Italian *cappuccino* or an Irish coffee—both popular in San Francisco.

Jefferson Street is one vast open-air fish market where you'll see rivers of steaming crabs and mountains of sourdough French bread. Try a "walk-away" seafood cocktail, sold in a disposable container. Beyond the seafood counters, activity centers around the fishing boats coming in with their catch. At the foot of Jones and Leavenworth, the boats stop while crates of fish are hoisted to the pier.

For thousands who come to the city, a San Francisco visit automatically calls for a meal at Fisherman's Wharf. The view is a big reason to go. If you get a window table, then below you are the bobbing fishing boats. In the distance are the tall orange red towers of the Golden Gate Bridge and beyond them the purple Marin hills.

At the seafood restaurants, specialties include fresh crab (during the season, early November to mid-June or July), cracked and served cold with lemon and mayonnaise; Crab Louis, the classic wharf salad, served with San Francisco's sourdough bread; abalone; and *cioppino*, the heroic fish and shellfish stew you eat with your fingers.

Restaurants elsewhere along the north waterfront are not easily categorized—however, if you're looking for Italian, Japanese, Mexican, or California food, you can find it here.

About two blocks east along the wharf is the permanent berth of the *Balclutha*, a handsome old three-masted sailing ship. Refurbished and restored, she looks like what she was: a Scottish-built, square-rigged ship that plied the seas between the 1880s and the 1920s and that was a veteran of 17 Cape Horn crossings. You can go aboard

**You stroll** *between steaming crab cauldrons and mounds of sourdough French bread to choose picnic ingredients at Fisherman's Wharf.*

**Board the Balclutha,** *a fine old three-masted sailing ship docked at Wharf. For a moderate fee, you can roam all over this popular Scot veteran.*

from 10 A.M. to 10 P.M. daily, inspect the wheel-house, the red-plush-upholstered chart house, the captain's cabin, and the ship's galley. There's a moderate admission charge.

At Pier 39 nearby, the replica of Sir Francis Drake's *Golden Hinde* sailing ship, which recently completed its voyage across the sea from England, is ready for viewing. Guided tours help tell the story of the historic vessel. It's open from 10 A.M. to 7 P.M. daily. You'll pay a moderate admission charge to board.

**Boat tours** offer striking views of San Francisco from the water. For a sightseeing tour of the bay, go aboard one of the trim ships of the Red and White Fleet. They leave from pier 43½ near Fisherman's Wharf. The route will take you close to the Golden Gate Bridge, past the grim rock that was Alcatraz Prison until it was abandoned in 1963, past Treasure Island, under the Bay Bridge, and along the waterfront. From shipboard you see San Francisco and the surrounding area as a dramatic rim around the bay. The city's buildings look higher than ever; its streets are wide strips running downhill to the water. To the north lie the gentle hills of Marin County, and to the east Oakland and Berkeley spread out along the shore and up into the hills. Because it gets chilly on the bay, take along a wrap and a scarf.

Boats for the 1¼-hour excursions leave frequently, beginning at 10 A.M. daily all year (weather permitting). Prices are moderate, and you can get snacks on board. You can also take excursions seasonally to Alcatraz (reservations required far in advance; call 398-1141). In summer and on winter weekends, excursion boats take picnickers to quaint Tiburon and then to a day's outing on Angel Island. Luncheon and dinner cruises go to Tiburon and Jack London Square from spring to early fall. For information on the latter cruises, call 391-2137.

**Aquatic Park,** only three blocks west of Fisherman's Wharf, encompasses the ship-shaped San Francisco Maritime Museum, with its fascinating collection of figureheads, sea anchors, shipwreck relics, and other remnants of the days when the edge of the bay was a forest of tall masts. There's no fee to visit this museum at the foot of Polk Street, open daily from 10 A.M. to 5 P.M. The most pleasant way to arrive is by Powell and Hyde street cable car, whose turntable is in little Victorian Park.

Five old ships, moored along the Hyde Street Pier just north of the museum, make up San Francisco's Maritime State Historic Park. The three-masted schooner *C. A. Thayer*, steam schooner *Wapama*, ferry boat *Eureka*, scow schooner *Alma*, and steam tug *Hercules* are all symbols of an era when wooden vessels were the coast's principal cargo carriers. Visitors may board the ships.

**Ghirardelli Square,** just south and west of San Francisco's floating maritime museum, covers the block bounded by Beach, Larkin, North Point, and Polk. First a woolen works and later the Ghirardelli Chocolate Factory, this red-brick building complex has been remodeled and restored to contain an enticing miscellany of shops, art galleries, theaters, and restaurants, as well as a radio station.

Ghirardelli Square includes a number of buildings (with names such as Mustard, Cocoa, and Chocolate), all of which are situated around an inviting plaza. The brick tower that marks the square was copied from one at the Chateau Blois in France. If you wish to rest, select one of the benches near the splashing fountain or one that affords a view of the bay and boats.

Shops in the square contain imports from such places as Africa, Holland, Ireland, the Orient, Finland, and Greece. Stores contain wearing apparel, toys, cutlery, flowers, jewelry, and leather goods.

Part of Ghirardelli's charm lies in the outdoor cafes and in the variety of food available here. For instance, you can watch thin crepes being made, sample Mexican, Chinese, Hungarian, or Italian food, or enjoy a Twin Peaks sundae or a Golden Gate Banana Split at an old-time ice cream parlor. And at the Ghirardelli Chocolate Manufactory and Fountain, you can watch chocolate being made.

An underground garage has entrances on Beach and Larkin streets; there is a parking fee.

**Infamous Alcatraz Island** *is highlight of bay boat cruise. Some tours visit former prison.*

**Ghirardelli Square** *plaza offers ship-ogling, multilevel restaurants, and intriguing shops.*

**Bayside walkers** *skirt shoreline along Golden Gate Promenade's 3½-mile walk from Aquatic Park to Ft. Point.*

**The Cannery** is similar to Ghirardelli Square in some ways. Bounded by Beach, Leavenworth, and Jefferson streets, it was originally constructed in 1894 to house the Del Monte Fruit and Vegetable Cannery. Today, the old brick building with its concrete walkways and arched windows has been restored and refurbished.

The Cannery contains three levels of shopping pleasures. You can buy an assortment of goods, from contemporary household furnishings to primitive art objects. Other shops feature such items as candles, fine foods and wines, apparel, flowers, linens, books, and pet supplies.

Outside escalators and stairs provide access to different floors, or you can take a glass-enclosed elevator from the ground floor to the top. From the third floor, you can see Alcatraz Island, the Bay Bridge, and Coit Tower.

On the west side of The Cannery is a plaza containing a small garden center, outside tables, and an oyster bar. Other restaurants feature Oriental, Mexican, French, and English food.

Across Leavenworth Street from The Cannery is a parking lot that provides one hour of free parking with your validated ticket from The Cannery.

## The Marina

Until recently it has been hard to do more than drive by the lovely homes in the Marina area, get-ting a peek now and then of the shoreline and a tantalizing glimpse of the boats on the bay. Now the Marina is a part of the Golden Gate National Recreation Area (encompassing lands on both the Marin and San Francisco sides of the Golden Gate), and you can walk from the northern waterfront to Ft. Point, huddled under the Golden Gate Bridge.

**The Golden Gate Promenade,** a 3½-mile shoreline walk between Aquatic Park and Ft. Point, may be one of the most spectacular walks in the world. The old military gates at Ft. Mason and Crissy Field are open, making the promenade now totally accessible.

En route you pass scores of historical sites and many of the city's most desirable amenities. You can see long-forgotten vistas and discover a broad driftwood beach. Most of the walk is within 50 feet of the bay, following the seawall beyond the St. Francis Yacht Club and the northern leg of the Marina Yacht Harbor.

**The Palace of Fine Arts,** along the route, was built for the Panama-Pacific International Exposition in 1915 and restored to its original stunning splendor in 1967. In addition to the Exploratorium focusing on science, technology, and human perception (open 1 to 5 P.M. Wednesday through Sunday; 7 to 9:30 P.M. Wednesday; there's no admission charge), there is a theater where the San Francisco International Film Festival is held each October.

**Bilingual street signs** *are topped by spring cherry blossoms at Japan Center.*

**Multicolumned Palace of Fine Arts,** *built for temporary use at 1915 exposition, was restored as arts and science center.*

Other cultural and entertainment events also take place here.

## Japan Center—Japan without a passport

One of the most surprising new developments in town is the Japan Center in Nihonmachi—Japantown. A string of handsome white buildings between Geary Expressway and Post, the center starts on the east at Laguna Street past Buchanan, boldly leaps Webster Street with a curved bridgeway of shops, and ends on the west at Fillmore Street. Street signs are in both Japanese and English.

Tenants include the Japanese Consulate, manufacturers with showrooms, and retailers selling goods ranging from bonsai plants to pearls. The 5-acre complex of shops, showrooms, theater-restaurant, coffee and teahouses, tempura bars, and a 15-story hotel gives the Japanese community a needed focal point and showplace in the cosmopolitan tradition of Chinatown and the Italian sector of North Beach. Main entrance to the large parking garage is from Geary.

The Peace Plaza, containing a five-tiered, 35-foot Peace Pagoda in the center of a reflecting pool, is the main setting for such colorful observances as the annual Spring Cherry Blossom Festival and the *Aki Matsuri*, an annual fall event.

## Golden Gate Park—a park for all seasons

San Francisco owes a great debt of gratitude to the late John McLaren, whose vision and perseverance in San Francisco's early years turned more than 1,000 acres of rolling sand dunes into a park. Today, Golden Gate Park is one of the really great metropolitan parks of the world.

Park visitors benefit from an enlightened policy of operation: the park is meant to be used. You can park your car along most of the drives—there are few "No Parking" signs. On Sunday, though, auto traffic is restricted along Kennedy Drive.

You can walk, play, or picnic on the grass anywhere except the small plot of lawn surrounding Mr. McLaren's statue in Rhododendron Dell. The bridle paths, equestrian field, and bicycle trails are for public use; you can rent horses at the stables at Kennedy Drive and 34th Avenue and bicycles just outside the park in the 600 and 800 blocks of Stanyan Street.

The M. H. de Young and Asian Art museums, the Academy of Science, the concessions, the Arboretum, and the Conservatory close at night; otherwise the park is open from dawn until 10 P.M.

**John F. Kennedy Drive** takes you by many of the park's attractions; it's the entrance from the northwest corner. The nine-hole pitch-and-putt golf course located a short distance inside the park is open every day. To get to the clubhouse, turn left at the first intersection of Kennedy Drive after you leave the Great Highway.

**The Chain of Lakes,** a series of three artificial lakes, runs from north to south across the park near its western end. Largest of the three is North Lake (north of Kennedy Drive), dotted with several landscaped islands. The banks of Middle Lake (south of Kennedy Drive), are planted with camellias and Japanese cherry trees. South Lake, smallest in the chain, hosts large numbers of wild ducks.

North of Kennedy Drive and just east of the Chain of Lakes, the fences of the Buffalo Paddock are so carefully concealed by artful landscaping that buffalo and elk within the enclosure seem to be roaming at large.

Anglers will find an ideal practicing spot at the Flycasting Pool south of the Drive. The cement-lined pool is divided into three sections—one for distance casting, another for accuracy, and a third for practicing difficult overhead casts.

As you approach Spreckels Lake, you'll pass some of the largest and oldest rhododendrons in the park. Planted on an island in the center of Kennedy Drive, they're at their best in May.

The lake itself is north of the drive. Its waters are usually dotted with wildfowl, and during summer the lake is used for sailing model boats. The San Francisco Model Yacht Club has its headquarters in the building just west of the lake.

Polo matches are frequently held on Sundays from April to October in the Polo Fields, located just east of the Flycasting Pool.

Continuing east on Kennedy Drive, you pass 25-acre Lindley Meadow and tiny Lloyd Lake. A gravel path encircles the lake, leading to the "Portals of the Past" on its shore. The six white marble pillars that form the portals were the entrance to the A. N. Towne residence on Nob Hill. All that remained of the house after the 1906 fire, the pillars were later presented by Mrs. Towne to the park.

Stow Lake, largest of the park's manmade lakes, is the central reservoir for the irrigation system and also a popular recreation spot. Tree-lined walks border the lake, a road goes around it, and there's a snack bar near the dock where boats can be rented. Two bridges lead to Strawberry Hill, a wooded island in the center of the lake. A 5-minute walk up a fairly stiff slope puts you on top of the hill. The view from the summit reveals not only

the park—a wide green swath through the west end of the city—but also the towers of the Golden Gate and Bay bridges, the surf pounding the shoreline and, on clear days, the Farallon Islands, 30 miles out into the Pacific.

The Rose Garden, just east of the Stow Lake Drive on the north side of Kennedy Drive, contains about 75 varieties of roses, including recent award winners. All are labeled.

**The M. H. de Young Memorial Museum** opened in 1895 after Michael de Young, publisher of the San Francisco *Chronicle*, proposed that the profits of the California Midwinter International Exposition of 1894 be used to house a permanent collection of art. The original museum buildings were torn down in 1926, and today's museum consists of two wings extending from either side of a 134-foot tower that faces a landscaped court. Both the Pool of Enchantment at the entrance and the bronze Sun Dial at the building's southeast corner are the work of sculptor M. Earl Cummings.

A special wing overlooking the Japanese Tea Garden was added in 1966 to house the Avery Brundage Collection of Oriental Art (now called the Asian Art Museum). On display are nearly 6,000 treasures covering 60 centuries of Asian civilization.

The museum houses extensive and varied art collections displayed in spacious galleries enclosing the court. Paintings include works by famous

**Golden Gate Park's Stow Lake** *offers idyllic boating sites. Rent boats at dock. Hikers can explore lakeshore along a tree-lined path.*

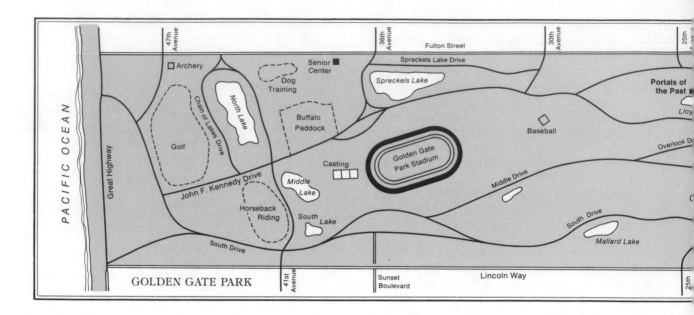

American and European artists. The doors are open daily from 10 A.M. to 5 P.M.

**The Japanese Tea Garden** just west of the museum is open daily from 8 A.M. to dusk. Created in 1894, this 3-acre exhibit of Oriental landscaping includes a moon bridge, a temple, Oriental gateways and lanterns, a large bronze Buddha, and a teahouse where Japanese girls serve green or jasmine tea and cookies. In spring the cherry trees make the garden a fairyland of delicate blooms. Blossoms are at their peak around April 1.

**The California Academy of Sciences** grouping includes the North American Hall, with its collection of American mammals and birds displayed in their natural habitats; the African Hall, featuring an African water hole with giraffes, gnus, impalas, gazelles, zebras, and hartebeests grouped realistically around it; the Steinhart Aquarium; and the Morrison Planetarium.

The academy and the aquarium are open daily from 10 A.M. to 5 P.M. (until 9 P.M. from mid-June to Labor Day); there's a slight admission charge. The planetarium presents spectacular outer-space shows every day on the great dome of its Theater of the Stars; admission is $1 for adults, 50 cents for children.

**The Music Concourse**, situated between the de Young Museum and the Academy of Sciences, is the setting for band concerts at 2 P.M. on Sundays and holidays (weather permitting). You can sit on terraces around the concourse or on benches.

**Strybing Arboretum** is a "must" for anyone interested in plants. Here in this self-contained, 60-acre world are about 5,000 species and varieties of plants from all over the globe, conveniently arranged according to geographical origin and carefully labeled.

Of particular interest are the *Sunset Magazine* Demonstration Home Gardens, designed to help homeowners with ideas for plant selection, planting design, and landscape construction.

The Arboretum, located along South Drive, is open from 8 A.M. to 4:30 P.M. on weekdays and from 10 A.M. to 5 P.M. on Saturday and Sunday; admission is free.

**Conservatory of Flowers** (open 8 A.M. to 4:50 P.M. daily) is like another world. The atmosphere is warm and humid, the plants lush and tropical.

The conservatory houses many fascinating collections — bright crotons, large-flowered hibiscus, rare cycads, graceful ferns, orchids. Along the path, among tall palms, are some of the largest and oldest philodendron plants under cultivation.

Be sure to look at the greenhouse itself. A replica of the conservatory at Kew Gardens, England, it was bought by James Lick, a San Francisco philanthropist, and its sections were transported from England around the Horn on a sailing ship. After the owner's death, the greenhouse was purchased by the city and erected in Golden Gate Park in 1878. The framework is wood, but the beams, unlike those of most greenhouses, are laminated. If you look closely, you can see how short pieces have been fitted together to form the dome.

In Conservatory Valley between Kennedy Drive and the conservatory are many formal beds of annuals and bulbs. On the slopes behind these beds are two floral features: a design in living plants that honors events of national or area importance and a blossoming clock presented to the city by the watchmakers of Switzerland.

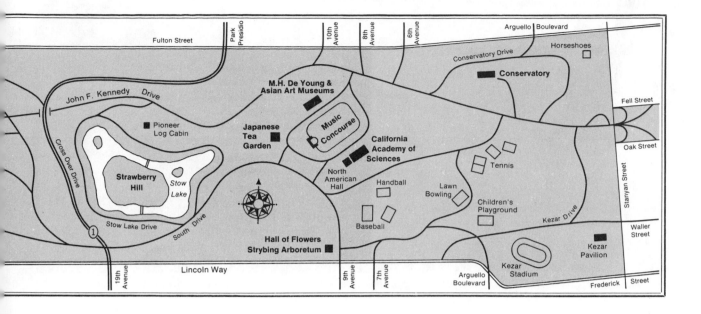

**Children's Playground,** in the southeast corner of the park adjacent to the Sharon Building, is devoted to recreation. Neighborhood mothers bring their offspring here during the week, and sightseers visiting the park find that an hour or so of play gives their own youngsters a needed diversion. There is also a small animal farm.

**Kezar Stadium,** a municipal field, is used principally by local high school football teams. Through 1970, Kezar was the home of San Francisco's professional football team, the '49ers. Kezar Pavilion, the indoor stadium, is used for sporting events, including professional boxing and roller derbies.

## The city's western perimeter

Fortunately for all of us, the Golden Gate National Recreation Area was created in 1972 to save the existing greenbelts on both sides of the bay. On the San Francisco side of the bay, a coastal fortification plan, developed in 1854, coincidentally protected much of the city's western edge from development by establishing a natural greenbelt from Ft. Mason to Ft. Funston.

San Francisco's ocean waterfront offers no swimming because of the dangerous undertow; however, several other recreational activities are available. You can sun or fish from the beaches; golf among cypress trees; visit an art gallery, zoo, or amusement park; or stroll through historic Ft. Point.

**Ft. Point,** huddling under the southern end of the Golden Gate Bridge, is reached from Lincoln Boulevard. Here Colonel Juan Bautista de Anza planted a cross in 1775. In 1853 the Americans, on the site of an old Spanish fort, started work on this massive brick, iron, and granite structure built roughly along the lines of Ft. Sumter in South Carolina. The fort, which never fired a defensive shot, has been abandoned since 1914.

Its most serious adversary proved to be the weather. Wind-driven salt water and fog have rusted out iron balustrades and spiral staircases and have eaten into the mortar. If the Golden Gate Bridge's imaginative chief engineer, Joseph Strauss, had not ordered construction of a special arch over the fort, it would have been torn down to make way for the bridge in the mid-1930s.

The fort is open from 10 A.M. to 5 P.M. daily. Guided tours reward visitors with unusual views of the bridge and the bay's shifting tides. Call the National Park Service at 556-1693 for information.

**Lincoln Park** is reached from El Camino del Mar, an extension of Lincoln Boulevard in the Presidio.

*Long-abandoned Ft. Point is tucked under Golden Gate Bridge. For touring, dress warmly here against the customary cold and wind.*

**Individualistic,** *frock-coated youth cavorts with gull under threatening skies on beach below Cliff House.*

Here you'll find a municipal 18-hole golf course and a fine art gallery—the California Palace of the Legion of Honor. You'll see works by the great masters, a special collection of graphic prints and, in the courtyard, Rodin's *The Thinker*. The museum is open daily from 10 A.M. to 5 P.M.

For a look at Mile Rock Lighthouse, the Golden Gate Bridge, and the Pacific Ocean, take the northern turnoff from Pt. Lobos Avenue to Land's End. Besides a view, you'll see the shelled bridge of the *USS San Francisco*, torpedoed in 1942 at Guadalcanal.

**San Francisco's Zoological Gardens** ranks among the top city zoos in the United States. Adults as well as children will enjoy a visit. It's out at the edge of Ocean Beach (turn off the Great Highway at either Sloat Boulevard or Park Road) and is open daily from 10 A.M. to 5:30 P.M. You can easily walk around the zoo, where you can look through the fences at animals roaming in surroundings similar to their natural habitat. Or you can take the motor-drawn "elephant train" which circles the entire zoo. Cars leave every half-hour near the main entrance, taking you on a 20-minute circuit.

Next to the zoo are Storyland, a special playground using themes from children's folklore, and the Children's Zoo, where boys and girls can feed and play with young animals. There are slight admission charges for the zoo and other attractions, which are open all year from 10 A.M. to 5 P.M.

# The City's Hills

San Francisco is famous for its many hills and the views which each affords. Some hills are more accessible than others (only a footpath reaches the summit of Mt. Davidson, for instance), some are more interesting physically, and some provide exceptional views. Nob, Telegraph, and Russian hills, along with Twin Peaks, are probably San Francisco's best-known heights.

## Telegraph Hill

At Lombard and Kearny streets, you pick up the road that climbs up Telegraph Hill to Coit Tower. Parking space at the top of the hill is limited, but with patience you can usually get a place. Or you can leave your car at the garage on the corner of Filbert and Grant and board the Coit bus at Stockton and Filbert. It will take you to the top and, if you prefer, you can walk down the footpath on the east slope of the hill.

Telegraph Hill gives good views of San Francisco's waterfront, Russian Hill, Nob Hill, the Bay and Golden Gate bridges, Alcatraz Island, Angel Island, Treasure Island and, on a clear day, some East Bay landmarks.

For an even loftier view, take the elevator (slight charge) to the top of Coit Tower (210 feet). Elevator operates from 11 A.M. to 5 P.M.

Coit Tower, dramatically lighted at night, is a well-known landmark against the city's skyline. It was built in 1934 as a memorial to the city's volunteer firemen from funds left to the city by Lillie Hitchcock Coit, a great fire buff. The shape of the tower is often said to resemble a fire nozzle. Inside the fluted cylindrical column are murals done by artists in 1934 under the Work Projects Administration.

If you choose to walk down from Telegraph Hill, take the pathway that curves down the eastern slope. You will come to two sets of steps, one leading to Filbert and the other to Greenwich. Either stairway takes you down to Montgomery, a short distance below, and then drops down a long, steep flight to Sansome at the foot of the hill.

## Russian Hill

Located west of Telegraph Hill, roughly between Hyde, Taylor, Vallejo, and Greenwich, is Russian Hill. In the immediate area you'll find small, green parks, quaint cottages, and skyscraper apartment buildings. Here you can drive on two of San Francisco's most interesting streets. Filbert between Hyde and Leavenworth is one of the city's steepest streets; Lombard between Hyde and Leavenworth is the crookedest—the brick road coils down in snakelike fashion amidst bright hydrangea gardens.

## Nob Hill

To reach the top of this hill, take the California or Powell Street cable car. Or if you prefer to drive, you'll find several parking garages on California, close to Mason.

The very top of the hill covers about three square blocks. Before the earthquake and fire of 1906, this small hilltop was the site of the city's grandest mansions. Only one survives: the imposing brownstone built by James C. Flood. Now the Pacific Union Club, it faces California, just west of Mason.

Two of San Francisco's most famous hotels, the Fairmont and the Mark Hopkins, stand atop Nob Hill at California and Mason. The luxurious Fairmont, the tallest building on the hill, has several restaurants, a spacious lobby, and a cocktail lounge at the top. You can reach the Crown Room in an outside glass-walled elevator or, if you prefer, in an inside elevator.

Across California is the Mark Hopkins Hotel, long known for the elegant Top of the Mark cocktail lounge. Panoramic views can be had from both the Crown Room and the Top of the Mark.

Next to the Mark Hopkins Hotel, at the corner of California and Powell, is the elegant Stanford Court Hotel, on the site of the Stanford mansion. Rebuilt and refurbished in turn-of-the-century decor, the new hotel has a dramatic circular driveway entrance, accented with a round fountain and topped by an opulent stained-glass dome. The lobby, with its potted palms, reminds you of an early 1900s photo.

Up the hill, at 1075 California, is the chic Huntington Hotel, with a superb restaurant (L'Etoile) in the same building.

Three blocks west, at California and Jones, is Grace Cathedral, the ultimate in Gothic architecture. Of particular interest are the interior murals, stained-glass windows, and the Ghiberti doors—gilded bronze panels that are a reproduction of the famous East Door of the Baptistry in Florence,

**Nob Hill's Flood Mansion** (*now Pacific Union Club*) *managed to survive 1906 earthquake.*

**Shaft of modern apartment** *contrasts with more modest, more familiar Coit Tower stub.*

Italy. Protected by guardrails, the doors are open only on special occasions.

Across from the cathedral is the Masonic Temple, a spacious auditorium used for fine arts and musical productions. It is open to visitors Monday through Friday. Of special interest are the heroic carvings on the California Street side of the marble temple, and the plastic translucent mural windows.

### Twin Peaks

Situated in the center of the city, Twin Peaks are noted for their sweeping vistas of the entire Bay Area. Now a 65-acre park, their crests are popular with sightseers. To reach the summit, take Upper Market Street to Twin Peaks Boulevard.

## Streets That Unlock The City

You'll make your own discoveries of some of San Francisco's most interesting byways. Here are a few of its famous (and some not-so-famous) streets, with an idea of what you'll find along them.

**Market Street.** San Francisco's best-known thoroughfare runs diagonally across the city from Twin Peaks to the Ferry Building. The strip of Market south of Union Square is a continuation of the downtown shopping area. Underneath Market runs BART, giving the street a new look—less traffic, wider sidewalks, new landscaping, and old-fashioned street lamps. At the foot of Market is the Ferry Building, partially obscured by the double-decked Embarcadero Freeway skirting the waterfront. Across the street is the Justin Herman Plaza, with its monumental free-form sculpture—the Vaillancourt Fountain, a walk-through design of 101 concrete boxes.

High-rise buildings accent Market Street's rejuvenation. The Crown-Zellerbach building, an impressive, 20-story green monolith, rises above a pleasantly landscaped park (popular with noon "brown baggers") at the corner of Market and Bush. At 555 Market you can stroll through colorful gardens at the Standard Oil Company Plaza; on weekdays you can go inside the 43-story building to view an exhibit on the history of petroleum. The Crocker Building (Post, Montgomery, and Market) towers 38 stories above its green mall.

At Market and New Montgomery stands a San Francisco landmark—the Sheraton-Palace Hotel. The reputation of this magnificent eight-story structure began with its opening in 1875. Originally built by silver king William Ralston, the building was severely damaged in the 1906 earthquake-fire; restoration was completed in 1909. The glass-roofed Garden Court dining room (a historical landmark) is a fine example of old San Francisco elegance—and a good place for lunch.

Where Geary, Kearny, and Market converge you'll see Lotta's Fountain, a reminder of Lotta Crabtree, who charmed San Franciscans during Gold Rush days.

**Geary Street.** A street of many faces, Geary runs west from Market, ending at Sutro Park near the ocean. On its way through town it passes by some of San Francisco's smartest shops, Union Square, the theater district, and the Japan Center.

**Mission Street.** Roughly paralleling Market through downtown, Mission takes an abrupt turn south after crossing Van Ness. Primarily a manufacturing

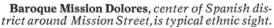

**Sumptuous glass roof** *of Sheraton-Palace's Garden Court draws diners to city landmark. Luncheon is chic tradition.*

**Baroque Mission Dolores,** *center of Spanish district around Mission Street, is typical ethnic sight.*

area from its beginning at the bay, it boasts one large tourist attraction—the historic U.S. Mint at 5th and Mission. Completed in 1873 and phased out of operation about 80 years later, the mint reopened as a museum in 1973. An outstanding example of Federal Classical Revival architecture, it's undergone extensive restoration and refurbishing. In the front section you'll see exhibits tracing the development of American money. The mint's special coins and medals division operates in the rear. The landmark is open from 10 A.M. to 4 P.M. Tuesday through Sunday.

*Se habla Espanol* signs appear around the Mission District, with Duboce, Castro, Harrison, and 28th streets forming the basic trapezoid. Walking around near Mission Dolores, you'll feel the strong Spanish influence. Mission Street once linked the village of Yerba Buena to this Franciscan outpost; now BART tunnels beneath it.

Mission Dolores, established in 1776, was the sixth of the California chain. Its ceilings are decorated with Indian art, and the original bell and altar from Mexico remain. Be sure to walk through the garden cemetery, final resting place of many San Francisco pioneers. An impressive statue of Father Junipero Serra stands in the courtyard.

**California Street.** Taking off from Market at the Embarcadero Plaza, California extends all the way through town, avoiding much of the business traffic and ending at Lincoln Park. Along the way, you'll climb from the canyons of Montgomery's "Wall

**Check the works** *in the refurbished U.S. Mint at 5th and Mission. Money was coined here for about a century.*

# Getting Around without a Car

Buses, trains, and ferryboats shuttle weekday workers between San Francisco and residential communities around the bay. With a few modifications, these same commuter networks operate on Sundays and holidays.

Wherever you live in the greater Bay Area, you can find public transportation departing frequently for San Francisco's downtown Transbay, Southern Pacific, or Greyhound terminals. There's also ferry service from Sausalito to the Ferry Building and from Tiburon to Fisherman's Wharf.

East Bay residents can bring their bikes along on a special "Pedal Hopper" bus from Oakland (write Transit Information, 508 16th St., Oakland, CA 94612, for schedules), and ferries from Marin allow passengers to bring their bikes.

Once you get into the city, you can take buses, streetcars, and cable cars of the San Francisco Municipal Railway to all recreation, dining, and shopping areas. The San Francisco Muni is not as glamorous as BART (which does not operate on Sunday and holidays), but its schedules are frequent and its cars head almost anywhere a visitor might want to go.

Special 50-cent Sunday-holiday Tour Tickets give you an unlimited number of rides over the entire system all day. You can buy the ticket from any cable car conductor or from starters at the Powell and Market turntable.

For a free copy describing every Muni route, send a request with a stamped, self-addressed, business-size envelope to San Francisco Municipal Railway, 949 Presidio Ave., San Francisco, CA 94115. A route map, descriptions of routes, and chart indicating frequency are at the beginning of the Yellow Pages in the San Francisco telephone directory.

If you haven't been on a bus recently, remember drivers no longer carry change or tokens. Present the exact fare (and ask for transfers) when boarding.

Street" through colorful Chinatown to the heights of Nob Hill, passing some of San Francisco's famous hotels, the Masonic Temple, and Grace Cathedral. It's a good street for catching outstanding views.

**Union Street.** Passing by the North Beach and upper Grant Avenue areas, Union becomes better known after crossing Van Ness. In pre-Gold Rush days, the district was known as Cow Hollow. It was, in fact, the city's dairyland. But its renaissance began in the late 1950s when ingenious merchants began reclaiming its vintage dwellings, cow barns, and carriage houses and converting them to a flourishing shopping area with odds-and-ends emporiums and an international array of restaurants.

**Clement Street.** A melting pot of ethnic life, Clement is practically a discovery. This shopping area, not really frequented by tourists, has a little bit of everything—almost all authentic. Best known as a Russian neighborhood, it also harbors other European and Asian nationalities. Women still carry shopping bags and haggle with shopkeepers for the best-looking vegetables for the evening dinner. This multiethnic neighborhood is trying hard to retain its identity. You can learn belly-dancing, eat at a vegetarian restaurant, or shop for fertilized red eggs, Indian pickles, or *piroshkis*. A number of good international restaurants (modestly priced) are sprinkled along both sides of Clement. You'll also find everything from furniture to flower shops in this 11-block area.

**Sutter Street.** Appropriately named for today's shopping prospector, this 1.8-mile street runs from the financial district to the residential uplands and includes a rich lode of treasure in eight blocks. Lined with grand and small hotels, specialty houses and sprightly boutiques, art and import emporiums, fashionable restaurants and small cafes, the thoroughfare is a rich slice of San Francisco.

**Outer Sacramento Street** has blossomed into a shopping sector reminiscent of Union Street (Cow Hollow) in its early Cinderella period. What was formerly a service area for Pacific and Presidio Heights residents is now a browsable, seven-block cluster of shops, galleries, and boutiques, many of them occupying turn-of-the-century clapboards. Interspersed among apparel, antique, art, gift, and home furnishings outlets are coffee houses, snack bars, and a theater featuring film imports. Most shopping is between Broderick and Spruce streets.

# The City's Cultural Side

San Francisco's cultural life began simultaneously with its financial history—in the 1850s. It is reported that the city's first classical concert was a trombone solo in 1850. From the beginning, local audiences were warm to actors and musicians; concert halls and theaters abounded, and performers were handsomely rewarded with gold. The

**After dark,** *bustling Union Street specializes in restaurant trade; in daytime, it's a shoppers' mecca.*

**Crocheted dress** *enhances model (or vice versa) in fanciful boutique. Fashions keep pace with the times.*

**Crowds flock** *to outdoor concerts in Stern Grove on summer Sunday afternoons.*

**Superb** *Palace of Legion of Honor* **(left)** *is modeled after 18th century Parisian building. In this art museum and cultural center, listeners* **(below)** *enjoy concerts.*

city has never lost its zest for the arts. Notice the abundance of street musicians.

## The performing arts

Music and theater are not limited to legitimate stages. Sunday afternoon outdoor concerts are held in Golden Gate Park and, in summer, in the Sigmund Stern Grove (along Sloat Boulevard near 19th Avenue).

**San Francisco Symphony's** regular season is December through May in the Opera House. Concerts are Wednesday and Friday nights, most Thursday afternoons, and some Saturday evenings. The symphony also plays pops concerts in July on Tuesday, Thursday, and Saturday nights in the Civic Auditorium. Try Sherman Clay Box Office for tickets.

**San Francisco Opera's** 11-week season opens in mid-September. Performances are Tuesday, Wednesday, Friday, and Saturday nights, as well as Sunday afternoons. "Spring Opera," in March at the Curran Theatre, features young American singers. "Dollar Opera" performances are held two weekends in early May at the Palace of Fine Arts Theatre.

**Companies on tour** also perform at the Masonic Memorial Auditorium, Grace Cathedral, the Legion of Honor, San Francisco State University, and the Cow Palace. Check the Sunday newspaper's "Datebook" for listings.

**Visitor scrutinizes** *identifying label on svelte statue of Venus at Legion of Honor.*

**California's only wine museum** *is located in San Francisco. Here the grape is king.*

**Contemporary Bay Area couple** *gaze at man and woman captured in oils at an earlier time.*

**San Francisco Ballet** has two principal seasons. In December (during the Christmas holidays) they perform the *Nutcracker* in the Opera House. Spring season in the Opera House is the ballet's major offering. Get tickets at Sherman Clay.

**American Conservatory Theatre,** a repertory company whose season runs from late October into May, also presents a long-running show for the summer. Performances are at the Geary Theatre nightly except Sunday (matinees Wednesday and Saturday). Special productions are held at the Marines Memorial Theatre.

**Civic Light Opera** productions start in April/May and continue into autumn at the Curran Theatre.

Matinees are held Wednesday and Saturday; dark on Sunday.

## A mélange of museums

Museum subjects range from history to wine; take your pick. Of the many museums in the city, here is a sampling.

**African American Historical Society** exhibits pertain to African and Afro-American history. Open Tuesday through Saturday from 1 to 5 P.M., it's at 680 McAllister; admission is free.

**Asian Art Museum's** collection of treasures spanning 60 centuries is internationally acclaimed.

You'll see bronze Hindu deities, sandstone Khmer figures, whimsical ivory and jade figures, fine porcelains, and silken scrolls. Open from 10 A.M. to 5 P.M., it's located in the M. H. de Young Memorial Museum, Golden Gate Park; small admission fee.

**California Historical Society's** 1896 red sandstone mansion seems an appropriate headquarters for an excellent library and small museum. The library is open from 10 A.M. to 4 P.M. Tuesday through Saturday, and the headquarters is open from 1 to 5 P.M. on Wednesday, Saturday, and Sunday. It's located at 2090 Jackson; there's a small charge.

**Chinese Historical Society of America,** in Chinatown, has displays of early California mining activity and the building of the transcontinental railroad, as well as personal memorabilia. It's open 1 to 5 P.M. Tuesday through Sunday, except Christmas and New Year's Day; admission is free. The museum is at 17 Adler Place, just off Grant Avenue.

**The Octagon House,** built in 1861 and restored in 1952 by the National Society of Colonial Dames, displays authentic furnishings. This elegant, unusual home is open 1 to 4 P.M. the first Sunday of each month and the second and fourth Thursdays. It's located at Gough and Union streets; donation requested.

**Wine Museum of San Francisco** is the first of its kind in the United States. Paintings, sculptures, artifacts, and historical exhibits all relate to viniculture. The striking brick structure opened in January, 1974. Located at 633 Beach Street near Fisherman's Wharf, it's open from 11 A.M. to 5 P.M. Tuesdays through Saturday and noon to 5 P.M. Sunday. There's no charge to visit this collection by the Christian Brothers and the Fromms.

## Looking at art

You'll find art galleries scattered throughout the city, but there are three main museums.

**San Francisco Museum of Art,** on the third and fourth floors of the Veteran's Building in the Civic Center, is the nucleus of modern art in the Bay Area. Traveling exhibitions add depth to the collection. Permanent acquisitions include works by Henri Matisse, Paul Klee, Alexander Calder, Jackson Pollock, and other noted artists. Admission is free; the museum is open Tuesday through Friday from 10 A.M. to 10 P.M. and closes at 5 P.M. on weekends.

**California Palace of the Legion of Honor** is one of San Francisco's most splendid museums and sites. This neo-Classical edifice, set among green lawns, dominates the height of Land's End in Lincoln Park in the city's northwest corner. Paintings span the 16th to the 20th centuries, with emphasis on 18th

---

# Don't Miss

**Broadway** (North Beach)—San Francisco's Bohemia; cabarets and cafes; a flavor of Italy blended with exotic nightlife; it comes alive after dark

**Cable cars** (downtown San Francisco)—bounding, bell-clanging trolleys providing the city's most unusual transportation; watch the turnaround at Hallidie Plaza; visit the Cable Car Barn

**Fisherman's Wharf** (waterfront)—stroll past the fish stalls; munch French bread; try a "walkaway" seafood cocktail; departure point for harbor cruises; nearby are Ghirardelli Square, The Cannery, and Cost Plus

**Golden Gate Bridge** (San Francisco to Marin)—fabled in story and song, it's a bridge you can walk across, observing ships coming and going from the busy harbor; good city-viewing spot

**Golden Gate Park** (western San Francisco)—a park for everyone in over 1,000 acres; museums, lakes, music concourse, arboretum, Conservatory of Flowers, and Japanese tea garden; rent horses or bikes

**Grant Avenue** (downtown San Francisco)—an eclectic street ranging from elegant Union Square through bustling Chinatown and North Beach to some out-of-the-way shopping

**Harbor cruises** (Pier 43½)—a scenic cruise around the bay gives best opportunity to view city skyline; tour goes near Angel Island and Alcatraz; other cruises to both

**Nob Hill** (California Street)—site of pre-earthquake Flood Mansion, four of city's finest hotels (Fairmont, Mark Hopkins, Stanford Court, and Huntington)

---

and 19th century French artists. The collection of Rodin sculpture is rated as one of America's finest.

Free docent tours of permanent collections are given at 2 P.M. daily. Organ recitals are held Saturday and Sunday at 4 P.M. The museum is open from 10 A.M. to 5 P.M. daily; slight admission fee.

**M. H. de Young Memorial Museum** is one of San Francisco's most popular art museums. You'll find Rembrandt portraits, Greco paintings, Flemish tapestries, and many works by other major artists. In addition to paintings and sculpture, you'll see displays of period furniture, porcelain, and silver. The newest exhibit is devoted to artifacts from Africa and Oceania.

Located in Golden Gate Park, the museum is open from 10 A.M. to 5 P.M.; there is a slight admission charge. Guided tours are given daily.

# Around San Francisco Bay

Many visitors to the San Francisco Bay area find Marin County the surprise treat of their visit. The bay side is one of the most photogenic shorelines in California. Two ridges project like stubby fingers, forming a narrow horseshoe enclosing shallow Richardson Bay. The main Marin peninsula, with Mt. Tamalpais in the background, faces across this small bay to the Tiburon peninsula and the low, offshore pyramid of Angel Island. Sausalito and Tiburon offer unusual shops, good restaurants, and lots of bay and boat watching. These two waterside centers have long been known as gathering places for artists, sailors, fishermen, commuters, and visitors.

Across the Bay Bridge, crowded into a narrow strip between the water of San Francisco Bay and the low hills that rise to the east, the East Bay communities parallel the shoreline, flowing into one another so that you scarcely know when you depart one and enter the next.

East Bay's attractions are not as well known as those of its neighbor across the bay, but visitors will find some surprising discoveries: Lake Merritt (in the heart of Oakland), glamorous Oakland Museum, fine waterfront restaurants, California's largest university, and some of the state's finest parks.

The narrow belt of land south of San Francisco is divided into two distinctly different regions by a forested ridge of mountains that runs down its length. The bay side of the mountains is crowded with cities; the ocean side is sprinkled with peaceful farms, unspoiled beaches, and lightly traveled country roads. One of the most scenic drives down the peninsula is on Interstate Highway 280, extending from San Francisco to San Jose. Marked exits direct you to major attractions along the way.

**Belvedere Island homes** *(foreground)*
*overlook Richardson Bay. Marin's gentle*
*hills and the towers of Golden Gate Bridge*
*rise in background.*

# Marin-on-the-Bay

Sausalito is a hill town; Tiburon includes 10 square miles of salt water; Belvedere was once an island. But you catch only tantalizing glimpses of these bayside areas from U.S. Highway 101. For a real look, you must follow the slow roads along the shore east of the freeway. So many people flock to this region that traffic jams are a regular weekend occurrence.

## Sausalito: A Mediterranean Transplant

Sausalito's setting has the quality of a southern European seacoast village. Its harbors are full of small vessels of varied sizes and shapes; its hillside-hung homes recall those found on the Italian Riviera. Shops and restaurants are concentrated at the water's edge.

Before the Golden Gate Bridge was built, Sausalito was the transfer point for Marin commuters. They came this far south by train and went on to San Francisco by ferry. These services stopped in 1937 with the completion of the bridge; however, ferry commuter service has been recently revived. Modern ferries now operate from the foot of Anchor Street.

A short distance north of the Golden Gate Bridge, the road to Sausalito (Alexander turnoff) branches to the east. As you descend you have superb views of Raccoon Straits and Angel Island. Then the road drops, with abrupt turns, to Bridgeway, the waterfront main street of Sausalito. Along the way you'll get your first good look at the stair-stepped hill houses rising above you.

You can get a good view of the Sausalito terrain and the bay from the dining deck of the historic Alta Mira Hotel on Harrison Street.

Sausalito is a town of small shops. Most complicated (and varied) shopping place is The Village Fair on Bridgeway not far from Plaza Vina del Mar. On its different levels are about 40 small specialty shops, some of which contain handcrafted goods and imports from Europe, Mexico, and India.

A walk south from The Village Fair along both sides of Bridgeway reveals one small shop after another, each usually in an old building repainted in cheerful colors. At the south end of town is a pier supporting several restaurants and a parking lot. From here, you get a marvelous view of Richardson Bay and the San Francisco skyline.

At the north end of town, on Bridgeway, is a curious industrial and maritime wasteland dotted with ship hulls, abandoned shipways, old buildings, and scraps of roadways. Here, too, is the colorful houseboat community.

Also on North Bridgeway, at the end of Spring Street, are the U.S. Army Corps of Engineers' San Francisco Bay and Delta models, open to the public weekdays.

## Turn to Tiburon

Tiburon sits on the shores of Richardson Bay, directly opposite Sausalito. To reach Tiburon, take U.S. 101 north from Sausalito to Tiburon Boulevard.

About a mile east from U.S. 101, keep watch for a handsome old Victorian house standing off to the right in a grove of cypress. This is headquarters for the 800-acre Wildlife Sanctuary managed by the Audubon Society. About 8,000 birds are residents; as many as 30,000 more may stop by at peak migratory seasons. The refuge is open to visitors Wednesday through Sunday from 9 A.M. to 5 P.M.

**Sausalito ferry** *loads passengers for commute run across San Francisco Bay to city offices.*

**Victorian home and grounds**
*(headquarters for Audubon Wildlife Sanctuary) attract Tiburon birdwatcher.*

**Modern interior** *of Marin's Civic Center, designed by Frank Lloyd Wright, looks out on rolling hills that inspired building's design.*

Follow Tiburon Boulevard down to the water and park your car in one of several parking areas. Main Street's first block is Tiburon's downtown: shoulder-to-shoulder shops, art galleries, and dockside, view-of-the-water restaurants.

Beach Road will take you over Belvedere Lagoon, past the yacht club and the old, shingled headquarters of the Belvedere Land Company, in business since 1889. Should you consider driving up and around and down Belvedere? Belvedere's roadways generally range from 14 to 16 feet wide. Our suggestion is to head your car up and keep to the right (west); road signs are confusing, but you will get around without getting lost.

Commuters use the ferry from Tiburon to San Francisco during the working week. In the summer, tourists can take dinner cruises to Tiburon (Thursday evening) and lunch cruises daily from San Francisco. Call Tiburon Cruises at 391-2137 for information.

## Roaming Through Marin

Small towns are grouped near Marin's main north-south thoroughfare—U.S. 101. Many are in canyons west of the highway. San Rafael extends down to the bay, and you can now take the bridge across the bay to Richmond, on its east side.

A historic old saw mill (from which Mill Valley got its name) still stands in skeleton form. The charming public square in the center of town evokes memories of England. From here you can see the meandering streets and the steeply gabled roofs of lovely homes nestled in the hills surrounding the town.

Marin's most traveled east-west road is Sir Francis Drake Boulevard. It threads its way from U.S. 101 west to the Pt. Reyes Peninsula. Along its route you'll pass the towns of Ross, a treasury of stately homes with an Art and Garden Center, and San Anselmo, once the junction for railroad lines throughout Marin. Like a medieval French castle, the San Francisco Theological Seminary dominates the southern hillside. Near Fairfax, to the west, are the lovely lakes of Bon Tempe, Lagunitas, Alpine, and Phoenix—ideal for picnicking, hiking, and horseback riding.

In San Rafael you'll find a replica of Mission San Rafael Archangel, founded in 1817; Boyd Park and Museum; the Marin Historical Society Museum; and to the east on San Pablo Bay, a fishing village and swimming beach.

Nestled in a group of hills just north of town is the imaginative, domed Marin Civic Center, designed by Frank Lloyd Wright. It's open daily and there's no charge to look around. Here, also, stands the recently completed Veterans' Memorial Auditorium-Theater, a center for performing arts.

Situated in the rolling hills of northern Marin County, Novato's residential areas reflect its early Spanish settlers.

Each fall the Renaissance Pleasure Faire, an Elizabethan festival, is held on the meadows south of State Highway 37. At this replica of an English country fair, you'll find food, drink, crafts, and entertainment—both on stage and off. For information, write to Renaissance Pleasure Faire, 3440 Clay St., San Francisco, CA 94118.

# High to Low: Marin's Parks

Ranging from an island in the bay to one of the bay area's tallest peaks, Marin's parks are a varied lot. Marin, curiously, has greater extremes of climate than the counties farther north, principally because Mt. Tamalpais and the high ridges leading up to it form a sharp barrier against sea fogs.

## Angel Island State Park

Part of the fun of going to Angel Island is how you get there. A tour boat of the Red & White Fleet

**Annual Renaissance Faire** *attracts merry crowds of costumed visitors to Marin's rural countryside.*

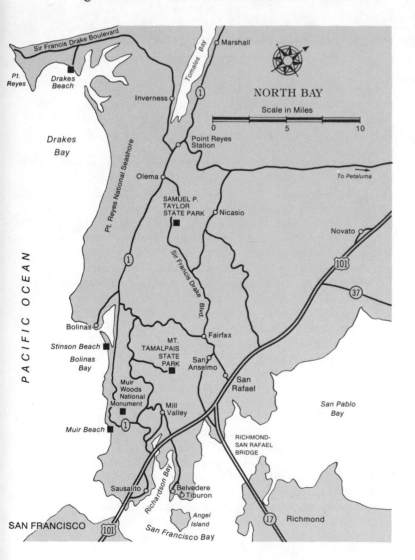

(pier 43½) at San Francisco's Fisherman's Wharf or a ferry from Tiburon will bring you to the island in the morning and pick you up in the afternoon. Or you can make the trip in a private boat.

At Ayala Cove, the entrance to Angel Island, you'll find picnic facilities, beaches for sunning (no swimming is allowed), and a grassy softball field. Bike rentals are available (summer only), or you can bring along your own. You'll find posted maps of hiking trails. If you take the sightseeing tour of the island, you'll pass through former military installations.

## Mt. Tamalpais—for the view

"Mt. Tam" is the keystone unit of four park units that have common boundaries. A finger reaches down to sea level at Muir Beach, but the main body of the park drapes across the upper slopes of the 2,571-foot mountain. Here you'll find a labyrinthine network of hiking and equine trails.

Picnic grounds are at the Bootjack area on the Panoramic Highway leading up from Mill Valley, near the park headquarters; campsites are at Pan Toll and still higher at East Peak. The large parking area at East Peak is as far as cars can go. Paths lead up the last couple of hundred feet to the summit.

**For campers:** Pan Toll Campground, with unimproved sites a short stroll beyond the parking area, is heavily booked from spring through autumn. Sites are scattered among shady groves.

**For hikers:** Trails offer endless variety of terrain and distance. You can pick up a trail map at the headquarters; the trails are clearly posted and well-groomed.

**Boats dock** *in quiet Angel Island cove for picnic in middle of San Francisco Bay. State park offers excellent views of San Francisco and Marin cities.*

**Dwarfed by tall trees,** *visitors pause near Bohemian Grove in Muir Woods National Monument, closest redwoods to San Francisco.*

Steep Ravine Trail follows the course of Webb Creek from Pan Toll (1,150-feet elevation) down to Muir Beach. Round-trip distance is 3½ tough miles. Any number of routes from Pan Toll cross the ridges to Samuel P. Taylor Park to the north. Although it's quite a hike and the summer heat is a factor, the terrain is relatively gentle.

For day-use, the park closes a half-hour after sundown and opens a half-hour before sunrise.

## Muir Woods: closest redwoods to San Francisco

Always cool and green, the 502-acre national monument named for the famous naturalist John Muir preserves a stand of virgin coast redwoods *(Sequoia sempervirens)* at the foot of Mt. Tamalpais.

For a leisurely walk, follow the ½-mile, sign-guided Bootjack Trail. Redwoods and Douglas fir

tower above the forest floor, and you will also find tanoak, alder, buckeye, and California laurel, from which one type of bay leaf finds its way into spice jars.

The central part of the park and most of its paths are on a relatively level stretch of forest floor. If you want to do some exploring off the main trail, consider the two trails that climb high up the canyon wall to lookout points and a panoramic view to either side of the Golden Gate.

Muir Woods is open daily during daylight hours. There's a slight admission fee. No camping or picnicking is allowed.

You can reach the woods by way of State 1 and the Panoramic Highway. The road into the park, like all those flanking Mt. Tamalpais, is narrow and winds tortuously up the long grade from sea level. Its innumerable blind curves require cautious driving. Passengers can enjoy the view.

# To the East Bay

Although the East Bay's "big city" reputation may not equal that of San Francisco, some of its attractions can match or even exceed those of the fabled sister in whose shadow Oakland and its surrounding towns dwell.

## Oakland: A City to Reckon With

The major East Bay city and the third largest city in Northern California, Oakland is an important industrial center and shipping port. Long eclipsed in prominence by across-the-bay San Francisco, Oakland has finally emerged as a city in its own right. In addition to containing several impressive recreational areas, Oakland prides itself on its international airport, its impressive sports complex, and its exceptional new museum. Here, too, is the headquarters of BART—the Bay Area Rapid Transit System.

For an overall view of the Oakland area (including the nearby cities of Alameda, Piedmont, and

**Escalators carry passengers** *down to BART's new subway platform at Oakland's Lake Merritt station.*

Berkeley), take a summer sightseeing bus tour. On the 2½-hour tour, which operates between Memorial Day and Labor Day, guides narrate historical features of the area. The tour begins at Jack London Square daily except Monday at 1 P.M.

If you wish to explore the area yourself by car, follow the bright blue "Scenic Tour Oakland" signs, starting with Jack London Square.

For more specific information on attractions, write to the Oakland Chamber of Commerce Convention and Visitors Bureau, 1320 Webster St., Oakland, CA 94612, or call (415) 451-7800.

**Riding BART** is an experience for anyone who equates a transportation system with New York City's antiquated subway. Moving from underground stations to elevated heights, shining BART cars range from Richmond and Concord on the north to Fremont on the south and underneath the bay through San Francisco to Daly City. Visit BART Headquarters (800 Madison St.) for a route map.

**Oakland's International Airport,** within minutes of downtown, is served by interstate and major U.S. carriers. Limousine and bus service is available to Berkeley, downtown Oakland, and San Francisco.

**The Port of Oakland** is Northern California's leading shipping center. It's a beehive of activity that is fun to drive through, watching cargo from all over the world being unloaded. The new 140-acre Seventh Street Terminal is probably the easiest to reach, though you can watch the ships pass in and out of the Oakland Estuary from Jack London Square.

## Highlights of a City

It's fairly easy to get around in Oakland—many of the city's chief attractions are located near the city center. You'll find a variety of activities to delight both children and adults.

### Lake Merritt's North Shore

A favorite recreational spot for Oakland and other East Bay residents, Lake Merritt is a 155-acre body of salt water right in the heart of the city. The Y-shaped lake is encircled by a park strip and a main thoroughfare. Green lawns and cool shade greet you as you turn off Grand Avenue and enter Lakeside Park to sample its variety of activities.

**Children's Fairyland,** an imaginative land of make-believe, is a collection of replicas of favorite nursery rhyme settings. To enter you step (adults stoop) through the "instep" in the dwelling of the Old Woman Who Lived in a Shoe. Paths through landscaped grounds lead you to the Sugar Plum Tree, Three Men in a Tub, the Walrus and the Carpenter, Chinese Tree House, and the Owl and the Pussycat. Noah's Ark is overloaded with animal passengers. When appropriate, the sets are animated with live pets that children may feed—Mary's lamb, the Little Red Hen, and cavorting sea lions outside the house of the carpenter.

Fairyland is open from 10 A.M. to 5:30 P.M. daily during the summer, weekends and holidays during the winter. Admission fees are minimal.

**The Lakeside Nursery Gardens,** just east of Fairyland, serve as a propagating nursery for the plants, shrubs, and trees planted in the Oakland parks and as an all-year floral show garden.

In the heart of the gardens is the Lakeside Park Garden Center, where garden club meetings and flower shows are held. The newest feature is a lush Polynesian garden in the greenhouse behind the center. The gardens are open daily to the public.

**The oldest waterfowl refuge** in the country is an area on the northeast arm of the lake. The refuge was set aside in 1870 for the protection of the ducks and other waterfowl that flock to the lake. Between November and April, the bird count here sometimes goes as high as 5,000.

You can buy a bag of grain and feed the birds or watch them any day at 3:30 P.M. being fed by park naturalists, who help you identify the migratory birds currently occupying the refuge. Some of the birds in residence are the whistling swan (the only wild swan in California), coot (or mud hen), pintail, mallard, and canvasback. Birds banded here have been traced as far away as Siberia.

**The Rotary Natural Science Center,** open daily, is adjacent to the duck feeding area. Its handsome and informative exhibits appeal to both amateur and professional natural scientists. Children will enjoy the glass beehive.

**Other activities** around the lake include lawn bowling and putting greens, summer band concerts, and boating facilities. The sailboat clubhouse near the wildlife refuge has launching ramps for sailboats and motorboats. Indoor storage areas for sailboats are also available here for a small fee. On the west shore of Lake Merritt is the main boathouse, where you can rent canoes, rowboats, and sailboats. Launch trips around the lake leave from here at frequent intervals during the day.

## Kaiser Center

The 28-story Kaiser Center, home of Kaiser Industries, covers the block bounded by Lakeside Drive,

**Twilight cyclists** *follow 3-mile path around Oakland's Lake Merritt.*

**Ever-hungry ducks** *get handout from girls at Oakland waterfowl refuge.*

20th, Webster, and 21st streets. Of particular interest is an attractive 4-acre roof garden atop the center's garage.

The garden is remarkable because all of the plants grow in artificial soil. Altogether there are some 5,000 cubic yards of this planting mix on the roof of the garage. In it are planted 42 specimen trees, 1,700 shrubs, and hundreds of flowers. The landscaping is completed by a lawn, a pool with 8,800 square feet of water surface, and three fountains. A restaurant featuring French cuisine overlooks the gardens.

## For excitement, try Oakland's museum

Oakland's grand new museum covers four square blocks and sits alongside and beneath an evergreen park. The three-tiered complex is so constructed that the roof of each level becomes a garden and terrace for the one above. To enter the museum at 10th and Fallon streets, on the south shore of Lake Merritt, you walk down, not up.

The basic concept of the museum is not only intriguing but, in many ways, unique. Three different disciplines—history, natural science, and art—are combined into one museum, and the museum displays its wares as environments. You'll see actual rooms—kitchens, parlors, offices out of the past—or vivid displays suggesting a historical period, such as the time of an election campaign, the gold rush era, or the 1906 earthquake.

In natural science each display presents some ecological message.

The museum is open daily except Monday with late closing on Friday evenings; small admission charge. In addition to streetside parking nearby, you'll find parking beneath the museum.

## Pause for history at Jack London Square

Oakland's waterfront, the birthplace of the city, centers around historic Jack London Square, a 10-block area located on the Oakland Estuary at the foot of Broadway. Here, around landscaped malls, shipping wharves, and marina docks, are some of Oakland's finest restaurants and shops.

Of special interest is the First and Last Chance Saloon, a weathered and rustic old building located

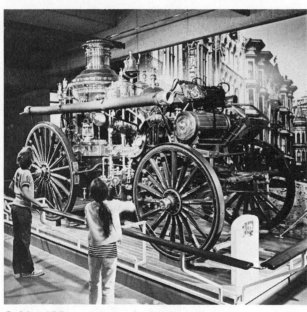

**Oakland Museum's** *meticulously restored American-La France fire engine intrigues youngsters. It was actually used in San Francisco's 1906 disaster.*

**Roof of Oakland Museum** *is terraced hillside park open to each gallery level and linked by wide stairway to courtyard below.*

**Famous saloon** *in Oakland's Jack London Square has memorabilia of author's visits, offers refreshments.*

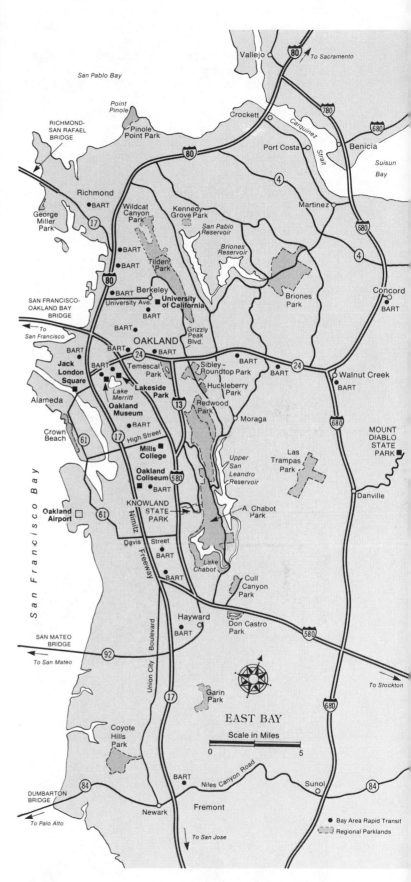

on the edge of the Square at 50 Webster Street. Built in 1880 from the remains of an old whaling ship, the building was first a bunkhouse for oystermen and later a saloon. A favorite boyhood hangout of California author Jack London, the saloon is filled with photos and mementos of London. It's open from 1 P.M. to 2 A.M. daily except Sunday. Ask the bartender about its interesting history.

Nearby is the replica of a Yukon cabin that sheltered London in the Klondike in the winter of 1897-98. Complete visitor information is available at the visitors' kiosk in the center of the square.

## Oakland sports complex

The Oakland-Alameda County Coliseum complex is two separate circular structures—an outdoor stadium and an indoor arena. At the outdoor stadium you can watch professional football and baseball; in the arena; ice hockey, basketball, stage shows, and civic and cultural activities take place. The Coliseum complex is well designed—every seat is comfortable and provides a good view of the attraction. Adjacent to the arena floor is an exhibit hall, where trade, boat, home, and car shows are held.

The coliseum is just east of the Nimitz Freeway. Take the Hegenberger or 66th Avenue exit to the spacious parking lot.

## Knowland State Park: home of the zoo

Animals—real ones and sculptured ones—welcome visitors to the Oakland Zoo, located at Knowland State Park. One observation point allows you to look a Bengal tiger right in the eye. From across a narrow moat, you can toss peanuts to Malaysian sun bears. Children are welcome to pick up the goat kids and piglets and to pet a baby llama.

A unique ape cage, 50 feet high, dramatically towers over the park like a giant inverted basket. For a good look at the entire zoo, ride the 1,250-foot-long chair lift that takes you high up in the East Bay hills. As you glide up the hill, you pass over the "African veldt" and on to the newest display area—the "high veldt," where deer, elk, and buffalo range. A child-scaled train also makes regular trips through the zoo, which is open daily.

To reach the zoo, take the Golf Links Road turn-off from MacArthur Freeway (Interstate 580).

## A look at Victorians

Many of Oakland's old homes have been torn down, and many are run-down, but a few choice examples of Victoriana remain.

**Bret Harte Boardwalk,** close to Jack London Square (at Fifth Street between Jefferson and Clay), has a one-block array of old Victorian houses and barns, renovated specialty shops, and tearooms. Bret Harte's home once stood across the street.

**Dunsmuir house,** in southern Oakland, is a notable product of Victorian wealth and taste. The 37-room estate cost a cool $250,000 in 1898. The house and its 48-acre grounds are open to the public on Sundays from noon to 4 P.M. Golden Gate Park designer John McLaren did the landscaping; that alone is worth a visit. There's a nominal admission charge.

## Some more visual treats around town

A few other buildings deserve at least a "pass-by." The Paramount Theatre of the Arts (2025 Broad-

**Concert-goers** *at Oakland's Paramount Theatre of the Arts descend staircase in restored 1930s lobby.*

way) was an opulent movie palace in the 1930s. Carefully restored, it is now a center for concerts and ballet. On the 4700 block of Lincoln Avenue are two architectural treasures: the Mormon Temple and the Greek Orthodox Church. For a parkside stop, visit the Morcom Rose Garden at Jean Street off Grand Avenue. And to view the stars, ascend Mountain Boulevard to the Chabot Science Center on Friday or Saturday evening for a 7:30 show (small admission charge).

# Berkeley Backs up to a University

A former factory town, Berkeley achieved both fame and notoriety from the world's largest educational institution—the University of California. It's an inviting place to park your car and walk around —especially if you're interested in the latest fad or food. Telegraph Avenue, just south of the campus, has a 4-block stretch (between Bancroft and Dwight ways) where street artists and craftsmen display their wares.

Facing San Francisco, Berkeley's new marina has a boat basin, sandy beaches, picnic areas, trails, lookout points, a fishing pier, and several new restaurants.

## University of California—Bear country

Spreading up into the hills and surrounded by sections of Berkeley, the buildings of the 720-acre Berkeley campus of the University of California stand out against the landscape, with the unmistakable outline of Sather Tower (the Campanile).

Parking on the campus is subject to control at all hours. Cars without parking permits are admitted to the campus only after 8 P.M. daily. The campus is always open to public foot traffic.

For a magnificent view of the campus, the whole East Bay area, and San Francisco across the water, take the elevator to the top of the 307-foot Campanile, open daily between 10 A.M. and 5 P.M.

Visitors to Berkeley can take a walking tour of the campus. Pick up a brochure outlining the nearly 2-mile walk (about 1½ hours) at the visitors' desk in the Student Union at the end of Telegraph Avenue. Escorted tours leave from the Student Union at 1 P.M. weekdays.

You'll want to see the California Memorial Stadium (it has a seating capacity of 78,000), where the Golden Bear football team plays out its fall schedule; pace across the 133-foot stage of the Greek Theatre, a beautiful amphitheater presented to the university by Phoebe Appersen Hearst in 1903; linger on the footbridges that cross Strawberry

University of California's *familiar Campanile rises above campus of state's largest school.*

In Berkeley *you can watch harbor action from waterfront restaurant* (above) *at new marina, or* (left) *can inspect crafts that vendors sell along Telegraph Avenue.*

Creek, a thin stream that becomes fairly boisterous after the first rains; and visit the Botanical Garden (located near the stadium in Strawberry Canyon), a 35-acre tract of plantings including many rare rhododendrons, cactuses, and succulents.

One architectural highlight is the university's new art museum—a sculpture in itself. A jumble of jutting balconies, staggered levels, interesting angles, open galleries, and ramps—all arranged around an open central gallery—the museum is open daily except Monday; it has late closing each Tuesday and Thursday.

## Lawrence Hall of Science— touch, don't look

This boldly designed complex, built as a research facility for science education, has exhibit areas housing dozens of colorful, do-it-yourself displays demonstrating scientific principles at children's level. Youngsters operate complex electronic equipment and control preprogrammed experiments.

Open daily, the Lawrence Hall of Science is located on North Canyon Road, reached from Gay-

ley Road on the east side of the campus or from Grizzly Peak Boulevard, a scenic route that follows the crest of the East Bay hills. There's a slight admission charge.

## East Bay Regional Parks: Something for Everyone

In the low hills that rise behind the East Bay cities, some 33,000 acres of beautiful countryside have been set aside for recreational use. About 1,000 acres of San Francisco Bay beach and swampland in Alameda and Contra Costa counties have also been incorporated into the East Bay Regional Park System. Some of the parks are small, some large; some are highly developed, some relatively untouched and primitive. Many miles of hiking and bridle trails lead through unspoiled woods and fields. Picnicking, swimming, fishing, boating, and archery are offered at most of the parks, which are primarily designed for daytime use.

Parks of particular interest are Tilden (Environmental Education Center, model railway, Little

Farm), Temescal (a unique entrance tunnel features walls that are brightly painted with interesting art designs), Redwood (redwood groves, heated outdoor swimming pool), Chabot (marina and horse rental), Crown (beachcombing), Pt. Pinole (biking and hiking), Shadow Cliffs (swimming), Coyote Hills (ancient Indian shellmounds), and Black Diamond Mines (historical area).

For detailed information and a free brochure on all the parks in the region, write to the East Bay Regional Park District, 11500 Skyline Blvd., Oakland, CA 94619.

## Up Mt. Diablo

Mt. Diablo's summit is an exceptionally fine view point. On a clear day you can see as far as the Sierra, Mt. Lassen, San Francisco, and the inland waterways of the Central Valley. Because such an expanse of California is visible, Mt. Diablo has been the surveying point for Northern and Central California since 1851.

Diablo's main peak is only 3,849 feet in elevation; however, it seems higher because it rises so abruptly. Occasionally during the winter the conical peak gets a coating of snow.

A state park covers a portion of the area with 80 campsites, group camping facilities and about 250 picnic sites. You'll find a number of good hiking trails. The park is open all year; day-use hours are

from 8 A.M. until dark. You can reach Mt. Diablo from Interstate Highway 680 at Danville.

## Along the Carquinez Strait

Pt. Costa, seen from the Carquinez Strait, is just a tuck in the rolling Contra Costa hills. Yet in the last part of the 19th century this town of 250 residents was a large wheat shipping port.

Pt. Costa's most interesting structures are the empty hotel, the old Chinese laundry, the warehouse-shops, and the charred stumps that mark the site of the docks. All are on Main Street close to the water.

At Martinez, east of Pt. Costa, is the John Muir Historic Site. You can follow Pomona St. from Pt. Costa or take Interstate 80 to State Highway 4. Follow State 4 to Alhambra Avenue and turn left under the overpass. The John Muir home is about 100 yards beyond the overpass to the left.

In the old, gray, 17-room house, John Muir, ardent conservationist and founder of the Sierra Club, and his wife lived between 1890 and 1914. The rooms are decorated with furniture, clothing, and memorabilia of the period.

Tours of the house start every hour from 1 to 4 P.M. Wednesday through Sunday. There's a small admission charge for visitors over 15 years of age.

Across the strait is Benicia, California's state capital in 1853-54. Once a thriving port, today it is quiet. Many of its weathered buildings house antique shops. The two-story State Capitol Building (built in 1852), still stands, now restored as a State Historic Park.

The Benicia Chamber of Commerce (737 First Street), open weekdays, has maps and a walking-tour booklet.

**Riders** in Briones Regional Park enjoy pastoral scene on network of trails through low East Bay hills.

**Capitol Building** in Benicia, erected in 1852, was home for legislature before Solons moved to Sacramento.

# Down the Peninsula

Geographically, Palo Alto lies at the end of the San Francisco Peninsula. But generally the cities of Mountain View, Los Altos, Sunnyvale, Santa Clara, and San Jose are considered as part of this region. This area at the southern tip of the bay is the scene of heavy industry. Moffett Naval Air Station is located here, along with many electronics and chemical firms and a variety of large and small businesses.

Several main routes run down the peninsula from San Francisco. State Highway 1 skirts the coast, Skyline Boulevard (State Highway 35) follows the ridge of the mountains, and Junipero Serra Freeway (Interstate 280) runs along the east side of the mountain spine. The Bayshore Freeway (U.S. Highway 101) and El Camino Real (State Highway 82) go through the population centers that edge the bay.

The Santa Cruz Highway (State Highway 17) offers a delightful, easy-to-drive connecting route from the southern end of the bay across the Santa Cruz mountains to the coast. The highway climbs in long, sweeping curves through beautifully wooded slopes. Traffic is generally light, except on summer weekends, when cars head toward the cool coastal areas and the popular beach parks around Santa Cruz.

A more northerly cross-peninsula route, State Highway 92, leaves Bayshore Freeway (and El Camino Real) at San Mateo and reaches the coast at Half Moon Bay. It intersects Skyline Boulevard at Crystal Springs Reservoir.

## Traveling the Bayshore

Originally, the peninsula cities grew as suburbs of San Francisco. But in recent years the ideal climate and pleasant living conditions of the area have attracted industry, business, and an ever-increasing residential population that works where it lives—on the peninsula.

Two main highways lead south from San Francisco through these urban areas. You can drive from San Francisco to the southern tip of the bay without encountering a stop light. But Bayshore is not a scenic route—much of the time it consists of bleak bay views and uninspiring subdivisions.

El Camino Real roughly parallels Bayshore Freeway all the way to San Jose. But whereas the freeway skirts along the edge of the bay, El Camino slowly passes through the towns. This is the route to take if you want a sampling of the peninsula's commercial and residential areas. Bayshore Freeway and El Camino Real are but a short distance apart, and frequently there is a connecting road.

A third express freeway—Interstate 280—is a highly scenic route that leads from downtown San Francisco to San Jose. Avoiding urban clutter, it winds through oak-studded foothills high above the bay.

**Candlestick Park** stadium huddles along the edge of Candlestick Point, on the bay side of the freeway. The stadium is in use almost all year: the San Francisco Giants play baseball from mid-April to late September, and the San Francisco '49ers play football from September to December. Candlestick is 8 miles south of San Francisco.

**The Cow Palace,** a huge, strangely named sports arena, is on Geneva Avenue in San Mateo County. This is the site of the Grand National livestock exposition, horse show, and rodeo, a very popular event that draws large crowds of spectators every fall. You can also attend basketball games, circuses, prize fights, and big conventions in its vast arena.

**Bay Meadows Race Track,** next to Bayshore Freeway in San Mateo, is where the horses run from September to June. Times and admission vary according to type of racing. Call (415) 345-1661 for information.

**San Francisco International Airport** spreads along the edge of the bay east of the highway near San Bruno. Two terminals accommodate the 15 million air travelers that pass through the airport annually.

The seven-story Central Terminal Building has restaurants, lounges, shops, and an observation deck. The South Terminal Building, an 800-foot, sweeping arc structure, also provides passenger facilities.

**Exclusive residential areas** are located in the hills south and west of Burlingame. A short side trip into Hillsborough takes you through beautiful grounds and past palatial homes. Atherton, a heavily wooded area south of Redwood City, also contains many large estates.

Woodside, set in the foothills, is another area of fine homes with more of a rural look. Many residents own horses, and riding trails and pasture land are an integral part of the community. The center of town, reached along Woodside Road west of El Camino Real, is actually quite small—little more than a village. The old one-room Woodside Store, built in 1854, is open as a county museum Wednesday through Saturday and on Sunday afternoons. South of Woodside many interesting homes are tucked into the hills of Portola Valley.

**Large shopping centers** invite browsing. You'll find well-stocked stores at Serramonte Center, Daly City; Hillsdale Mall, San Mateo; Stanford, Palo Alto; Town and Country Shopping Centers, Palo Alto and west San Jose; Eastridge Mall, east San Jose; and the Pruneyard and the Factory, Campbell.

## Special stops along the way

A few of the main peninsula attractions deserve a special stop or make rewarding destinations. Plan to spend a couple of hours for maximum enjoyment.

**Marine World/Africa USA** is located on a 60-acre stretch of tidal flats east of Bayshore Freeway in Redwood City. This sprawling, well-landscaped refuge seems to be owned by the animals who kindly let people in to applaud their acts. And there is plenty to applaud: six spectacular shows featuring aquatic and land animals and 50 other attractions, including a rubber-raft cruise winding through facsimiles of the Amazon and African veldt—created as much for the animals populating the shores as for the people viewing them. A single moderate admission price allows you to spend the day. Marine World is open daily during the summer and, depending on the weather, most of the winter. For information on features, transportation, and hours, call (415) 365-7446.

**Sunset Magazine and Sunset Books,** in Menlo Park, welcome visitors to their editorial and business offices. The two buildings are located at Willow and Middlefield roads (between Bayshore Freeway and El Camino Real). Hostesses are on hand Monday through Friday for conducted tours at 10:30 and 11:30 A.M. and 1, 2, and 3 P.M. You will see the kitchen where all recipes are tested before they are published, and you can stroll through the extensive demonstration gardens of outstanding trees, shrubs, and flowers native to all sections of the Pacific Coast from the Northwest to Mexico.

**Allied Arts Guild,** at Arbor Road and Creek Drive in Menlo Park, offers a glimpse of the early, more leisurely Spanish California. The 3½-acre site that the guild occupies is part of the once vast Spanish land grant, El Rancho de las Pulgas (Ranch of the Fleas). The original barn and sheep sheds of the old ranch still stand but now house the shops of craftsmen. New buildings, containing a variety of shops, preserve the Spanish Colonial theme of the original ranch. In the dining room, luncheon and tea are served; advance reservations are needed. The Guild is open daily except Sunday from 9:30 A.M. until 5 P.M.

**Petting a tiger** *is a thrill for children visiting Marine World/Africa USA.*

**Hostess offers tours** *through* Sunset's *Menlo Park offices and grounds.*

# Business Tours Around the Bay

Many industries offer free tours to visitors. Some require advance notice. Here is just a sample of the variety you will find:

**Marin French Cheese Co.** Watch cheese being made. The factory is the busiest—and most interesting—weekday mornings. Guided tours are daily at 7500 Red Hill Rd. in Petaluma.

**California Maritime Academy.** Weekdays at 1 P.M. you can tour the Vallejo headquarters of the American Merchant Marines. You'll see training facilities and some ships. (Children must be in the 6th grade or higher.)

**Shasta Beverages.** Hour-long tours of bottling plant with free refreshments. Call 783-3200 at least 2 weeks in advance for appointment to visit the Hayward plant.

**Leslie Salt.** Located on Central Avenue in Newark, the refinery offers 1-hour tours including a film on harvesting salt. Call 797-1820 to visit.

**Rod McLellan Co.** Daily tours at 10:30 A.M. and 1:30 P.M. of the world's largest hybrid orchid grower. You'll see scientific labs and lush tropical grounds at 1450 El Camino Real in South San Francisco.

**Ames Research Center.** Tours go through the big wind tunnel, flight simulation facilities, and flight operations hangar at Moffett Field weekdays at 9:30 and 10:30 A.M. and 1 and 2:45 P.M.

**Edelweiss Dairy.** By booking a month or more in advance, you can tour this dairy Monday through Saturday at 9 A.M. It's located at 17717 Old Mt. View-Alviso Rd., Santa Clara; phone 984-8484.

## Stanford University—the elegant "Farm"

University Avenue, Palo Alto's main business street, crosses El Camino Real on an overpass southeast of Menlo Park. West of El Camino Real, University becomes Palm Drive, the approach to Stanford.

At the entrance of the Quadrangle at the end of Palm Drive, the Stanford Guide Service Information Center has an assortment of maps (one outlines a tour of the campus) and descriptive material. The center is open daily from 10 A.M. to 4 P.M. Guided tours leave daily at 11 A.M. and 2 P.M. from the center.

An easily visible campus landmark is the 285-foot tower of the Hoover Institution of War, Revolution, and Peace. An elevator goes to the top where you get a visual orientation of the campus. Call 497-2053 for visiting hours.

You'll want to see the Memorial Church, dedicated in 1903 and completely rebuilt after the 1906 earthquake. The large cruciform church is decorated with Venetian mosaics, most striking of which are reproductions of "The Sermon on the Mount" on the front facade and Rosselli's "Last Supper" in the chancel. Except when services are in progress, the church is open to visitors from 10 A.M. to 5 P.M. daily.

Northwest of the general campus buildings on Quarry Road is the Stanford University Medical Center. It is best known for its pioneering work in the development of uses of the atom for treatment of cancer, basic techniques of heart transplantation, and programs for understanding basic causes of mental retardation. A tour of the medical center leaves from the information desk in the hos-

**Hoover Tower,** *Stanford University landmark, houses political science library. East Asian Library is near.*

pital lobby; call 497-6389 for times.

Located on Lomita Drive and Museum Way, northeast of the Medical Center, is the Stanford University Museum of Art. Among the museum's permanent exhibits are galleries of ancient Oriental, Egyptian, and primitive art, baroque paintings, and early Californiana. Of particular interest is the Rodin exhibit—a "working" collection designed to teach rather than entertain—and the Stanford Collection, with exhibits of family photographs and paintings, Leland Stanford Jr.'s boyhood collection of toys and artifacts, and other memorabilia.

Hours are weekdays except Mondays from 10 A.M. to 4:45 P.M., weekends from 1 A.M. to 4:45 P.M. Admission is free.

# Metropolitan San Jose Area

Spreading out from the tip of San Francisco Bay, the Metropolitan San Jose area has undergone an industrial explosion which transformed the northern section of the Santa Clara Valley from an agricultural region to a big manufacturing center. Small semi-rural communities have expanded into side-by-side urban areas. The San Jose region is composed of a multitude of housing subdivisions and many industrial parks; however, there are also some interesting attractions. For a taped message on what to see and do, call 293-4678.

## San Jose: a growing city on the bay

One of the nation's fastest-growing cities, San Jose originated in 1777 with a population of 66. It remained a small town, taking a back seat to the famous city farther north, until the early 1950s when industry moved in and opened up the area. Although many orchards were removed to provide housing for the growing population, San Jose is still a major canning and fruit-drying center.

**Kelley Park** is one of the city's most popular spots. Here is a 2-acre zoo with almost a hundred animals on view in 14 exhibit areas. One of the best exhibits is the abovewater and underwater river otter section. The zoo is open daily. Take the Story Road exit off U.S. 101 and continue 4 blocks south to the zoo. Also at Kelley Park are the Japanese Friendship Gardens and the popular children's playground—Happy Hollow, open daily in summer.

**The Winchester Mystery House,** 4 miles west of the city at the Winchester Road exit off Interstate 280, is a State Historical Landmark. Sarah Winchester, heir to her father-in-law's gun fortune, was an eccentric who believed that, if she stopped adding rooms onto her house, she would die. The 160-room house, now being refurnished, is a memorial to her

obsession. Tours cover 6 acres of Victorian splendor—the house, museum, and extensive gardens—daily from 9 A.M. for a moderate charge.

**Other attractions** in San Jose include the 5½-acre Municipal Rose Garden at Naglee and Dana avenues; San Jose State University at 125 So. Seventh St.; Alum Rock Park at the end of Alum Rock Road in the foothills; Egyptian museum (a library, art gallery, and planetarium at Rosicrucian Park at 1342 Naglee Ave.); and Frontier Village, just south of the city on Monterey Road.

**A new attraction,** opening in the spring of 1976, is Marriott's Great America, a 600-acre theme park. Five historical areas open up from the Carousel Plaza (with the world's largest, two-level merry-go-round): Hometown Square, Country Fair, Yukon Territory, Yankee Harbor, and Orleans Place. Emphasis is on live entertainment and spectator action. To reach Great America, take the exit marked with its name from both Bayshore and State Highway 237. Admission fee includes all attractions.

## Mt. Hamilton's Lick Observatory

Twenty miles southeast of San Jose, the University of California's Lick Observatory is reached by a winding narrow road that climbs to the summit of 4,209-foot Mt. Hamilton.

Visitors are welcome every Saturday and Sunday (except national and university holidays) from 1 to 5 P.M. Guide service is provided at no charge. Of particular interest is the 120-inch reflector telescope (second largest in the world) that you view from a small gallery in the dome where it is housed.

## Mission Santa Clara de Asis

Eighth in the chain of California missions, Santa Clara de Asis, founded in 1777 along the banks of the Guadalupe River, had several locations and structures. The present site was selected and the church constructed in 1825. One hundred years later, fire practically destroyed the mission; however, in 1929 a concrete replica was completed.

You'll see a few original remnants: a cross, dating back to the founding, stands in a protective covering of redwood in front of the church; a bell, given by the King of Spain in 1778, still tolls in the tower; and a magnificent crucifix hangs above a side altar. Now part of the campus of the University of Santa Clara (on The Alameda), the mission is open daily.

## Los Gatos and Saratoga—two foothill charmers

Los Gatos is a popular shopping stop. You'll also find parks for picnics, charming old residences,

**Old Town** *in Los Gatos—an old schoolhouse transformed into a cluster of small shops and restaurants.*

**Delighted antiques shopper** *discovers wicker-wood perambulator by browsing through Main Street stores in Los Gatos.*

and a winery to tour. To reach this attractive foothill city, take the State 17 turnoff southwest from U.S. 101 in San Jose.

**Old Town**—a lively collection of shops, studios, restaurants, and theaters housed in a converted elementary school—is the best-known attraction. Most stores are open Tuesday through Sunday; most restaurants serve lunch and dinner daily.

Other galleries and antique stores are scattered around the town's main streets. You'll find excellent examples of carpenter's Gothic architecture on homes between Pennsylvania and Hernandez avenues and around Fairview Avenue.

**The Novitiate Winery** is the spot for wine touring. Turn toward the mountains from Main Street onto College Avenue, which leads to Prospect Avenue and the winery. The Novitiate produces sacramental wine for much of the Jesuit order and also sells aperitif, dessert, and a few table wines.

Tours of the hillside winery take place Tuesday and Friday from 2 to 3 P.M. You can taste and buy wine every day except Sunday from 10 to 11 A.M. and 2 to 4 P.M.

Tiny Saratoga's business section (at the intersection of State 85 and 9) is only a few blocks long—but they are blocks of intriguing shops for browsing.

**Hakone Gardens,** tucked into the hills just behind Saratoga, is an unexpected bit of the Orient. Formerly a private garden established in 1917, it is now a city park, open daily from 10 A.M. to dusk. Follow Big Basin Way west about a mile.

**The Paul Masson Champagne Cellars,** at 13150 Saratoga Ave., welcomes visitors daily. Most of the vineyards are farther south at Pinnacles, but Saratoga is where the wine comes for bottling. After your tour, plan to do some sampling in the tasting room. Masson's original winery is the site of "Music in the Vineyards." On weekends in July and August, chamber groups and soloists appear in afternoon programs with a champagne intermission.

# Through the Mountains

Skyline Boulevard (State 35) will take you along the mountain spine of the peninsula. Interstate 280 runs just east of the mountains. The Santa Cruz Mountains, a spur of the Coast Range, stretch from the Crystal Springs area down just below Santa Cruz, east of Monterey Bay. Standing 2,000 to 3,000 feet high, these mountains receive heavy rains in the winter, which help to produce the forests of Douglas fir, pine, madrone, maple, alder, bay, and the towering, shadowy redwoods that make this a shady retreat.

Here you can revel in the fine mountain scenery and enjoy the thrill of catching a glimpse of the ocean on one side and then switching your glance to a grand view of San Francisco Bay on the other.

## What's to see?

You'll pass by Crystal Springs Reservoir, which holds the water supply for San Francisco. Toward the southern end of the reservoir, Interstate 280 intersects Canada Road. If you take Canada north, you see the Pulgas Water Temple at the southern tip of the reservoir. The temple marks the end of the Hetch Hetchy aqueduct, a 162-mile pipeline that begins at an impoundment on the Tuolumne River in the northern section of Yosemite National Park. It's a good place for picnicking, strolling, or just watching the waters surge past.

Some 25 miles south of San Francisco, Skyline Boulevard intersects Kings Mountain Road, a winding, 5-mile route to Woodside. About 2 miles east of Skyline is San Mateo County Huddart Park, with nature trails, a horse-training ring, campsites, and areas for horseshoe pitching, volleyball, and softball.

Parks farther south include Sam McDonald Park, San Mateo County Memorial Park, Pescadero Creek County Park, and Portola State Park. All are to the west of Skyline; some have overnight camping.

## San Lorenzo Valley

Where Skyline Boulevard meets Saratoga Gap, a left turn on State 9 will take you to Saratoga, or you can turn right and take State 9 through the San Lorenzo Valley to the coast, where it meets the

**Girls on ponies** *proudly pass craft shop along State Highway 9 in Santa Cruz Mountains.*

**Roaring Camp & Big Trees steam train** *passes by picnickers along trestle near Felton.*

Coast Highway (State 1) at Santa Cruz.

Shady, wooded San Lorenzo Valley near Santa Cruz offers rich fare for the auto explorer. In the valley and the land that flanks it, you'll see 100-year-old vineyards, lovely mountain streams, handsome ranches, and orchards. You'll wind through groves of giant redwoods and along roads where the evergreen madrones reach across and shut out the sky.

The San Lorenzo River starts near the junction of Skyline Boulevard and State 9, cutting a crooked course diagonally across the west slope of the Coast Range and emptying into the sea at Santa Cruz. State 9 follows the river all the way and is the "main street" of the valley. The valley's towns and most resorts are along this road.

Drive slowly so you won't miss the charm of Boulder Creek, Brookdale, Ben Lomond, Bonny Doon, and Felton—centers for artisans and craftsmen.

Big Basin Redwoods State Park, the first preserve of redwoods ever set aside as a state park, is today one of the most visited forest parks in California. The Big Basin junction is about 6 miles down State 9 from Skyline; it's 8 miles from the junction to the park.

Here you will find magnificent stands of redwoods, over 35 miles of hiking trails, picnic sites, campgrounds, and a couple of streams good for wading. From Big Basin you can hike all the way down to the ocean. Planned summertime recreation includes guided nature hikes and a campfire program. At the nature lodge, open all year, are excellent exhibits of plant and animal life.

A trail has recently been completed connecting Big Basin with the newer Castle Rock State Park, just south of the junction of State Highways 35 and 9.

## Take a ride on the Roaring Camp & Big Trees Railroad

One-half mile south of Felton, you can board a steam train at a quaint old depot for a 5-mile loop trip through thick redwood groves. If you wish, you can stop over at Bear Mountain for picnicking and hiking and return on a later train.

Roaring Camp offers picnic sites, trout fishing, a full-scale replica of a covered bridge, a general store dating back to the 1880s, and an old-fashioned caboose turned restaurant.

Steam passenger trains leave Felton daily on the hour from 11 A.M. to 4 P.M., June through Labor Day; Saturday and Sunday the rest of the year. Fares are moderate.

## Henry Cowell Redwoods State Park

Roaring Camp trains run right alongside this lovely redwood park—their whistles the only disquieting

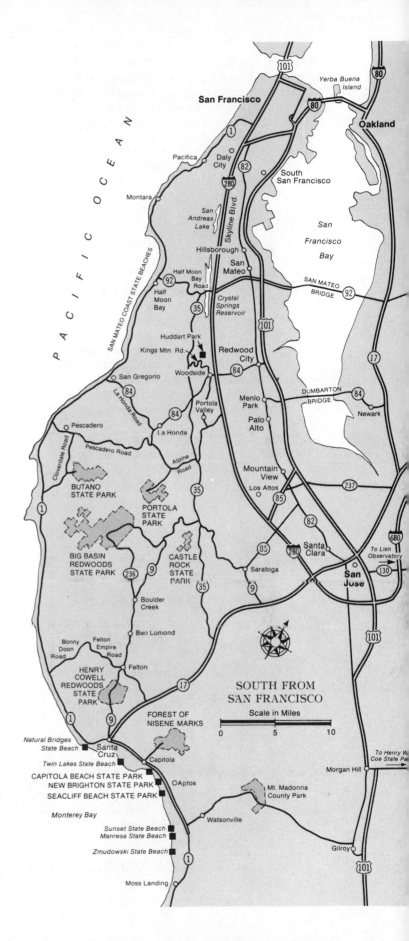

SOUTH FROM SAN FRANCISCO

Scale in Miles

0    5    10

note in the cathedral-like stillness of a mature grove of redwoods and Ponderosa pines. The 4,000-acre park has two streams, good for winter steelhead fishing and inviting for summer swimming and wading.

Although Cowell has a campground, its major use is by daytime visitors, who come to walk the excellent self-guided nature trail. A large redwood sign on State 9 south of Felton marks the park's entrance.

## The Scenic Coast Highway

The most picturesque route down the peninsula is State 1. This Coast Highway follows the shoreline closely, staying away from the larger cities. You won't make good time on this road, but if you enjoy the ocean, beaches, hills, and windswept bluffs, this will be the most enjoyable route.

Several public beaches along the coast are in various stages of development. The most developed areas are invariably the most crowded.

One unpredictable factor about this coast route is the fog that rolls in from the ocean. Sometimes you can see it from San Francisco or peninsula cities as it rolls in over the mountain ridge. On other days, the east side of the peninsula will be sunny and warm, but the minute you reach the top of the mountains, the fog reaches up to you from the other side.

If you continue down the coast as far as Santa Cruz, you can take State 17 back across the mountains and then return to San Francisco by the faster State 101 inland.

**The San Mateo Coast State Beaches,** with headquarters at Half Moon Bay, are a collection of nine beaches scattered along 50 miles of the San Mateo County coast and administered as a single park unit. Though often foggy in summer, these narrow beaches, lying below low coastal bluffs or steep cliffs, are popular for strolling, picnicking, sunbathing, shallow wading, and surf and rock fishing. The currents are too dangerous for safe swimming, though.

North to south the beaches are Thornton, Gray Whale Cove, Montara, Half Moon Bay, San Gregorio, Pomponio, Pescadero, Bean Hollow, and Ano Nuevo (a sea lion reserve). All beaches except Thornton are accessible from State 1.

**Butano State Park** is 7 miles from Pescadero Beach. Here, you can hike, picnic, or camp. Easiest access is from State 1. In addition to dense forests of Douglas fir and redwood, you'll find a creek and a small fern canyon. Three major trails traverse the park's 2,186 acres; from Outlook Trail you get a good view of Ano Nuevo Island just off the coast.

### Santa Cruz has a Victorian soul

The town of Santa Cruz, at the north end of Monterey Bay and at the mouth of the San Lorenzo

**Mimes** *leave Cooper House, former Santa Cruz courthouse now a shopping complex.*

**Sculptured by waves,** *rocky arch is part of Natural Bridges State Park near Santa Cruz.*

River, has undergone some real cultural ferment since the Santa Cruz campus of the University of California was established here in 1965. Santa Cruz is also a repository for much stunning Victorian home architecture. And the city is a good base for exploring the beaches along this section of the California coast.

At the Santa Cruz waterfront, you can fish off the long municipal pier, go deep-sea fishing, enjoy the ocean beach, or try the attractions and rides of the boardwalk.

Pacific Avenue, the main street of the downtown area, is a shopping delight. Now a tree-shaded mall, it's full of crafts shops and interesting restaurants. A star attraction is Cooper House, the former County Courthouse that is now a restaurant-shopping complex.

Seven miles north of Santa Cruz on Highway 17, small fry (and their parents) will enjoy Santa's Village, a make-believe community spreading over 33 wooded acres of Scotts Valley. You'll see Santa's house and his workshop; there's a good chance that Santa himself will be about. Santa's Village is open daily during the summer, weekends and regular school holidays the rest of the year.

Tree-Sea Tour, a 29-mile sightseeing route, has signs marking principal points of interest. Before following the blue and white markers, you should get the Santa Cruz County Convention and Visitors Bureau's accompanying pamphlet, with map, many interesting facts about way points, and motel and restaurant listings. Copies are available from the bureau's office at Church and Center streets.

You'll visit Mission Hill—site of California's 12th mission, founded in 1791—where the city began and where you'll find the largest concentration of "gingerbread" architecture. At the Reliquary (a small museum) attached to the replica of the mission, you can get a pamphlet on the history of Mission Santa Cruz and the surrounding buildings. The oldest building in town is across School Street from the mission. This adobe once served as a guardhouse for Spanish soldiers accompanying the clergy.

At the University of California at Santa Cruz (on High Street in the sloping hills above the city), stop and take a walk through this innovative campus in the woods. You can have lunch at the Whole Earth Restaurant weekdays during the school year. There's a visitor information kiosk just inside the entrance where you can pick up free, detailed campus maps and directions for guide-yourself tours through the forested campus.

## The beach parks

The coast in the Santa Cruz-Capitola area is dotted with excellent beach parks. Most of them have

---

---

clean, wide beaches and are popular with swimmers and surf fishermen. The water is warmer here than along the coast farther north, and the surf is usually gentle.

Three miles west of Santa Cruz, Natural Bridges Beach State Park is an excellent surf fishing, swimming, and picnicking park, and its beautifully arched bridges are a favorite subject of painters and photographers.

Twin Lakes Beach State Park, within the Santa Cruz city limits, is a favorite with local residents. Camping is not permitted, but there are firepits. One lagoon in the park is a wildfowl refuge; a second has been developed into a 350-berth small craft harbor.

Capitola Beach State Park is a small park operated by the city of Capitola. There's a swimming beach, and the city also maintains a fresh-water pool at the mouth of Soquel Creek. Visit the begonia gardens at 2545 Capitola Road. Peak season is in August and September.

Campsites are available at New Brighton and Sunset state beaches. Seacliff State Beach offers trailer hookups and fishing from a unique pier—a 435-foot cement ship, *Palo Alto*. Zmudowski and Manresa state beach parks are day-use-only parks.

# Monterey, Carmel, & Southward

Characterized by white sandy beaches, huge craggy rocks, pounding surf, and twisted cypresses and pines, the Monterey Peninsula juts out into the Pacific Ocean south of Monterey Bay. Not only can you view here one of the most memorable shorelines along the Pacific coast but also you can explore carefully preserved historic Monterey, browse through the shops of charming Carmel, and drive through the densely wooded Del Monte Forest.

The peninsula's ocean setting conditions its weather. Summer months are apt to be overcast; you can expect morning or late evening fog to roll in. In autumn, the days are warm and the sky crystal clear. Rain is frequent from December to March; but even in January, the wettest month, there will be crisp, sunny days.

On the peninsula you'll find numerous accommodations, ranging from old hotels to modern motels. For a listing of places to stay, write to the Monterey Chamber of Commerce and Visitors and Convention Bureau, P.O. Box 1770, Monterey, CA 93940 (telephone (408) 649-3200).

State Highway 1, from north or south, takes you directly through the heart of the Monterey Peninsula. If you want to follow the coastline, exit from the highway and follow the 17-Mile Drive (see page 64).

South of the peninsula, on State 1, the area is almost unpopulated. On your way to San Simeon, site of Hearst Castle, you'll pass through Big Sur country, with the ocean on one side and the Santa Lucia Range on the other. Inland, U.S. Highway 101 will take you to Soledad, Pinnacles National Monument, Salinas, San Juan Bautista, and up to Gilroy and Morgan Hill—new sites for the winegrowing industry.

Plan to extend your visit for several days so you won't miss any of the numerous attractions of one of California's most captivatingly scenic areas.

**Dramatic Big Sur coastline** *where Santa Lucia Mountains sweep down to the sea is a photographers' favorite. Here State Highway 1 crosses inlet on scenic Bixby Bridge.*

# Monterey:
# Mexico's Last Bastion

Juan Rodriguez Cabrillo, a Portuguese explorer sailing for Spain, discovered Monterey Bay in 1542, and Sebastian Vizcaino visited the bay in 1602. But it was not until 1770 that the area was settled. On the south shore of the bay, Gaspar de Portola and Father Junipero Serra established the first of Spain's four California presidios and the second of the Franciscans' 21 Alta California missions. One year later Father Serra moved the mission to its present site on the Carmel River.

Until the middle of the 19th century, Monterey was California's liveliest and most important settlement. It began that century as the Spanish capital of Alta California; in 1822 it became the Mexican capital and in 1846 the American capital. After the discovery of gold in 1848, San Francisco took over as California's number one city. Monterey's 20th century role centers around its tourist and waterfront attractions.

You will find many echoes of the old Spanish and Mexican village of Monterey in today's modern town of 29,000. Many buildings constructed before 1850 still stand, most in good repair. Eleven of them are preserved as historical monuments by the state of California. In downtown Monterey you can follow the dashed red line that guides you past many of these old structures.

## Along the waterfront

The Municipal Wharf extends out into Monterey Bay from the foot of Figueroa Street. Here you can watch commercial fishing boats unload anchovy, cod, kingfish, herring, salmon, sole, and tuna. Seven fish-processing plants share space at the end of this wharf. If you don't mind getting your feet damp, you can watch from doorways as workers clean and pack fish. Municipal Wharf is the best place for pier fishing (the catch ranges from sunfish to tomcod) and for viewing Monterey fronted by its crescent-shaped bay.

**Fisherman's Wharf,** around the Monterey Marina four blocks west of Municipal Wharf, has novelty shops, a commercial aquarium, an art gallery, excursion boats, several restaurants, and a broad, expansive plaza reminiscent of old Monterey. Sport fishing boats leave from here early every morning.

**Cannery Row's** old canneries are still there, monuments to the sardines that mysteriously vanished from Monterey Bay near the end of the 1940s. But the Row is not the same street Steinbeck described in *Cannery Row* as "a poem, a stink, a grating noise."

Today as you enter Cannery Row, you drive under the covered conveyor belts which once carried the canned fish from the canneries to the warehouse. Many of the old buildings have been renovated, and you can browse through art galleries and antique shops, eat at one of several restaurants, or watch a film at the Steinbeck Theater. Some reminders of Steinbeck's novel remain—at 800 Cannery Row are the weathered clapboards of Doc Rickett's Western Biological Laboratory; across the street is Wing Chong's, the "Lee Chong's Grocery" of the book; and down the block is the Bear Flag Inn.

## Presidio of Monterey

Founded in 1770 by Gaspar de Portola, the Monterey Presidio is a subpost for the 22,000-acre Fort Ord Area; the site of the Defense Language Institute, West Coast Branch (where 24 foreign languages are taught); and the Training Center Human Research Unit.

The main gate is at Pacific and Artillery streets, near the site where Sebastian Vizcaino landed in 1602 and Father Junipero Serra and Captain Portola founded Monterey in 1770. A drive up the Corporal Ewing Road to the motor pool will take you to a life-size statue of Father Serra and a splendid view of Monterey Bay.

**Classic Monterey waterfront scene:** *fishing boats, wharf, and pier. City edges hills in background.*

**Converted cannery shops** *carry variety of crafts — handmade purses to dulcimers.*

**Catwalk crossing Cannery Row** *in Monterey was used by canning company to link cannery and warehouse.*

**Flags flying** *in Simoneau Plaza have flapped over city of Monterey since its birth.*

West of the Father Serra monument is a memorial to Commodore John Sloat, who in 1846 declared Monterey a possession of the United States. Stone from every county in California was used to make this memorial. A bust of Sloat is carved in the stone pedestal of the monument; an eagle overlooks the bay.

## Naval Postgraduate School

Just east of downtown Monterey, alongside State 1, are the grounds of the old Del Monte Hotel, once one of the most elegant resorts in California. In 1947 the hotel was purchased by the U.S. Navy and in 1951 it became the Naval Postgraduate School.

Visitors are welcome to stroll through the campus daily between 9 A.M. and 4 P.M. The grounds contain more than 1,200 exotic trees, Del Monte Lake, and landscaped gardens. The hotel buildings remain, although they have been converted into classrooms and offices. Herrmann Hall boasts handpainted ceilings, wrought iron chandeliers, and a now-unused fountain that extends along one wall from floor to ceiling.

# Monterey's Path of History

Many Spanish-style adobes were constructed during the early 1800s to accommodate the 2,000 residents of Monterey. When New England seamen arrived, they modified the Spanish colonial design and created the "Monterey style"—two-story adobes with a balcony. Although many of the old buildings have disappeared, 12 buildings have been preserved and are maintained as the Monterey State Historic Park; most of them are open daily.

These historical structures are close to the downtown area and the harbor. A good place to start is at the Custom House near Fisherman's Wharf.

**The Custom House,** at 1 Custom Plaza, is the oldest government building on the Pacific Coast. Here the United States flag was officially raised for the first time by Commodore John Sloat in 1846. This building was the collection center for revenue from foreign shipping until 1867, when it was abandoned. Today, the interior has been restored; inside is a display of early ships' cargo. The plaza with its adobe walls and benches is reminiscent of early California.

**The Pacific House,** at 8 Custom House Plaza, dates back to 1847. This building was first used by the U.S. Quartermaster for military offices and storage; later it housed a tavern; now it's a museum. The first floor contains exhibits of California history and the second floor a collection of American Indian artifacts.

**Casa del Oro** is so named because of the unverified story that the building was once used as a gold depository. A general merchandise store in the 1850s, Casa del Oro stands at the corner of Scott and Oliver streets and displays trade items from early Monterey days.

**California's First Theater,** built in 1846-47, at the corner of Scott and Pacific streets, is open daily except Monday. Once weekly a theater group presents 19th century plays. The old bench seats are still there, and walls of the barroom are lined with old theatrical mementos.

**Casa Soberanes,** at 336 Pacific, is a private residence not open to the public. But it is an excellent example of "Monterey-style" architecture.

**Colton Hall,** on Pacific Street, was built in 1847-49 and is the largest and most impressive of the old buildings. A museum on the second floor displays early government documents.

**The Larkin House,** which dates back to 1835, is an excellent example of "Monterey-style" architecture. The two-story adobe, surrounded on three sides by a balcony, was built by Thomas Larkin, U.S. Consul. Many of the furnishings are original pieces. This home, at the corner of Jefferson Street and Calle Principal, is open to the public. Visitors are taken on a 35-minute guided tour daily except Tuesday.

**Casa Gutierrez,** at Calle Principal near Madison, is a typical adobe home of the Mexican period. Now it's a Mexican restaurant.

**The Cooper-Molera Adobe,** at the corner of Polk and Murray, is the former home of Captain John Cooper, a trader and half brother to Thomas Larkin; it is not open to the public.

**The Stevenson House,** named for Robert Louis Stevenson, who lived in this building during his short sojourn in Monterey in 1879, dates back to the late 1830s. At 530 Houston Street, the restored building devotes several rooms to Stevenson's personal mementoes. The house is open for guided tours.

**The Royal Presidio Chapel of San Carlos de Borromeo** was founded in 1770 by Father Junipero Serra. The original, hastily constructed mud structure was rebuilt with a baroque facade by Father Serra's successor in 1794. A simple wooden cross sits atop the chapel. Inside are several statues and Stations of the Cross dating from the founding of the chapel. The chapel, on Church Street, is still in use; visitors are welcome.

**The U.S. Army Museum,** in the Presidio of Monterey, exhibits military items from early Spanish days to the present. The museum is open Wednesday through Sunday.

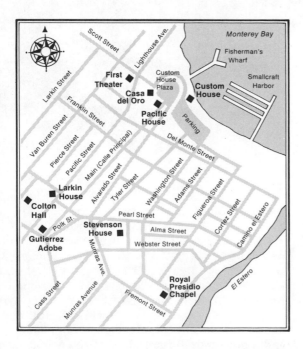

To reach the school, turn onto Aguajito Road from State 1; then turn right on 3rd Street to the main entrance.

# Pacific Grove–A Butterfly Town

The Methodists founded Pacific Grove in 1875 when they held the first of many seashore camp meetings here. Incorporated in 1889, the town was corseted with ordinances strictly regulating dancing, drinking, and public bathing. Today's Pacific Grove is more relaxed.

The Monarch butterfly *(Danaus plexippus)* is the Pacific Grove symbol. Starting in October thousands of Monarchs fly in to winter in a 6-acre grove of "Butterfly Trees" (follow the signs at the end of Lighthouse Avenue). Their fall arrival is celebrated with a big annual parade. Two other interesting events are the Victorian House Tour in April and the Feast of Lanterns in July.

**Pt. Pinos Lighthouse,** just north of the intersection of Lighthouse and Asilomar avenues, has stood at the entrance to Monterey Harbor since 1855. On the first floor of the lighthouse is a Coast Guard historical museum open to the public from 1 to 4 P.M. Saturday and Sunday. Surrounding the light station is a Coast Guard reservation, where deer roam protected and fishermen fish from the rocky shoreline. The original lighthouse of granite and mortar was rebuilt of reinforced concrete after the 1906 earthquake. Automation is planned for the future so the two-man crew will no longer have to check hourly on the light, radio, and foghorn.

**The Museum of Natural History,** at Forest and Central avenues, displays animal, vegetable, and mineral life of the Monterey Peninsula. Of particular interest is the relief map of the peninsula and bay. You can see the great chasm of Monterey Bay, which goes down 8,400 feet, deeper than the Grand Canyon. The museum is open daily.

**At Municipal Beach** along Ocean View Boulevard is Lovers Point. Here is a protected beach, a heated salt-water pool, and a good place to picnic. A short distance east of the beach is Pt. Cabrillo, where Stanford University maintains the Hopkins Marine Laboratories. Ideal weather and water conditions make possible extensive research in hydrobiology. The laboratories are not open to the public.

**Asilomar Beach State Park** fronts the ocean side of the Monterey Peninsula and is often used for large group conferences. If you cannot find hotel space on the peninsula, rustic and comfortable rooms are sometimes available at Asilomar. The beach here is perfect for hiking and games.

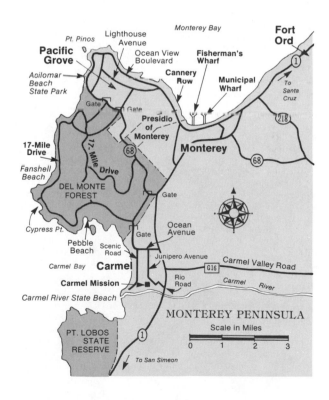

**Many-peaked Green Gables,** *corner of 5th Street and Lighthouse Avenue, is now Pacific Grove guest house.*

## 17-Mile Drive

Wholly contained within 4,280-acre Del Monte Forest, the 17-Mile Drive is an exceptionally scenic route. For 17 miles you drive through thickly wooded areas, see spectacular views of Monterey Bay, and swing along the breathtaking, rocky shoreline. At any of the four entrance gates (fee is $3 per car), you'll be given a map of the route showing points of interest. It's easy to drive this 17-mile route—just follow the yellow line.

Along the drive stand weathered Monterey cypresses, whose branches and foliage have been dramatically distorted by the sea winds. At Seal and Bird Rocks are black cormorants, sea ducks, sea gulls, and Leopard or Harbor seals. Between the shore and the rocks are the sea lions.

Though overnight camping is not allowed within the Del Monte Forest, you can picnic in specified areas. Fishing is permitted from Fanshell Beach north; hunting is not allowed. Within the forest are more than 100 miles of bridle trails.

Along the peninsula's south shore is Pebble Beach. Here are the famous Pebble Beach Golf Course (one of six within the forest), Del Monte Lodge (resort hotel), and exclusive homes.

# Carmel-by-the-Sea

Since its first settlement, Carmel has prided itself on remaining a simple village by the ocean. Even today houses have no street numbers, and mail delivery is nonexistent (everyone goes to the post office). Downtown there are no billboards, no large retail signs, and at night no flood lighting and almost no street lighting. On the side streets you see no curbs, no sidewalks.

Unfortunately, this lack of commercialism attracts tourists. The sidewalks are crowded on weekends, and the main street is jammed with cars. Now Carmel's motto seems to be, "If you can't beat 'em, join 'em."

This is a village of shops—more than 150 of them, mostly small. And the shopping is good. Specialties are casual clothing for both men and women, often from Scotland, England, or Italy; art and craft work of all kinds, much of it produced locally; decorative imports from Mexico, Sweden, France, Italy; basketry, pottery, furniture from Japan and Hong Kong. Shopping is a pastime in Carmel.

Carmel is a village in a forest, and the forest is encouraged. The village forestry commission, busy with reforestation, has planted new street trees (mostly Monterey pines) between older trees.

Carmel has always respected its artists, writers, and craftsmen. Many serious artists who live here display their works in several downtown galleries. The Carmel Art Association maintains a sales gallery on Dolores Street.

One of the yearly attractions here is the Bach Festival, a week-long program of concerts held each July in Sunset Center.

Carmel has several hotels and a large number of motels, inns, and guest cottages; yet advance room

**Wide, sugar-sandy Carmel Beach,** *spiked with Monterey cypress, is grand for walking, dangerous for swimming.*

**Doll house architecture** *of Carmel's Tuck Box provides cozy, picturesque atmosphere for lunchers.*

# Fore!

Few places in the world have as many beautiful golf courses as the Monterey Peninsula. No wonder it's called the "golf capital of the world."

Some of the courses are by the shore, some in the valleys; all offer a great adventure for player or spectator. The 16th hole at Cypress is one of the most talked-about in the world; golfers must drive over 220 yards of undulating ocean to reach the green. Del Monte is the West's oldest golf course. Each course has individual challenges.

Most famous of the golf events on the peninsula is the Bing Crosby National Pro-Amateur Championship. Watched by thousands of spectators, it is also seen by millions on television.

Peninsula hotels and motels often offer golf packages. Check with your travel agent for details. Below is a listing of courses:

**Carmel Valley Golf & Country Club,** Rte. 2, Box 2300, Carmel, CA 93921; (408) 624-5323; 18 holes; 6,756 yards (championship), 6,401 yards (regular); reciprocal arrangements with members of other private clubs.

**Corral de Tierra Country Club,** Corral de Tierra Rd., Salinas, CA 93901; (408) 484-1112; 18 holes; 6,532 yards; reciprocal arrangements with members of other private clubs.

**Del Monte Golf Course,** 1300 Sylvan Rd., Monterey, CA 93940; (408) 373-2436; 18 holes; 6,175 yards; public.

**Ft. Ord Golf Course,** North-South Rd., Ft. Ord, CA 93941; (408) 242-5651; two 18 hole courses; 6,966 yards (bayonet), 6,239 (blackhorse); military and guests only.

**Laguna Seca Golf Ranch,** Box 308, Monterey, CA 93940; (408) 373-3701; 18 holes; 6,310 yards; public.

**Monterey Peninsula Country Club,** Box 2090, Pebble Beach, CA 93953; (408) 373-1046; 36 holes; 6,400 yards (shore course), 6,300 yards (dunes course); reciprocal arrangements with members of other private clubs.

**Naval Postgrad School Golf Course,** Box 665, NPS, Monterey, CA 93940; (408) 646-2167; 18 holes; 5,680 yards; military and guests only.

**Pacific Grove Municipal Golf Course,** Box 627, Pacific Grove, CA 93950; (408) 375-3456; 18 holes; 5,493 yards; public.

**Pebble Beach Golf Course,** Del Monte Lodge, Pebble Beach, CA 93953; (408) 624-3811; 18 holes; 6,815 yards (championship), 6,345 yards (regular); semiprivate (2 weeks reservation required for busy periods).

**Peter Hay Par 3 at Pebble Beach,** Del Monte Lodge, Pebble Beach, CA 93953; (408) 624-3811; 9 holes; public.

**Rancho Canada Golf Club,** Box 5336, Carmel, CA 93921; (408) 624-0111; 36 holes; 6,613 yards (west course), 6,401 yards (east course); public.

**Spyglass Hill Golf Course,** Box 787, Pebble Beach, CA 93953; (408) 624-3811; 18 holes; 6,810 yards (championship), 6,277 yards (regular); public.

**It's a sure putt** *into the cup for this golfer at the Monterey Peninsula Country Club course.*

reservations are advisable in summer, especially during such events as the Bach Festival.

In exploring Carmel, you'll see a variety of architecture. The early rough summer cabins have given way to Hansel and Gretel-type structures and Monterey-style adobe homes. Fronting the ocean are some very modern homes, including a Frank Lloyd Wright design.

## Carmel's beach was made for walking

Carmel's classically beautiful beach is for walkers and, in good weather, sunbathers. The beach is unsafe for swimming, but most bathers find the water too cold anyway. On Scenic Drive, which runs along the water, you will see dark, gnarled cypresses, sparkling white sand, and crashing surf. At the southern end of the beach, the shoreline becomes rocky and has many tidepools.

South of the village limits, at the end of Scenic Drive, the beach becomes Carmel River State Beach. Here you can picnic around a beach fire or splash in the lagoon of Carmel River.

## Carmel Mission Basilica

South of the town proper just off State 1 at Rio Road (or follow Junipero Avenue south) is Basilica

San Carlos Borromeo del Rio Carmelo. Fully restored through the efforts of craftsmen, benefactors, and clergy, the mission provides one of the most authentic and picturesque links with early California history. The mission is open to visitors Monday through Friday from 9 A.M. to 5 P.M., Sunday from 1 to 5 P.M.

In the mission museum are the original silver altar pieces brought by Father Junipero Serra from Baja California and the restored refectory of Father Serra. Behind the mission is a cemetery where 3,000 Indians are buried. Inside the mission is Father Serra's final resting place.

### Point Lobos State Reserve

On State 1 just south of Carmel, 1,500-acre Point Lobos State Reserve, one of the most beautiful spots on the California coast, is more than just one point. Its 6-mile-long broken coastline encompasses many points. At this magnificent meeting of land and sea you can hike, picnic, explore tidepools, sun on the beach, or fish.

Around the headland and shoreline, low tides expose rocky pools teeming with marine creatures. Colonies of sea urchins, sea anemones, starfish, and scuttling hermit crabs are a few of the more conspicuous inhabitants. Remember that Point Lobos is a nature reserve; tidepools are for looking only. On prominent rocks you will see sea gulls and, on Bird Island, cormorants and brown pelicans.

If you visit Point Lobos in November, you might see the California gray whale, which travels close to shore here on its annual 12,000-mile migration to Lower California.

Point Lobos is open only during daylight hours. There are picnic sites, but camping and fires are not permitted.

# Carmel Valley

South of Carmel, the Carmel Valley Road turns east from State 1 and heads inland along the Carmel River. Driving through the valley, you'll pass artichoke fields, fruit orchards, strawberry patches, and rolling hills on which cattle graze.

Carmel Valley is a vacationland. Its weather is sunny, warm, and clear—ideal for such outdoor sports as fishing, hunting, horseback riding, tennis, and swimming. Near the mouth of the Carmel Valley, spanning both sides of the Carmel River, are two championship golf courses—available for public play. The Carmel River holds an abundance of trout, and, during the annual spawning season, steelhead fishing is excellent. In the nearby Santa Lucia Mountains, you can hunt wild boar and deer.

Hotels and motels are more than places to spend the night; all offer a variety of interesting activities. For a list of accommodations and facilities available, write to the Carmel Valley Chamber of Commerce, Box 288, Carmel Valley, CA 93921.

If you're in the Carmel Valley, you might want to visit the most-unusual Thunderbird Bookshop in Valley Hills Shopping Center. Farther east are the Carmel Valley Begonia Gardens where 15,000 begonias are a massive wheel of color in the summer. The Korean Buddhist Temple welcomes visitors. It lies just west of the Farm Center off Robinson Canyon Road.

You can camp at Riverside Park and Saddle Mountain Recreation Park. Along the highway you'll find several fruit and vegetable stands.

# South Along the Coast

The dramatic 30-mile drive along State 1 to the town of Big Sur takes about an hour from the Monterey-Carmel area. The road south dips and rises, clinging precariously to the seaward face of the Santa Lucia Mountains as it follows the rugged coastline.

As you drive south from Carmel, you cross Bixby Creek Bridge, 260 feet above the creek bed. Park your car and walk out to observation alcoves for a view of the surf, beach, and headlands. You'll pass a cliff-perched eating place—Rocky Point Restaurant—and Pt. Sur Lighthouse, rising on a headland of rock. Every 15 seconds a warning is flashed that can be seen 25 miles out to sea.

Though the road is two lanes with narrow shoulders, scenic turnouts are numerous. You can stop for a roadside picnic (Big Sur has a few small

**Carmel Mission facade** *draws admiring tourist glances. Father Serra, founder of mission chain, is buried here.*

grocery stores) or a leisurely lunch at one of Big Sur's restaurants, take a stroll in the redwoods or a walk on the beach, do some shopping or gallery browsing. The Coast Gallery (center for local artisans) recently opened two showrooms inside redwood water tanks. You can lunch or dine at Ventana restaurant, a resort with rental condominiums and a gift shop. For a free list of commercial establishments in the Big Sur area, write to the Chamber of Commerce, Big Sur, CA 93920. Enjoy Nepenthe, 3 miles south of Pfeiffer-Big Sur State Park. The redwood pavilion, designed by a student of Frank Lloyd Wright, sits 800 feet above the sea and affords a superb view of southern Big Sur. The original core building was the honeymoon "cottage" built in the 1940s for Rita Hayworth by Orson Welles. Nepenthe opens every day at noon. In addition to being a restaurant, it has become an informal social-cultural center for the Big Sur region.

## State Parks Along the Way

Some of the finest meetings of land and water occur in three state parks along the coast. Two of the parks offer camping, but you have to walk in to one.

**Andrew Molera State Park** has 2,088 acres encompassing the lower section of the Big Sur River. Because it's closed to motorized vehicles, you park your car off the highway and walk in to a designated camping area. Here you'll find somewhat primitive arrangements for about 50 campers. A network of fire-control roads makes it easy to get around in this preserve of redwoods, rocky bluffs, meadow land, and beach.

**Pfeiffer-Big Sur State Park** is one of the most popular of the state's nonbeach parks. Though the park isn't too large, its trails give access to 300,000 acres of back country in Los Padres National Forest and the Ventana Wilderness. (Permits to enter the wilderness should be requested at least 2 weeks in advance from the District Ranger, Los Padres National Forest, 406 S. Mildred, King City, CA 93930.)

The park's campgrounds are apt to be crowded, especially in the summer or on weekends. You can picnic, hike, swim, or fish upstream in the river. Hotel-type rooms and housekeeping cabins are available at Big Sur Lodge, Big Sur, CA 93920.

Pfeiffer Beach, south of the park entrance, is reached by following narrow Sycamore Canyon Road from State 1. A scenic gem, the beach is open daily from 9 A.M. to 6 P.M.

**Julia Pfeiffer Burns State Park's** attractions include a dramatic waterfall, redwood groves, and vantage points for viewing gray whale migration. You'll also find 2 miles of scenic coastline and high country extending up canyons laced with trickling creeks. There's no camping, but you can

**Castlelike Hearst mansion,** *now a State Historical Monument, sits regally on San Simeon hilltop.*

picnic, hike, or stroll along the beach. The park is open in summer, and spring and fall weekends.

## San Simeon: A Castle Fit for Kings

The Hearst San Simeon State Historical Monument, a collection of mansions, terraced gardens, pools, sculpture, and exotic trees, occupies 123 acres atop a spur of the Santa Lucia Mountains. The focal point is *La Casa Grande*, a 137-foot-high structure resembling a Spanish cathedral. Its imposing ridge-top position gives it the aspect of a castle when viewed from afar.

In 1922, construction began on *La Casa Grande*, William Randolph Hearst's private residence. Hearst called the estate *La Cuesta Encantada—The Enchanted Hill.* Money was no object—Hearst imported furniture, antiques, Gothic and Renaissance tapestries, fine wood carvings, French and Italian mantels, carved ceilings, silver, Persian rugs, and Roman mosaics. The publisher also imported wildlife, and today zebras, tahr goats, and Barbary sheep still roam on the grounds.

San Simeon is located on State 1, about 96 miles south of Monterey. Three separate tours, each about 2 hours long, are conducted through the estate. For reservations (always required during the busy season) write to the Reservations Office, Department of Parks and Recreation, P.O. Box 2390, Sacramento, CA 95811. Tour prices are moderate. Each tour begins at the foot of Enchanted Hill; you park your car in the parking lot and board a bus for the ride up the hill.

# Inland Side Trips

Two inland routes parallel the coastal highway and offer sights well worth seeing. U.S. 101 heads south through the valley of the Salinas River; State Highway 25 crosses the San Benito River in the coastal range.

## Pinnacles National Monument

At Pinnacles National Monument, spires and crags —remains of a volcanic mountain—rise to 1,200 feet above the canyon floors and present a sharp contrast to the surrounding smooth countryside.

The best way to appreciate fully the extraordinary features here is to hike on some of the trails. On the east side, short and easy trips lead through the cave area around Bear Gulch, where the visitor center and picnic area are located. The High Peaks Trail is more strenuous, and a new trail (Juniper Canyon) makes it easier to reach High Peaks from Soledad.

On the Soledad side of the monument, you walk into the narrow defile between the overhangs of Machete Ridge and The Balconies. Huge boulders close the caves to natural light (be sure to carry a flashlight). You will have to crawl, stretch, duck, and squeeze along for a few hundred feet until you come to daylight and the other end of the cave. Children should not go in the caves alone; in the dark, slippery places, low ceilings and dropoffs are hazardous.

Pinnacles National Monument is just off State 25, 32 miles south of Hollister. You can also reach the Pinnacles along U.S. 101 by turning onto State Highway 146 at Soledad and following the narrow, winding road 14 miles to the camping and picnic area. Fall through spring are the best months to visit the monument; the summer months are hot.

Campgrounds are at Chalone Creek and Chaparrel, with group camping at Chalone Annex.

## Soledad Mission Ruins

A turn westward off U.S. 101 just south of Soledad will take you past a frame and adobe building on your right. This is Los Coches, former headquarters of a large ranch, part of the lands of Mission Nuestra Senora de la Soledad.

A half-mile drive west of Los Coches and a turn to the north will take you to the windswept beet fields on which are several crumbling walls, all that remain of the original mission. A modern chapel has been erected.

From the mission ruins, you can backtrack to U.S. 101 or take the back roads to Carmel and Monterey. Drive south up the steep Arroyo Seco Road, following its turn in a westerly direction to Paloma Creek Road. This is a dirt road—unsatisfactory within 24 hours after rain. After 18 miles of winding through range land dotted with oaks, eucalyptus, sycamores, and pines, you'll be back on the paved Carmel Valley Road.

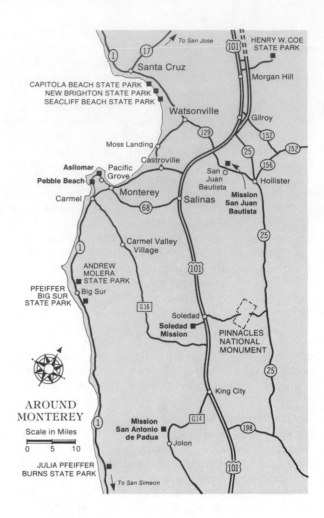

AROUND MONTEREY

Scale in Miles

0   5   10

## Mission San Antonio de Padua

One of the most completely restored of all California missions, Mission San Antonio de Padua still remains somewhat isolated. To reach it, exit off U.S. 101 at King City and follow the road for 18 miles to Jolon. Visitors are welcome.

Mission San Antonio de Padua is reminiscent of the missions as they were during the days of the padres. In place of the crumbling adobe walls are buildings considered to be replicas of those that existed in the prosperous years between 1771 and 1830. Some of the original tiles still cover the roof.

Besides the mission itself, you'll see a water-powered grist mill, a tannery, the original wine vat, and exhibits of early mission art and replicas of mission equipment. In spring, carpets of purple lupine, golden poppies, yellow wild pansies, and scarlet Indian paintbrush cover surrounding slopes.

# In and Around Salinas

Salinas, the heart of the "salad bowl of the world," is the birthplace of John Steinbeck. His home (now a restaurant) stands on the northwest corner of Central and Stone streets, and the surrounding locale provided the geographical setting for many of his books. The city is also the home of California's largest rodeo, held the third weekend in July.

From Salinas it's only a few miles to the Monterey Peninsula or to Castroville (the artichoke capital) and Watsonville on State 1.

## Mission San Juan Bautista

About 21 miles north of Salinas, 3½ miles off U.S. 101, San Juan Bautista State Historic Park presents a carefully restored chapter of early California history. Once a crossroads of stagecoach travel, the old mission village declined after the railroad pushed south from San Francisco. But in 1933 San Juan Bautista was named a state historic park, and the flavor of old San Juan was preserved. The history of the San Juan Valley centers around the mission, founded by the Franciscans in 1797. Construction of the present mission building began in 1803 and reached completion in 1814. The carefully restored buildings still overlook the valley much as they did. Down in the town, though, new shops, galleries, and other attractions are moving into the old frame buildings that stand shoulder-to-shoulder along Third Street.

At La Calavera, on Washington Street, a resident troupe presents plays stocked with early California history on Friday and Saturday evenings.

Mexican holidays begin in December. The typical *Las Posadas* procession and fiesta takes place nightly from mid-December until Christmas Eve.

**Stop for lunch** *at author John Steinbeck's home in Salinas. The Victorian is open weekdays only.*

Nearby camping spots include Fremont Peak State Park, a rich historic and botanical area 11 miles south of San Juan Bautista on the San Juan Canyon-State Park Road. Fourteen miles east of Morgan Hill on East Dunne Avenue is Henry W. Coe State Park, little known and usually uncrowded. Seasonally blessed with good wildflower displays, the park is at its best in spring and in autumn after the first rains.

## Try the Hecker Pass wineries

Clustered around State 152 like grapes on a stem, a handful of wineries extend west of Gilroy toward Hecker Pass. All these wineries are small; two are tiny.

Tasting is leisurely, and you may get a chance to go on an informal tour. Most wineries offer a few varietal as well as generic wines. If you go in October, there's a good chance of seeing the picking and crushing.

To reach the wineries, leave U.S. 101 at Morgan Hill; just south of town, take Watsonville Road roughly 5 miles to Bonesio Winery. Just over 2 miles past Bonesio is the junction with Hecker Pass Highway (State 152), where you'll find the other wineries. Bertero and Bonesio have picnic areas, and you'll also find good picnicking in Mt. Madonna County Park a few miles farther west.

# To Mendocino & the North Coast

Stretching almost 400 miles from San Francisco Bay to the southern border of Oregon, the virtually unspoiled Northern California coastline delights visitors. Photographers record the beauty of whitecapped waves pounding against rugged shores; anglers contest with fighting steelhead in mighty rivers emptying into the sea; campers choose between parks ranging from sandy dunes to dense forest; and crowds of urbanites flock to unique rural festivals.

Heading north across the Golden Gate Bridge, you can reach the coast either by way of U.S. Highway 101, an inland route until meeting the ocean at Humboldt Bay, or by the slower, scenic route—two-lane State Highway 1. Numerous back country roads connect these two major highways before they join at Leggett, just south of the Avenue of the Giants.

It would be impossible to list the chief attractions of this section of Northern California; everyone makes his own discovery. Hikers might want to roam the vast open spaces of Pt. Reyes National Seashore. California's history takes on a new dimension when you view the wooden outpost of the Russian fur traders—Fort Ross. The charms of artistic Mendocino and its bustling fishing and lumbering neighbor, Fort Bragg, outrank everything else along the central portion of the coast. To the north the mighty coast redwood makes spectacular daytime viewing; herds of Roosevelt elk munch in meadows fringed by titans.

Weather is usually foggy and cold along the coast during the summer; surprisingly, winter brings clear, warm days. Old-fashioned inns with modern accouterments seem to offer even more warmth when fog horns bellow and rain rattles against your windows. Any month of the year, the North Coast provides a pleasing change of pace.

**Sonoma County sea stacks** (*rocky islets*)
*are typical of Northern California
coast. State Highway 1 dips close to the
shore, offering views of tumbling hills.*

# The Marin Beaches

As far as mariners are concerned, the Marin County shore from Pt. Reyes to the Golden Gate has very little to recommend it. For them it's a treacherous obstacle to San Francisco, composed equally of sea fogs, howling winds, reefs, and shoals. But for those who are shorebound, it is something else: good rock fishing, good wave-watching, good rock-hounding, and good clamming. In its shallow bays, the hardy enjoy good swimming.

Only one remote beach is more than an hour from San Francisco. Some of the shore is hardly 15 minutes away. In spite of its proximity to the city, Marin's coast has not been subjected to any permanent overcrowding, mainly because the terrain slopes skyward in many places. Lack of further development has been somewhat assured by the recent creation of parks along all but a handful of miles of shoreline.

## North from the Headlands

Marin's shores from the north end of the Golden Gate Bridge are now practically all open to the public. Divided between the Marin Headlands State Park and the Golden Gate National Recreation Area (which extends as far north as Olema), the land is a mixture of former army forts, ruggedly undeveloped open areas, and once-private ranch lands.

### From Marin Headlands—a bay view

Plummeting from bare-crested hills into deep water all along its length, the westerly section of Marin Headlands stretches from the bridge to Pt. Bonita. (One pocket beach a few hundred yards west of the bridge is the exception.) A loop road running high along the face of the headlands is first-rate for kite flying, poppy watching, and panoramas of San Francisco. The beach, backed by a row of abandoned artillery bunkers, is merely a pleasant resource for short strolls; it's a stiff hike down and back.

**Pt. Bonita Light Station** (closed to visitors) perches on the eroding tip of the Golden Gate's north side. A prime weather station and warning point for the bay, it's a reliable check point for the comings and goings of the summer fog bank. The first sounding device installed here in 1856 to help befogged mariners was an army sergeant, charged with firing a muzzle-loading cannon at half-hour intervals whenever the weather demanded. At the end of two months, he was exhausted and had to petition for relief. An unearthly electronic racket does the job now.

**Ft. Cronkhite** is the outermost of three sentinel forts on the north side of San Francisco Bay, the only one outside the Golden Gate, and the only one with publicly accessible beaches. The reasons for visiting are several: rockhounds roam Cronkhite's gravelly shore in search of jadeite and jasper, especially in winter; the summer crowd comes to bask in the lee of bluffs that offer some protection from the prevailing westerlies; and people who like to watch seabirds fly have a superior arena.

The headlands, Pt. Bonita, and Cronkhite are all accessible on the same spur road. After crossing the Golden Gate Bridge, take the first turnoff (Alexander) from U.S. 101. To reach the western end of the loop, turn left on the road almost immediately at the mouth of a tunnel. (Wait for the green light before proceeding into the tunnel.) Beyond that, forks lead to each of the three areas. If you want to go only to the headlands overlooking the Golden Gate, turn left after taking the Alexander turnoff (at the sign reading "San Francisco"), cross underneath the freeway, and take the unmarked road that shoots up the hill. Watch carefully or you'll end up heading back across the bridge. From the north take the last (unmarked) exit to your right before crossing the bridge.

**Stinson Beach** is the name of a town and a day-use state park. The park runs mostly south of town. Fishermen do well with ling cod, cabezone, and blenny at several rocky points toward its south boundary. Just opposite the town entrance is a summer swimming beach, its water warmed by the shoal of Bolinas Bay to a tolerable if not exactly tepid state. (In winter, strong currents make swimming perilous, and cold water makes it foolish.) The park attracts more than a half-million visitors annually, surprising in view of the one lone road leading to it.

**Audubon Canyon Ranch,** 3 miles north of Stinson Beach, is a good place to watch the courtship

**Sampling** *coastal activities a few miles from San Francisco might include exploring Duxbury Reef* **(left)** *or enjoying a family outing* **(below)** *at Marin Headlands.*

**Audubon Canyon Ranch** *bird watchers* **(left)** *point telescopes and binoculars at a regal gathering of egrets* **(right)** *who appear ready for wide-winged takeoff.*

rituals of the great blue herons, who rendezvous here every March. Bring binoculars or use the ranch telescopes to watch these, along with graceful white egrets. Most birds are gone by August.

## Bolinas . . . a tiny tourist town

Sitting just across the mouth of a small lagoon from Stinson Beach, Bolinas is a tiny town that does not try very hard to attract visitors but gets them anyway. Duxbury Reef, a principal cause of Bolinas's popularity, sets up the proper conditions for surfing, tidepooling, clamming, and rock fishing. Striped bass feed at the mouth of the lagoon. Each end of the town's east-west main street dips down to a beach access. The one nearest Stinson Beach serves bass fishermen and surfers; the westerly end is closest to the foot of Duxbury Reef, an area rich in tidepools and cockle beds.

# Pt. Reyes - the National Seashore

U.S. Weather Bureau statistics cede to Pt. Reyes the twin honors of foggiest and windiest station, bar none, between Canada and Mexico. But the point is only one outcropping of rock in a magnificently rumpled landscape, and its weather differs considerably from milder Inverness, only 11 miles away on Tomales Bay.

An ideal place for an August, September, or October outing, the peninsula reaches another peak of attractiveness in May when wildflowers bloom. In midsummer, chances are you'll be shrouded in fog. Limited lodging restricts the peninsula as a vacation spot. Bear Valley has a few campgrounds, or you can camp at Samuel P. Taylor State Park (about 6 miles southeast of Pt. Reyes Station) or at a private campground near Olema.

Natural history takes a few unusual turns here—even a few unique ones. Most of them stem from the peninsula's having sprung up as the result of earthquakes. Recorded history is thin but unusual enough to include Sir Francis Drake's arrival in 1579 aboard the Golden Hinde. The area's dramatic background led to its being named Pt. Reyes National Seashore in 1962.

Straight up the coast about 50 miles from San Francisco, Pt. Reyes can be easily reached from U.S. 101 and Sir Francis Drake Boulevard or State 1. It's divided into two distinct areas. You reach major beaches and dairylands through Inverness to the north; the Bear Valley trails and hilly forest of Inverness Ridge through park headquarters near Olema off State 1.

## Drake's Bay: home for the Golden Hinde?

A long and gentle curve facing almost due south, this bay has a wide, flat, sandy beach abutting steep sandstone bluffs all the way from Pt. Reyes on the west to a point right next to Bolinas on the east. The one break in the arc is the mouth of Drake's Estero, a clutching hand of water that cups oyster beds in its palm.

Although some historians believe Drake brought his ship into Bodega Bay, Bolinas Bay, Tomales Bay, or San Francisco Bay, the prestigious Drake Navigators Guild claims a stronger case for Drake's Bay. Whether or not the argument is ever resolved by some dramatic new turn (like the recent discovery in Bolinas Lagoon of what might have been Drake's fort), the bay is a pleasant place to pass a long summer's day.

**Drake's Beach Visitor Center** adjoins the parking lot. Sheltered picnic tables allow you to sit and watch waves when the weather gets too raw to permit lazy strolls along the beach. On good days, beautifully symmetrical plunging breakers cream ashore. Lifeguards are on duty during the summer. The light station on this point is closed to visitors.

**Limantour Beach and Estero** (east of Drake's Beach) is the other spot on the seashore where wading and swimming are usually safe. Sun and stroll or watch the bird life; the estero is one of the few Pacific Coast marshes not seriously altered by man. On summer weekends (July 4 to Labor Day) a shuttle bus runs between the Limantour parking area and the Bear Valley trailhead, making it possible to hike and ride through this region.

**Pt. Reyes Bird Observatory** is the only full-time ornithological field research station on the continent. Year-round you'll see land birds, shore birds, and waterfowl on the south end of the peninsula. Take Mesa Road from Bolinas.

**Pt. Reyes Beach,** southwest of Inverness on the Sir Francis Drake Highway, is ruler straight, steep faced, current ridden, wind scoured; it has a haunting, austere beauty. Solitude and astonishingly high surf are rewards for your visit. Sometimes big waves roll up from distant storms during a spell of

**Hikers** *returning from Pt. Reyes overlook at Chimney Rock walk past small fishing station on Drake's Bay.*

freakish warm weather that comes nearly every February. Oddly enough, picnicking then is better than during almost any other month of the year. Water and rest rooms are available. Pounding surf at Pt. Reyes and McClure's beaches makes them too dangerous for water activities.

**McClure's Beach,** at the northern end of the peninsula, is usually almost deserted because the access trail is steep and narrow. There's no swimming here but plenty of driftwood for fires and rocks for shelter from the wind.

## Bear Valley trails

Gateway to the national seashore is a mile west of Olema at the old Bear Valley Ranch. The Information Center, open daily from 8 A.M. to 5 P.M., has maps and schedules of nature programs. Its most fascinating attraction is the seismograph, registering any quiver of the San Andreas Fault. Behind the big red barn nearby, you can see, pet, and photograph Morgan horses or visit the working blacksmith shop.

Hikers, horsemen, and bicycle riders enjoy more than 50 miles of trails—some nearly level through fir groves and meadows to the sea, others steep, leading up to panoramic vistas of the entire peninsula. You can spend an hour or a day just roaming.

## To Tomales Bay for gapers

Its own skinny profile and the sheltering bulk of Inverness Ridge make Tomales Bay a tranquil alternative to the oceanic edges of Pt. Reyes.

**Tomales Bay State Park,** just north of Inverness, is not a part of the national seashore but includes some fine stretches of pleasant sandy bottom coves —Shell, Pebble, Heart's Desire, and Indian—offering the warmest and quietest salt-water swimming on the Marin coast. Rockier stretches below sandstone bluffs support fair-sized populations of rock cockles. In addition to its shoreside charms, the park is a preserve for the Bishop pine, which flourishes on the peninsula but is not found on the adjacent mainland.

Around on the east side of the bay is a county boat launch just south of the point where State 1 bends inland toward the town of Tomales. Beach areas all along the bay are accessible for cockling or the winter run of herring. You can buy oysters from one of the commercial growers in the town of Marshall.

**Dillon Beach,** a raffishly charming commercial establishment and summer village right at the mouth of Tomales Bay, is almost due west of Tomales on a spur road. Clamming for gapers on a low-tide island, fishing of various sorts, and swimming (for the hardy) are popular.

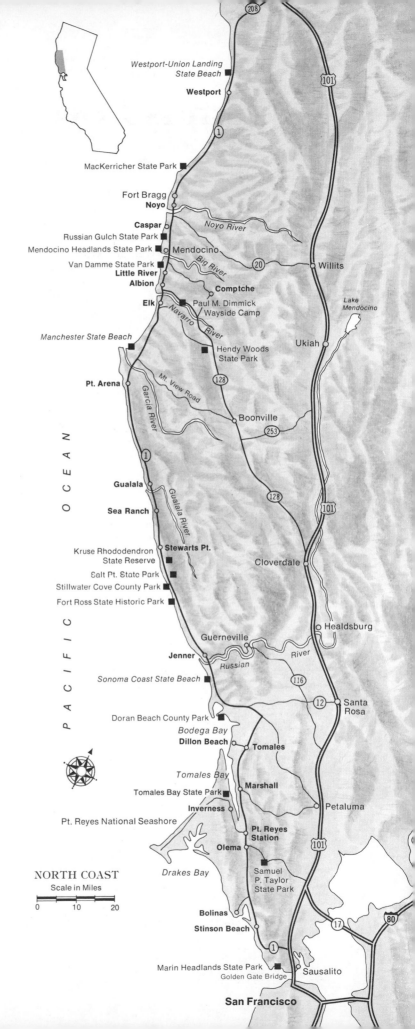

NORTH COAST
Scale in Miles

0    10    20

# Sonoma's Lovely Coastline

Shorter and less developed than the Mendocino coast, its more famous neighbor to the north, the Sonoma coastline begins at Bodega Bay and runs north to the mouth of the Gualala River. Its principal attractions are a series of beach parks, awesome scenery, and Fort Ross, last surviving sign of the 19th-century Russian incursions into California. Terrain divides the whole into three distinct parts: Bodega Bay to Jenner, Jenner to Fort Ross, and Fort Ross to Gualala.

## Around Bodega Bay

The Bodega Bay-Jenner segment of the Sonoma Coast is the most developed and easiest to view. A gently sloping shelf permits State 1 to run right along a series of sandy beaches, only a little over an hour from San Francisco by way of Petaluma.

**Bodega,** an old commonsensical fishing port, clings to the east edge of a lagoon, providing the only suitably protected small boat anchorage of any size between San Francisco and Noyo in Mendocino County. Both charter and commercial boats operate out of Bodega, chasing salmon from May to October and bottom fishing when salmon are scarce.

Perch feed in the lagoon shoals, especially along the west shore. A few gaper clams lurk along the shores, but most of them cluster offshore on a low-tide island. Outside the lagoon surfers can get up and ride toward the spit, starting at a point 400 yards east of the breakwater. Rock fishermen work the jetties and exposed side of Bodega Head. Parents with hyperactive children can be fairly sure of wearing them out in the rolling sand dunes that run all the way from the Head north to Salmon Creek.

**Doran Beach County Park** occupies most of the curving sand spit that reaches across the bay toward Bodega Head, forming the inner lagoon where the moorages are. The outer beach is good for long strolls, sometimes for surfing. Inside, a boat launch adjoins the U.S. Coast Guard station. Camping is toward the tip.

**Westside County Park** adjoins a moorage in the lee of Bodega Head. In essence, it is a pair of parking lots, one for boaters and one for campers. Along with its launch ramp, it offers shore fishing for perch and quick access to Bodega Head's scenic beauties. You'll find picnic tables and trails down to open beaches.

## Sonoma Beaches–for Variety

Small beaches, rocky headlands, and massive offshore rocks characterize Sonoma Coast State Beach. A collection of beaches and coves extends along State 1 from the village of Bodega Bay to the mouth of the Russian River, with over 11 miles of ocean frontage. Beachcombers and fishermen find this stretch of coastline fascinating.

**Bodega Head's** southernmost unit has a new campground—Bodega Dunes. From here you can view the coast north as far as Fort Ross cove, south to Pt. Reyes.

**Salmon Creek** is 1½ miles north of the town of Bodega Bay. Near the parking lot, Salmon Creek forms a summer wading pond. After fall rains break down the bar, it becomes a spawning stream for salmon and steelhead. Local surfers, night-smelters, and surf fishermen use the outer beach. Sand dunes roll away to the south, crisscrossed by walking and bridle paths.

Other beaches unfold in quick succession. All are essentially similar: pockets of sand interrupted by outcrops of rock, good for surf or rock fishing.

**Duncan's Pt.** is a dangerous section of coast. A large sign looms up in front of a barbed wire fence, noting that a number of persons have been swept off the point to their deaths in a pounding sea. For all of that, there's plenty of safe rock fishing in these parks. On the sandy beaches, surf fishing and dip-netting for smelt are good. Duncan's Cove, just in the lee of the point, is one of the most productive day smelt beaches in the region.

**Wright's Beach,** on the north side of the point, is the camping unit of Sonoma Coast State Beach and a picnicker's favorite, as much for the broad, sandy strand as for facilities.

**Goat Rock Beach** is more than one thing—a protected cove, a long, sandy beach reaching out to form the mouth of the Russian River, and a sandy

Stout wooden walls *and gates surround 19th century Russian outpost at Fort Ross, now a state historic park.*

**Weathered barns** *and wavy fences enhance the pastoral Sonoma scene.*

**Clammer** *is up to his nose in pursuit of a gaper; friend keeps an eye out for incoming tide.*

length of river bank. The road to it forks off State 1 near a long, upgrade crest and descends across nearly a mile of meadows to arrive at sea level. The northern end of the park is a popular daytime beach offering good smelt fishing in summer and steelheading in the winter.

## A Russian Fort

Fort Ross is 13 miles north of Jenner, where State 1 finally comes down from elevations that are either awe-inspiring or terrifying, depending on the density of the sea fog and the reliability of the driver. You see the stout, wooden buildings sitting high on the headlands before you reach them. The

parking lot turnoff is just beyond the park.

Now a state historic park and national monument, Fort Ross was originally the American outpost for Russian fur traders of the 19th century. During their reign the Russians and their Aleut hunters wiped out the sea otter herds to the point of extinction, with minor help from American and British competitors. The Aleuts, who learned their trade by hunting Alaskan otter herds, were deadly efficient. Working from two-man kayaks, they hunted in fleets. Several canoes would form a circle and then start constricting the perimeter. When the animals surfaced to breathe, they were harpooned. Or hunters would take a live pup and use its distress cries to lure adult otters into range.

These days, friends of sea otters or enemies of

Russians keep burning down the wooden fort. In 1970 the Commander's House caught fire; within a year, two more fires had damaged the seven-sided blockhouse, devastated the little chapel, and severely damaged the stockade. Painstakingly restored, the fort now looks as it once might have. A small museum within the Commander's House contains relics of the Indian-Russian-American historical eras.

Today you can walk by the Call Ranch, home of the owners of Fort Ross from 1873 to 1903. From here you get a beautiful view of the beach below, once the site of a profitable shipping business. Now rockhounds forage in the gravelly shore, and divers work the rocks north and south in quest of abalone. There's a slight fee for visiting the historic buildings and using the adjacent picnic area. Park hours are 9 A.M. to 5 P.M. daily; to 6 P.M. during the summer.

## The Northern Beaches

From Fort Ross to Mendocino, the coastal shelf is generally narrow but gently sloping, sometimes wooded but mostly covered by meadow grass. It's wise to carry a picnic basket; eating places are few.

Immediately north of Fort Ross the land is privately held as part of the Timber Cove develop-

# Old Inns Are In

Mellow old inns offer a warm welcome to North Coast visitors. Most center around the Mendocino area and serve as bases for exploring the countryside. Varying from the intimate home to the sprawling cottage, each hostelry has charm. Most operate on American (full meals) or modified (breakfast and dinner) plans.

A sampling of inns appears below. Plan to make reservations well in advance and note closed periods. For rates and additional information, write or call the inn directly.

**Vintage North Coast inns** *invite visitors to linger; this is the entrance to Heritage House.*

**Elk Cove Inn,** Box 367, Elk, CA 95432; (707) 877-3321: Old Victorian home with about 7 rooms furnished in "comfortable nostalgia"; guests enjoy reading around the fireplace or wandering on beaches behind the house.

**Harbor House,** Elk, CA 95432; (707) 877-3203: Lovely redwood home in Bernard Maybeck style and cottages (7 rooms total) on the ocean side with path to the beach; open all year; advance reservation only.

**Heritage House,** Little River, CA 95456; (707) 937-5885: Original farmhouse built on the cove in 1877 by relatives of present owner; interesting names and architecture for all 46 units; beautiful living room, lounge, and dining room; notice plantings on sod roofs; closed December and January.

**Little River Inn,** Little River, CA 95456; (707) 937-5942: Maine-style mansion, vintage 1853, forms heart of complex offering "attic rooms," casual cottages, or contemporary hilltop rooms; 9-hole regulation golf course; open all year (lounge and dining room closed for a few weeks before Christmas).

**MacCallum House,** 740 Albion St., Mendocino, CA 95460; (707) 937-0289: Landmark house sold with treasure of contents is now enticing new inn; fruit bowls highlight breakfast in your room; dining room on premises.

**Mendocino Hotel,** Mendocino, CA 95460; (707) 937-0511: Lone survivor of hotels once lining Main Street; extensive recent renovation lends air of opulence; costumed staff.

**Benbow Inn,** Garberville, CA 95440; (707) 923-2124: Tudor English inn in redwoods; Eel River forms lake and beach; 9-hole regulation golf course; large living room, restaurant, and lounge; season runs from April 1 to November 1.

**Modern architecture of Sea Ranch** *rises beyond swamp grass to give a touch of luxury along State 1.*

ment. Walk around to the seaward side of the hotel to take a look at sculptor Beniamino Bufano's last finished work—a monument to Peace—that overlooks both land and sea.

**Stillwater Cove,** a county park 3½ miles north of Fort Ross, opened its cove and creek-front location for day use in 1975.

**Salt Pt. State Park,** midway between Jenner and Stewarts Pt., is worth a stop, whether or not you plan to camp, picnic, or comb the beach. The shore, steep in some places and almost flat in others, provides fine wave action and superior tidepools. This rich environment made Salt Pt. a pioneer unit in the state's marine park system, which preserves the underwater area along the shore for divers.

**Kruse Rhododendron State Reserve** is at its best from April to June when plants are in bloom. You can wander along paths through more than 300 acres set aside to preserve shrubs as high as 20 feet. Sorry, no picnic facilities.

**Stewarts Pt. and Sea Ranch** architecture differ widely. Stewarts Pt.'s general store, hotel, and schoolhouse are clearly late 19th or early 20th century. At Sea Ranch, a private development just up the road, you'll see some striking examples of modern design. Sea Ranch also has a motel, restaurant, and golf course.

**Gualala** is an old lumber port between Anchor Bay and Sea Ranch. The county park occupies the headland and spit, forming the south side of the Gualala River and marking the northern boundary of Sonoma County. You can camp beside the river in which Jack London liked to cast for steelhead. The town's hotel is decorated in late Victorian.

**Salt Pt. State Park,** *unique marine preserve, is noted for superior waves and rich tidepools. Enjoy choice views while camping.*

# Mendocino's Magnificent Coast

The spirit of independence still flourishes in Mendocino County. On December 31, 1974, some citizens of Mendocino "seceded" from the state and formed their own "state"—Northern California. The news elicited no official comment from Sacramento except one wry remark by a veteran observer that "the county's departure, if it ever goes, would scarcely be noticed, at least not until the fog lifted."

Foggy it may be during the summer, but Mendocino's 19th century charm and scenic beauty draws many thousands of visitors yearly and a regular influx of new residents. Urbanization doesn't threaten yet, though; narrow, crooked roads help preserve its relative remoteness, and towns are still small and spaced well apart.

Blue sea and white surf contrast with deep green forests and weathered gray barns. In the 100 miles from Gualala to Rockport, the mood changes around every headland, making this a photographer's field day. Even the gap-toothed fences are appealing.

For most visitors the heart of this rugged coast is the short distance from Mendocino to Fort Bragg. At either end of this stretch, you'll find less deep sea fishing, less Victoriana, and less tourism but more expansive beaches for driftwood hunters and surf fishermen.

**Highways and byways** are more prevalent on this part of the coast than farther south. The southern boundary of the county lies only 125 miles north of San Francisco, the northern edge only 250 miles. And yet a weekend can often mean more hours on the road than on the beach. (For a delightful loop drive, head east from Mendocino to Comptche, north to State 20, and west to Noyo, just below Fort Bragg.) Most visitors find it comforting to have at least three days on hand to linger in comfortable old inns, browse among art galleries, and picnic on pebbly beaches.

State 1 clings to the seaward edge of Mendocino County. Much of it is two lanes, within a mile of the sea and almost always in sight of it. Dipping and twisting across sharply ridged country and around deep coves, the highway takes you across the mouths of Mendocino's many rivers and creeks. Forty miles an hour is average speed.

To reach the Mendocino coast you can join State 1 at its Leggett junction with U.S. 101 north of Fort Bragg or come up the Sonoma coast.

Two other routes provide easy access. State 128 meanders north and west from Cloverdale on U.S. 101, passing through miles of rolling orchard and vineyard country before becoming a winding path through towering redwood forests. You pass through several hamlets along the 57 miles of well-paved, two-lane highway. State 20 is more direct and the area it passes through less inhabited. The highway leaves U.S. 101 at Willits and joins State 1 just south of Fort Bragg-Noyo. Paralleling the route of the Skunk train, you'll travel 35 miles through fine stands of redwoods and Douglas fir. Watch for logging trucks on any road.

**Accommodations** center around the Mendocino-Fort Bragg area of the coast. You have your choice of old-time establishments or modern motels.

Inns in Little River and Elk, as well as a hotel and several inns in Mendocino, recall the nostalgia of the past (see page 78). If you wish to stay at one of these places, reservations are essential. Reservations are also advisable, especially during the summer and on weekends, at motels in Fort Bragg and Mendocino. For a list of accommodations, write to Fort Bragg-Mendocino Coast Chamber of Commerce, P.O. Box 1141, Fort Bragg, CA 95437.

**Weather** is variable. Your best chances for a good outing are in May and early June when the azaleas and rhododendrons are in bloom and summer traffic is not, or during September and October when the weather is balmy and the roads and campgrounds are less crowded. Tourist season runs from Memorial Day to Labor Day, even though the coastal fog bank often descends during summer months.

The rainy season begins around mid-October; most of the annual rainfall of 35 inches occurs between December and May. Most winter days are in the 40° to 50° range; summer temperatures often get into the 70s.

## Beach Parks and Campgrounds

Getting down to the shore or back into the forest is mainly a matter of getting to the public beaches scattered along the coast from Gualala to Fort Bragg. Ranging from flat, sandy coves to tunneled headlands, most of them have fine camping or picnicking facilities and abundant scenery.

**Manchester State Beach** has the first generous sand beach in Mendocino County and the last one south of Fort Bragg. Almost 7 miles of wide shore, it runs most of the distance between the Garcia River and Alder Creek. Middling good for sand castles, the beach is far roomier than its minimally developed campground, sheltered behind dunes from the frequent winds. To the south you see Pt. Arena's lighthouse; open weekends.

**Van Damme State Park,** on scenic Little River, offers campsites, reasonably safe (but cold) swimming, and biking or hiking trails. One trail leads to an ancient pygmy forest of stunted conifers in the southeast quarter of the park. Its beach is a pleasant wayside stop but only a minor introduction to the main park on the inland side of the highway.

**Mendocino Headlands State Park,** whose splendor needs no real development, begins at the mouth of the Big River as a sandy beach, loops west beneath the bluffs as a wall of rock, and then broadens out to cover the flat fields of the headlands, as well as their wave-swept edge. Heeser Drive, a loop road west of Mendocino town, circles along the edge of the bluff and down to the beach. This is a highly sculpted shore, with wave tunnels, arched rocks, narrow channels—even a few lagoons. Tidepoolers are expected to develop a "look but don't touch" attitude, and skin divers fare well. The easiest activity is scrambling around the rocks to watch an unusually picturesque surf pound its way ashore; the outermost point contends for honors as the finest wave-watching spot on the coast. Because offshore rocks or shoals temper the fury of on-rushing swells, safe vantages are only a few feet away. At the north end of Heeser Drive, a public fishing access adjoins calmer seas.

# Next Time, Try the "Skunk"

Linking Fort Bragg on the Mendocino coast with Willits, 40 miles inland on the Redwood Highway (U. S. 101), the California Western Railroad "Skunk" trains take you through the heart of towering redwood forests along a spectacular route inaccessible to auto travel.

For nature fans and camera addicts, the trip offers an opportunity to enjoy some of Northern California's most magnificent wilderness scenery at a leisurely pace. For train buffs and children, the train experience alone is thrill enough.

Originally a logging railroad for the Union Lumber Company of Fort Bragg, California Western traces its history back to 1885. The self-powered railcars—affectionately called "Skunks" for their original gas engines—were inaugurated in 1925. Service is casual, with stops made on passenger request to deliver mail and groceries to residents along the route or to let off fishermen and picnickers.

In 1965 an authentic old-time passenger train called the "Super Skunk" joined the line. Powered by a 2-8-2 Mikado steam locomotive half a century old, the popular addition fills up quickly, so make reservations well in advance. Another steam locomotive joined the line in 1970, alternating with the Super Skunk during peak load periods. Making just one stop on the way, the steam trains take about 2½ hours one-way; the Skunks make the crooked run in 2 hours.

A round-trip ticket for adults costs around $8, but prices and schedules change. To ensure a ride, write to the California Western Railroad, Box 907-B, Fort Bragg, CA 95437.

**Puffing across bridge** *over Noyo River, the "Super Skunk" travels through dense redwood groves between Fort Bragg and Willits.*

**Waves carve bluff** *in picturesque Mendocino headland. View to south is replay of pocket cove.*

**Sheepish smile** *signals delight at shedding heavy coat during Boonville's annual shearing.*

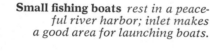

**Small fishing boats** *rest in a peaceful river harbor; inlet makes a good area for launching boats.*

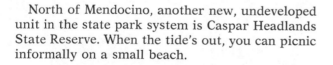

North of Mendocino, another new, undeveloped unit in the state park system is Caspar Headlands State Reserve. When the tide's out, you can picnic informally on a small beach.

**Russian Gulch State Park** looks back across a broad bay at Mendocino town from the next headland to the north. It offers a compacted replay of the sheltered beach at Van Damme and the exposed headlands at Mendocino. A creek cutting out of the namesake gulch pauses in a low, sandy spot so children may splash around in safety, and then slips into the sea in the lee of an especially craggy, lofty headland. A blowhole just north of the main overlook only works right during storms.

From its dramatic edge, the main body of the park runs deep inland; protected campsites nestle in the mouth of the canyon. It's an easy hike upstream to a lacy waterfall set amidst a forest underlaid with fields of ferns.

**MacKerricher State Park,** most versatile of the string, begins north of Fort Bragg where Pudding Creek empties into the sea. Greatly enlarged in 1972, it has headlands, beaches, surf, heavily forested uplands, and even a small lake for fishing and boating. A road wanders down to the shore between a rocky beach to the south and sandy beach to the north, which runs all the way from the main parking area to Ten Mile River. Chief reasons for heading out along the dunes would be smelt in season or all-year driftwood-hunting. You can get to the Ten Mile River end of the beach from an old logging road off State 1.

Like Van Damme and Russian Gulch to the south, MacKerricher is popular and, despite three campgrounds, rarely has campsite vacancies in summer. For information on any of these parks, write to the Area Manager, Mendocino Area State Parks, P. O. Box 127, Mendocino, CA 95460; call Ticketron for reservations.

## Inland to Boonville

About 30 miles inland from the windy Mendocino coast lie the quiet ranches and hillside pastures of the Anderson Valley. Boonville, largest town on State 128 between Cloverdale and the ocean, was settled in the 1850s. The people of the town and surrounding ranches still make their living from growing apples and raising sheep, cattle, and hogs.

**Events** are scattered throughout the year. In the spring when apple blossoms and native western azaleas color the valley pink and white against sheep-cropped, green hills, it's time for the local art show (March), the wildflower festival (April), and "Buck-a-roo Days," a rodeo in June. In July, sheep raisers gather to exchange gossip, compete for prizes, and feast on barbecued lamb. Held under tall shade trees at the Mendocino County Fairgrounds, this event attracts many visitors.

In the fall and winter, steelhead run in Navarro River, and roadside stands sell the valley's fine apples. September is the month for the County Fair and Apple Festival; reminiscent of old-time fairs, it draws visitors from all over the West.

**Camps and parks** dot the roadside. Paul M. Dimmick Wayside Camp, a 12-acre redwood park between the highway and the river, makes a handy base for both trailer and tent campers. Forested Hendy Woods State Park has two camping areas, a stream for summer swimming and fishing, and two stands of virgin redwoods.

## Mendocino to Fort Bragg

From Little River on the south to Fort Bragg on the north, Mendocino County reaches a sort of high point. These miles are the most populous, the most popular with tourists, and contain the two principal towns and the major fishing harbor. Progress is so complete that State 1 has been straightened and widened, bringing Mendocino and Fort Bragg within 15 minutes of one another. However, the best plan is not to hurry. There's variety to savor.

### Mendocino: New England revisited

Almost startlingly in contrast to its time and place, this small cluster of wooden towers and carpenter's Gothic houses contains a fully contemporary society of artists and artisans. They share a view south across the mouth of the Big River and west across the grassy headlands to the sea. It's instructive to amble through the numerous galleries and see how resident artists translate such scenes in oils, wood blocks, and water colors.

## Smile, If You Call a Man a *Haireem*

Like the Hawaiians with their pidgin and the cockneys with their rhyming slang, some of the people of Boonville speak a dialect quite their own. It's called Boontling, and when a real Boonter speaks it, there's an uneven lilt and a touch of humor that runs all through the more than 1,000 words of vocabulary that make it up.

Boontling grew up in Boonville in the late 1880s when the men would meet in town and try to *shark* (stump) each other with a new Boont word. Origins of some words have been lost, for Boontling developed as a spoken language and has only recently been written. But the old-timers have passed along most of the words to the new generations, and several logical patterns are apparent in word formation.

All through Boontling, names have become descriptive nouns, and a spirit of fun prevails. Those who speak it today do so strictly to entertain each other. These are some of the words they use:

A *Charlie Walker* is a photograph, after the one-legged photographer from Mendocino who took Boonville family portraits. A big mustache is a *Tom Bacon*—named for the man who could reputedly wrap his handlebar around his ears. Horace Greeley's name is used for any journalist, but especially to signify a newspaperman.

A *relf* is a rail fence, a *hairk* is a haircut, a *haireem* is a "hairy mouth" or dog, and *skipe* is a clergyman, from sky pilot. If you add the word "region" to these, a *hairk region* becomes barbershop and a *skipe region*, a church.

The remainder of Boontling is made up mostly of words or phrases whose connotation is immediately clear to a Boonter. *Featherlegged* means a know-it-all and comes from the strutting barnyard cocks. *Trashmovers* (big storms) tell something of winter problems in a rural community.

It's not easy to hear Boontling because Boonters speak it mostly to each other. But if you buy a cup of coffee or a sandwich in town, take a good look at the receipt. Across the bottom may be written: "Our Gorm is Boll, our Zeese is hot; some regions de-Hig you, but we will not." One hint: *Boll* means good.

**Headland offers** *a panoramic view of quaint Mendocino. Once a lumber town, it now shelters artists.*

**Mendocino visitors** *tread wooden sidewalks past old buildings hiding new art galleries and shops.*

A Cape Cod-style village, settled as a mill town in 1852 by timber baron Henry Meiggs, Mendocino may look like a relic, but its weathered buildings are bursting with life. Park your car as soon as you get to town. Streets are short, narrow, and easily jammed by vehicle traffic. It's good biking terrain.

Pick up a *Mendocino Gallery and Shop Guide* from any store. It will lead you to the Mendocino Art Center (heart of the coastal renaissance), past homes of long-dead lumber barons, to art galleries, book stores, unusual shops, and coffee houses. Be sure to notice the Old Masonic Hall with its intriguing rooftop sculpture of Father Time braiding a maiden's hair.

## Fort Bragg—for fish and flowers

Just up the road is the harbor town of Noyo, sportfishing center of Mendocino County. Charter boats operate out of a deep cove just inside the mouth of the Noyo River. Private boats go in here at a free public launching ramp; standard rate is about $15 for a half-day of salmon fishing. Fishing season runs from June until the first week in October (weekends only after school starts). Some of the best seafood restaurants are on the Noyo flat.

Fort Bragg, largest city on the coast between San Francisco and Eureka, was first settled as an army post in 1857, then resettled with the construction of its first sawmill in 1885. Paul Bunyan Days (Labor Day weekend) bring big crowds to watch modern loggers perform axe throwing, pole climbing, and log rolling. You can tour the Georgia-Pacific Company on Redwood Avenue, one block west of State 1, hop aboard the strangely named "Skunk" train (see page 81) for an 80-mile round-trip junket through redwood groves to Willits on U.S. 101, picnic and fish (slight fee) at the Fort Bragg Trout Farm pond from noon to dusk, or visit the Mendocino Coast Botanical Gardens, a lavish, 47-acre color display of plants and bulbs. (Gardens are open daily 8:30 A.M. to 6 P.M.; there's a moderate charge.)

Beyond Fort Bragg the coastal shelf narrows to next to nothing, then nothing. Weathered Westport's New England-style houses have changed little since the heydays of lumbering. Shore fishing is productive at Westport-Union Landing State Beach and South Kibesillah Gulch Coast Angling Access Area. A pair of unpaved parking lots alongside the highway give access to several hundred yards of vertical shore.

# The Redwood Highway

Before the Gold Rush brought a surge of new population to Northern California, a vast forest of the world's tallest trees—the coast redwood or *Sequoia sempervirens*—blanketed an area up to 30 miles wide, ranging 450 miles from the Santa Lucia Mountains south of Monterey northward into a corner of Oregon. The oldest known coast redwood was 2,200 years old when cut in the 1930s.

Civilization's demands have left only small parts of the forest primeval. The majority of the remaining redwoods are located along U.S. 101 from Leggett north to Crescent City. One of California's unique attractions, these giants grow naturally in no other part of the country.

**The Avenue of the Giants,** a 30-mile, alternate scenic route, roughly parallels U.S. 101. Winding leisurely between 300-foot-high trees, it offers a closer view of these "ambassadors from another age." The entrance is at Sylvandale, about 6 miles north of Garberville. The avenue ends about 5 miles north of Pepperwood (30 miles south of Eureka). Numerous turnouts and parking areas allow for "neck-craning"; trails lead strollers through tranquil glens and along river banks. By zooming along U.S. 101, you'll miss these sylvan glades, public campgrounds, picnicking and swimming facilities, and a few small towns on the way.

Logging still goes on, and visitors are not encouraged at harvesting areas. But you can visit demonstration forests, stop by reforestation displays, or visit the Pacific Lumber Company (one of the world's largest mills) at Scotia. At the main headquarters you get passes for self-guiding plant tours on weekdays.

Private displays include the popular drive-through trees: for 50 cents or a dollar you can drive your car through a living redwood. Since not all cuts were made for today's wider cars, pickup campers, and wide trailers, make sure there's room to squeeze through.

**Weather** is variable in redwood land. The finest season is autumn; then the crowds thin out, the air turns brisk, and the seasonal show of color brightens the countryside. Wildflower season along the coast often extends from March until August, but April to June is the best period. Because redwoods grow best along the cool coast, expect rainfall and summer fogs.

Eureka, the major city in the redwoods, is one of the cooler places in the nation from June until October. From this city north to the Oregon border, the weather is much the same as that experienced along the Mendocino coast. South of Eureka, after U.S. 101 cuts behind the coast hills, you get an entirely different kind of climate. Because the mountains screen out the cooling ocean air, summers can be warm and dry.

**Accommodations** in redwood country are somewhat limited. Many more motels and hotels line this highway than appear along the Mendocino coast, but traffic is correspondingly heavier. Eureka and Arcata have a number of motels between them, but during summer's tourist peak, it's wise to have advance reservations. Without reservations you'll have a better chance of finding a place to stay in Orick (gateway to the Redwood National Park) or in Crescent City. Roadside motels and inns are scattered along the road between Willits

**Wooden tavern sign** *is one of many handcrafted Mendocino touches. Some carvings sit atop roofs.*

and Eureka. Ukiah, at the southern extreme of the area, also offers a number of motels. Camping is very popular during the summer.

## Pick a Park

The best of the remaining coast redwoods are preserved in the Redwood National Park and in several state parks along the Redwood Highway (U.S. 101). Parks are busy throughout the summer, offering informative naturalist programs, nature hikes, and evening campfires. If you're of the school that believes a family visiting the redwoods ought to have a square mile or so to itself, plan your trip in the off season.

South of Eureka, the best groves, most of the state parks, and the highway all stay close to the South Fork of the Eel River. Sprawling Humboldt Redwoods State Park is the main attraction, but there are other good spots for campers. Several of the smaller parks contain awesome stands of old-growth redwoods and are frequently less crowded than the more publicized Humboldt groves. Standish-Hickey State Recreation Area, just north of Leggett, has plenty of camping but only one mature redwood among dense forest. Picnicking is popular at Smithe Redwoods State Reserve, a little farther north. You can hike to a waterfall or take a footpath down to the Eel River.

**Richardson Grove State Park** is relatively small (about 800 acres), but you can't fail to find it—the Redwood Highway goes right through it. Here are swimming holes along the Eel River's South Fork and highly developed campgrounds. Ten miles of trails make good hiking. Although it can be wet and chilly in the winter, Richardson Grove is open the year around. In winter, silver and king salmon and steelhead trout attract many fishermen.

**Humboldt Redwoods State Park** is scattered along most of the length of the Avenue of the Giants and the Eel River. Acquired piece by piece, the park complex now ties together more than 70 memorial groves. It begins unobtrusively at the Whittemore Grove across the river from the highway; take Briceland Road at Redway. Beyond Miranda, the groves are fairly continuous to the junction of the South Fork and the main Eel, with major breaks at Myers Flat, Weott, and the freeway overpass that has cut a tremendous swath between Founders Grove and California Federation of Women's Clubs Grove. At Burlington, in a dark copse of second growth, an all-year campground adjoins the park headquarters. Rangers on duty give information on camping and picnic facilities in other parts of the park and, in autumn, tell where to see the best color display.

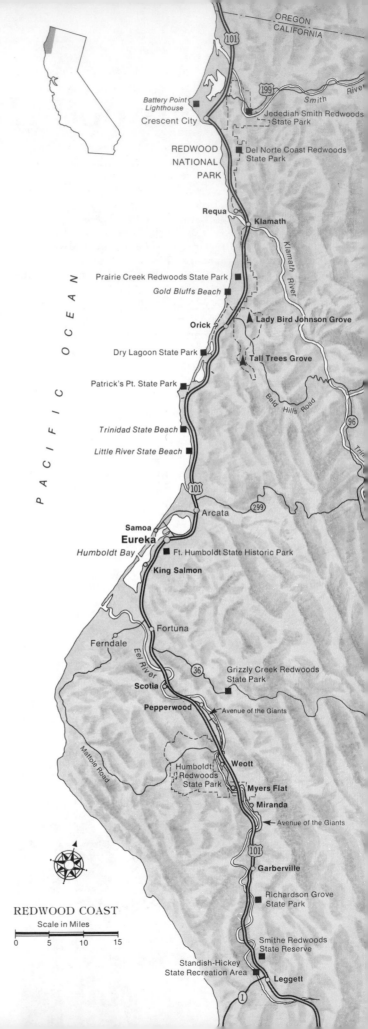

Highlights of the park include the Founders Tree, for many years considered the world's tallest (364 feet before a broken top brought the figure down to 347); the solemn depths of the Rockefeller Forest; the wide pebble beach of the Eel, where you can stand back and look at redwoods from top to bottom instead of being encircled and overwhelmed; and Bull Creek flats, where you can sit underneath the soaring trees and listen to the silence or stroll down to the site of the present "tallest" tree, Giant tree, and Flatiron tree.

For further information on both parks, write to the Area Manager, Richardson Grove State Park, Garberville, CA 95440.

**Grizzly Creek Redwoods State Park,** a small, secluded area along the Van Duzen River, is highly prized by picnickers and campers because of its climate, often warmer and less foggy than parks right along the coast. Its 234 acres include a virgin redwood grove, more than a mile of river front, hiking trails, and 30 improved campsites—but no grizzlies. Summer trout fishing is fair to good; steelheading is good from mid-February to mid-April. The park is 18 miles east of U.S. 101 on State 36.

# Eureka: A Victorian City

Lumbering and fishing built Eureka, largest city in Humboldt County, and are still its main industries. Sniff the air: the odors come from waterfront docks along Humboldt Bay or pulp mills south of town. Eureka is a midway point between San Francisco and Portland; you'll have to get off the main highway and drive through town to enjoy its charms. Here you'll discover many motels, a delightful Victorian hotel, and several fine restaurants particularly well known for their seafood. For maps, stop by the Chamber of Commerce, 2112 Broadway, on your way into town. During the summer, the chamber offers a 5-hour bus tour, including lunch and a bay cruise; price is moderate and reservations are a must.

**Ft. Humboldt State Historic Park,** constructed in the 1850s and abandoned in 1865, is a half-mile off U.S. 101 on the southern edge of Eureka. Open daily from dawn to dusk, a small museum behind the park headquarters gives a brief history of the fort where Ulysses S. Grant spent several months just prior to his resignation from the army. On display is a selection of equipment used for turn-of-the-century logging near a reconstruction of a typical logger's cabin. On a clear day the view of Humboldt Bay is outstanding.

**Sequoia Park** (Glatt and W Streets) is a woodland oasis in the heart of Eureka. On these 52 acres,

you'll find one of the best forests in this region. You can walk leafy trails past ferns and streams, stop at a zoo and children's playground, or feed the ducks the remains of your picnic lunch. A shady haven on rare warm days, it's equally pleasant when the weather is cool and foggy.

**Victorian-sighting** is excellent in Eureka. Except for downtown thoroughfares, the town still retains much of its original character. Brightly colored turrets, spires, and gables show up well against the often-foggy sky. Most homes are well preserved or being renovated. The largest concentration of Victorian homes is south of Seventh Street between C and K streets. Some will be moved as construction proceeds on the freeway through town. Fortunately, they will be preserved in a Victorian quarter near the much-photographed Carson Mansion (between Second and Third streets on M Street).

Now a private men's club, the "mansion" looks much as it did when completed by lumber baron William Carson in 1886. Decide for yourself whether it is "the finest example of Victorian Gothic architecture ever built" or an "architectural monstrosity." The smaller house across the street was also built by Carson as a wedding gift for his son. A carriage house, connected by a walkway, houses an interior decorator's studio.

Downtown, "Old Town" is being refurbished. A new park at Second and F streets is finished, and

**Immaculate, gaily painted** *Victorian home on Eureka's G Street is one of many in this northern coastal city. Viennese-curtained, double bay windows are striking.*

additional landscaping and face lifting go on. Clarke Museum (Third and E streets) has outstanding collections of mounted birds, Indian artifacts, and pioneer relics.

## Humboldt Bay

Just beyond the waterfront section of downtown Eureka and almost concealed from the highway is Humboldt Bay, largest deep-water port between Portland and San Francisco. You can explore the harbor on an old ferry, study the bay's birdlife, go boating and fishing, or beachcomb over the long stretches of sand guarding the harbor's narrow entrance.

**Getting around the bay** is easy when you take a narrated boat cruise leaving several times a day from the foot of Commercial Street. You'll see bay highlights and hear a brief history of the area. Watch the commercial fishing fleet coming into the harbor with nets still dripping from their catches or the large ocean freighters loading pulp on the peninsula.

Six boat ramps and two hoists make it easy to put your boat into the water. You'll find public ramps at several points: at the Eureka Mooring Basin, on the North Spit before the Coast Guard station, and at Fields Landing on South Bay. You can rent a skiff or charter a boat at King Salmon and use hoists and a ramp for a nominal fee.

**Crossing the bridge** to Samoa takes you over Woodley and Indian islands. Marshy Indian Island, part of the Humboldt Bay National Wildlife Refuge, is the site of the northernmost egret/heron rookery along the Pacific Coast. In a small grove of cypress, you may see hundreds of roosting birds, massed like a feathery white cloud. A sign at Samoa marks the turnoff to the Cookhouse, where you dine family style at one of the last lumber camp cookhouses still operating in the West.

From Samoa you can continue along the North Spit across Mad River Slough to Arcata, where a self-guiding architectural tour takes you back to the time of Bret Harte and the heydays of gold mining. A few miles north of Arcata, the Azalea State Reserve bursts forth into bloom around Memorial Day. Trails lead you among masses of overhanging blossoms. Take the North Bank Road from either U.S. 101 or State 299.

## A valley loop

A 73-mile loop trip through pastoral Mattole Valley to the sea and back into the redwoods can begin at Ferndale, about 15 miles south of Eureka. You can find ingredients for a picnic in one of its several stores—the last well-stocked shops you pass until your return to the highway. Fresh-as-paint

**Bridge leads** *across stream into the quiet stillness of virgin redwood grove in Redwood National Park.*

Ferndale is a study in carpenter's Gothic. A Mendocino of yesteryear, the village is full of artisans. At the annual art festival in May, displays of arts and crafts line Main Street. The village also hosts the county fair in August. For an overall town view (and a steep uphill climb), try 30-acre Russ Park. Take Ocean Avenue east from Main Street; your hike starts just west of the Catholic cemetery.

Continue your drive on the road over Bear River Ridge; you'll coast downhill through manicured pastures and finally reach the shore.

Heading back inland you'll pass through Petrolia, site of California's first drilled oil wells, and Honeydew, one of California's smallest towns. The village consists of a general store, gas station, and post office—all under one roof. Back in the redwoods, the road slants down to Bull Creek through Rockefeller Grove, meeting U.S. 101 about 2½ miles north of Weott.

## Redwood National Park

A representative segment of old-growth redwood and the outstanding coastal scenery in Northern California are now being protected so that, generations from now, people will be able to view the magnificent trees and the plant and animal life which they nurture. Redwood National Park is 46 miles long (extending from Crescent City south to a point on Redwood Creek opposite Big Lagoon) and 7 miles wide at its greatest width. Information centers are at Orick and Crescent City.

Klamath, at the mouth of the river, is well known for its fine salmon and steelhead fishing. You can take a 64-mile jet boat trip up the river just to view the scenery. Boats leave the Requa dock at 9 A.M. and return at 3 P.M. The cost is moderate.

**Lady Bird Johnson Grove** is located along the Bald Hills Road 2 miles east of U.S. 101 (just north of Orick). A half-mile trail will take you to the site where Mrs. Lyndon B. Johnson dedicated the national park on November 25, 1968.

**Tall Trees Grove,** home of the sky-scraping sequoias, can be reached by an 8½-mile trail beginning along Redwood Creek just west of Bald Hills Road. The tallest tree is 367.8 feet high and 14 feet in diameter. Primitive camping is available.

## Three Parks within a Park

Included within the Redwood National Park are three long-established state parks (Prairie Creek, Del Norte, and Jedediah Smith). In addition to being the nucleus of the national park, at present these parks have the only established camping. Federal recreation permits are not valid in the state parks, and summer reservations are a must for the 350-plus campsites.

Much of the redwood forest acreage of the state parks consists of memorial groves purchased by the Save-the-Redwoods League with donations from private individuals. Supplemented by state funds, this money is used to acquire more redwood groves and enlarge the parks.

**Prairie Creek Redwoods State Park** is a favorite of many campers. It does have more than its share of special wonders: a handsome creek, a herd of native Roosevelt elk, Gold Bluffs Beach, and scenic Fern Canyon. About 100 inches of rain falls on Prairie Creek most years, giving it rain-forest overtones; but high ground to the west protects it from most of the chilly ocean winds and fog. Hiking the more than 40 miles of trails (including one for the blind) is the best way to explore the park's interior. Two campgrounds offer a total of 100 sites.

**Del Norte Coast Redwoods State Park** lets you enjoy both a drive through rugged inland forest on U. S. 101 and vistas of rugged Pacific shore from high turnouts south of the wooded section. Damnation Creek Trail will take you on foot through the dense forest to the ocean where the giant redwoods grow almost to the shore. From April to July, you'll see outstanding displays of rhododendrons and azaleas. Del Norte has excellent camping facilities at Mill Creek Campground.

# Don't Miss

**Avenue of the Giants** (U.S. 101 bypass north of Garberville)—shady retreat from freeway traffic takes you into groves of 300-foot redwoods; has plenty of "pull-outs" for picnics or quiet hikes; a foretaste of the Redwood National Park to the north

**Fort Ross** (State 1)—remnant of the Russian fur trading days, this fort still stands, although burned several times; you can visit the restored stockhouse, commandant's house, and chapel; beach is open and picnics are popular

**Gold Bluffs Beach** (Prairie Creek Redwoods State Park)—wide expanse of sand once sifted for its gold makes for exciting hiking; at the north end you'll discover Fern Canyon and a secret waterfall; watch for elk frequenting the beach

**Mendocino** (State 1)—New England architecture with overtones of modern art mark this picturesque former lumbering port; at the Headlands you can walk, fish, or enjoy wave-watching

**Pt. Reyes National Seashore** (Marin County)—long, lonely, windswept beaches contrast with grassy, forested slopes; at the visitor center, you'll find a Morgan horse ranch and a blacksmith shop to explore

**Skunk** (Ft. Bragg to Willits)—a strangely named little train chugs along a 40-mile track, winding around spectacular curves and crossing dozens of trestles and bridges; trips along the Noyo riverbed last about 2 hours each way

**Jedediah Smith Redwoods State Park** is 9 miles northeast of Crescent City on U.S. 199. At the northernmost end of the Redwood National Park, Jed Smith presents views of skyline ridges still tightly furred with giant redwoods. The highway runs through hilly Tyson Grove and the National Tribute Grove (just two of ten memorial groves in the park) and then out onto a magnificent flat, where some of the most imposing redwoods soar above vine maple, salal, Oregon grape, and ferns.

The Smith River provides good salmon, steelhead, and trout fishing in season and sandy beaches for sun-bathing. There are numerous campsites and trails. Crescent City, at the gateway to the park, sits alongside a captivating harbor. Information on the area is available from the Chamber of Commerce and the Visitor Information Center for the national park.

Battery Pt. Lighthouse, built in 1856, stands on a small island approximately 20 yards from shore. Visitors may walk to it several hours each day at low tide. Though your target is a museum inside, most of the fun lies in getting there.

# Four Wine Valleys

 The growing appreciation of wines in the United States has uncorked a new flow of visitors to California's vineyards and tasting rooms. Between 1½ and 3 million people visit the Napa and Sonoma wineries (backbone of the North Coast wine district) each year. Here you see vinous works of art created and sample the results of the creativity—a delicious way to increase your knowledge of wine.

Winery architecture is intriguingly diverse. Handsome traditional buildings from the late 1800s show their European heritage; California ingenuity adds a variety of touches, ranging from mission to modern.

You could visit as many as 20 cellars in a day, if you planned your route with care. But you would miss the details—and details are what make wine. Don't try to visit more than three or four wineries in one day. Do plan to stop and visit other attractions in the area. The wine country lends itself to lazing; bring a picnic basket along or stop at one of the bakeries and cheese factories along the way.

When to go? The best time to visit the wine country is the most active period—late September and early October—when the crush (the initial fermenting of the new year's wines) takes place. The heady aroma of newly crushed grapes charges the warm afternoon air. Vines, stripped of their clusters of grapes, are tinged with gold and scarlet. Inside the wineries, in spite of hurried labor over the grapes, amiable guides welcome visitors as nonchalantly as they might in the still days of winter when the wines take care of themselves. Local harvest festivals add to the conviviality.

Divided into regions, this chapter points out typical wineries, lists main attractions, and offers a cool look at water sports, hiking, and camping locations.

*Rutherford, in the Napa Valley, looks much like other wine-growing areas, but veteran vintners say they can detect special taste from grapes.*

# Napa Valley:
# for Touring and Tasting

Many people consider the Napa Valley synonymous with "The Wine Country"—and with good reason. The vine-covered floor of the valley, flanked with tall hills and dotted with evocative wineries, may have its peers, but it has few superiors.

Easy to get to, Napa Valley is most accessible from Sacramento, San Francisco, and Oakland on a combination of Interstate Highway 80 and State Highway 29 from Vallejo. Another slower, hillier, and prettier route from San Francisco goes across the Golden Gate and then north on U.S. 101, State 37, and State 121. From the north, take U.S. 101 and State 128 for a pleasant drive.

The greatest concentration of wineries open to visitors flanks State 29 north and south of the unhurried town of St. Helena. A parallel road, the Silverado Trail, is a more leisurely route at the foot of the east hills, elevated enough to give panoramic vineyard views. Most of the old stagecoach route has been widened and straightened to suit the modern automobile. Crossroads among the vineyards tie the two together and make it easy to cover the entire valley and poke up into the hills.

## Touring the Wineries

Napa Valley's microclimatic characteristics are highly desirable for fine grape growing; today, 22,500 acres are under cultivation. Much of the valley has been declared an "agricultural preserve." Although you could drive through the valley in less than an hour, you'd miss visiting wineries dating back to the 19th century, learning of traditional and new processing methods, and sipping the results.

Presented alphabetically, the wineries listed in this chapter are only a smattering of what you'll see. For a free booklet listing wineries that welcome visitors, write the Wine Institute, 717 Market St., San Francisco, CA 94103. A free "Guide Map to Napa Valley Wines" is published by the Napa County Development Council, P.O. Box 636, Napa, CA 94558. The *Sunset* book *California Wine Country* gives a brief description of all California wineries, locator maps, and visitor hours. Most wineries close at Easter, Thanksgiving, Christmas, and New Year's Day. You'll notice some wineries have places to picnic; others offer dining rooms.

**Beaulieu Vineyard** (Rutherford), familiarly known as BV, has ivy-covered buildings dating back to 1885. Owned by a French family until 1969, it's now part of Heublein Corporation. Open daily 10-4; guided tours and new tasting room.

**Beringer Wines** (St. Helena) was started by a German family and operated by the family's descendants until sold to Nestle in 1971. A guided tour includes ascent into unique old hillside aging tunnels. Open daily 9:30-4; tasting room is Gothic Rhine House.

**The Christian Brothers** cellars are at Mont LaSalle (along with novitiate and vineyard) west of Napa, and at mammoth Greystone in St. Helena. Both locations open daily 10:30-4, with tours and tasting.

**Inglenook** (Rutherford) appeals to romantics. The original building's stone facade supports arched doors and windows, cupolas, and other frills; it's draped with ivy. On the tour you'll see 19th century oak casks and hear the story of the gravel floors. Open 9:30-5; tasting room.

**Hanns Kornell Champagne Cellars** (Larksmead Lane north of St. Helena) represents a one-man success story. You'll get a fine tour of bottle-fermented champagne making and be invited to taste-test sparkling wines. Open daily 10-5.

**Charles Krug** (St. Helena) founded his winery in 1861, building one stone structure to keep wines and another to keep horses (both at a constant temperature of 59°). Bought by the Mondavi family in 1943, it has handsome grounds where the August Moon Concerts are held on Saturday evenings. Open daily 10-4; the tasting room looks onto the vineyards.

**Louis M. Martini** (St. Helena) is considered one of the valley's most deeply rooted family-owned wineries. Winery tours are especially instructive here because all working parts of the winemaking equipment are exposed. Open 10-4; handsome tasting room.

**Robert Mondavi Winery** (Oakville) crushed its first grapes in 1966 while designer Cliff May was still completing the mission-style building. On the lawn beneath the open arch separating the two wings, summer concerts, art shows, and special tastings take place. Open daily 10-4:30; tasting room; lunches and dinners by appointment.

**Nichelini Vineyard** (11 miles east of Rutherford on State 128) offers a change from formal tasting and touring. This family winery, open 10-6 weekends and holidays, welcomes informal visits; tasting will probably occur on the terrace just outside the cellar door.

**Sterling Vineyard's** (south of Calistoga) Aegean church-style architecture high atop a hill can

**Winery architecture** *varies from traditional to modern throughout wine valleys. Sterling Winery* **(above)** *is Grecian in design; Beringer* **(left)** *offers tasting in Gothic Rhine House.*

# How to Become a Wine Snob

Though wine tasting is fun, there's no short course in becoming a "pro." The complexities of enology take years to learn. Most wineries run tasting rooms with wines organized in a sequence so each sample shows off to advantage: dry whites first, followed by rosés, reds, appetizers, then desserts; sparkling wines come last.

Here are a few basic tests which may help make you more knowledgeable:

**Sight**—look for color and clarity. The liquid should be clear. Table wines should not have brownish tints (whites range from pale gold to straw yellow, reds from crimson to ruby or slightly purplish, rosés from pink orange to pink). Most dessert wines will have a brownish or even deep amber tint, depending on type.

**Smell**—is it fresh and fruity? Don't confuse *aroma*, the smell of the grapes, with *bouquet*, the smell of fermentation and aging. New wines seldom have bouquet; appetizer and dessert wines have little aroma and substantial bouquet.

**Taste**—it can range from sweet to sour, bitter, and salty. Most "taste" is an extension of smell. Some qualities can be perceived only after the wine is on the taster's palate: acidity (liveliness versus flatness), astringency (young red wines will have a tannic puckeriness in all but the most mellow), and weight or body (light versus rich).

**A last note.** "Dry" simply describes the absence of sugar. Dry wines are sometimes thought sour because acidity and tannin are more evident.

hardly be missed. A tram ride (small fee) lifts you to the handsome building where you take a self-guided tour, ending up at the tasting room. Listen to the bells of St. Dunstan's, an audible extra. Open daily 10:30-4:30.

# Napa Valley's Villages

Though the city of Napa is by far the largest in the valley, its charms must be sought out. Free brochures on Victorian walking tours are available from the Napa Community Redevelopment Agency, 1559 First St., Napa, CA 94558. Notice the town square's clock tower and carillon.

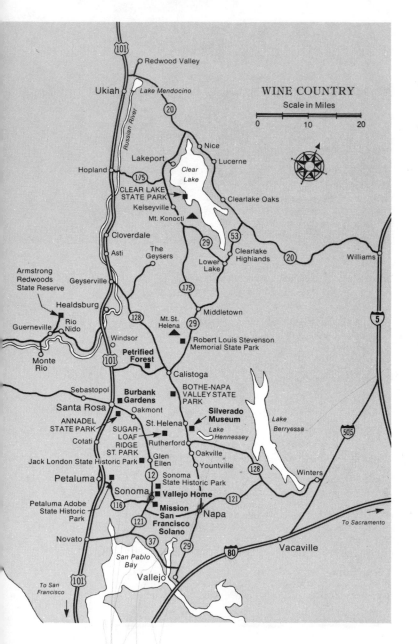

Smaller towns, with their valley-of-vines setting, contain intriguing art and crafts shops and colorful cafes and taverns. Prim, New England-style St. Helena is the wine country's central community, Calistoga its health center. Along State 29 you'll find other vineyard villages.

## St. Helena—the Wine Center

Activity—wine-oriented and otherwise—centers around St. Helena. The '90s look of its main business street is proudly maintained, as is the public library with its specialized collection of wine books and other material, much of it donated by local winemakers.

**Napa Valley Wine Library Association** helps stock the library and also offers special Wine Appreciation courses on several summer weekends. The faculty of this "liquid library" comes from surrounding wineries. Annual association dues are $5, but the waiting list may be long. Write the Library Association, Oak and Adams streets, St. Helena, CA 94574, for more information.

**The Silverado Museum and The Hatchery** (an art center and clearing house for local artists) share a lovely old example of stonemasonry on Railroad Avenue a block east of Main Street. The museum houses a large display of Robert Louis Stevenson memorabilia, including original manuscripts and letters, portraits and photographs of the writer, and a desk he used in Samoa. It is historically fitting to find this museum here because the peripatetic author honeymooned in the abandoned bunkhouse of the defunct Silverado Mine on Mt. St. Helena in 1880. In 1883 he celebrated that experience in his book *Silverado Squatters*.

**The Napa Valley Olive Oil Manufactory,** on Charter Oak Avenue, is a grand place to pick up picnic fixings to go along with your wine tour. Not only do they feature fragrant olive oil; you'll find cheeses, pastes, dried mushrooms, breadsticks, and other beguiling victuals.

**The Hurd Candle Factory,** in Freemark Abbey, is the center of a complex of shops offering foods, cookware, and wine accessories. Beeswax candles hang near good wine sleeping in adjoining cellars.

## To Calistoga for mud baths and geysers

St. Helena's life centers around grapes, Calistoga's around health. Situated at the foot of Mt. St. Helena, Calistoga is famous throughout the country as a health spa.

**Mud baths** bring thousands of tourists to this year-round resort. Visitors have been arriving ever since Samuel Brannan built his opulent spa in 1859. In addition to bath houses—where swimming

**"Old Faithful" geyser** *near Calistoga erupts on 50-minute cycle; steam, vapor rise for 3 minutes.*

pools may be mineral or hot spring water—motels, hotels, and resorts abound. Calistoga is a mecca for glider pilots. And you can take the scenic drive to the Petrified Forest, west of the city.

**Napa County Historical Society Museum** is located in town. History buffs will find some fascinating facts on the life of the wealthy of the late 1800s.

**California's "Old Faithful" geyser,** impressive spectacle in a region of hot springs and fumaroles, spews a 60-foot shower of steam and vapor at 50-minute intervals. The eruption continues for about 3 minutes, after which the geyser retreats until its next performance. A visit teaches a lot about the origins of geothermal steam. Located just north of town on Tubbs Road (turn east from State 128), the grounds are open from 8 A.M. to dusk; there's a slight admission charge. If you'd like to learn more about harnessing steam, you can view the outside of the new Pacific Gas & Electric plant, a major venture in the use of alternative power. (The sulfurous smell of subterranean gases might discourage you from emerging from your car.) To reach the plant, take State 128 about 17 miles north from Calistoga; turn right at signs for The Geysers.

## Yountville

Named for Napa County's first white settler, George Yount, this sleepy town has experienced a renaissance. Once geared to the pace of the nearby veterans' home, it is fast becoming a rural Ghirardelli Square.

The local cemetery is the final resting place of Yount, western mountain man, who planted his first vineyard on a land grant originally made to Salvador Vallejo by the Mexican government. Vintner Groezinger built a winery here in 1870.

The rebuilt winery, now located on 20 acres, houses Vintage 1870, a collection of shops, galleries, and eating spots. In the original buildings—somewhere among the intricate corridors, odd nooks, crannies, and pergolas—is the Napa Theatre Co., which performs during the summer.

# Hiking and Camping Spots

Beautiful weather, along with a variety of attractions, makes the Napa Valley an ideal place to spend more than a day. Fortunately you'll find a number of areas where you can pitch a tent, park a trailer, or throw down a sleeping bag. Hiking and biking are good ways to get around on the valley floor; heading up into the surrounding hills provides plenty of exercise. Swimmers, boaters, and fishermen will find natural and manmade lakes.

## Bothe-Napa Valley State Park

More than 1,000 wooded acres of broad-leafed trees and conifers and second-growth redwoods extend west into the hills. Facilities include camping and picnicking sites, hiking trails, and a swimming pool. The park is on the west side of State 29 about 4 miles north of St. Helena.

## The Old Bale Mill

A short distance south of Bothe-Napa, the mill was recently added to the park. Set in motion in 1846 for the convenience of nearby residents who needed their grain ground into meal, the grinding stones were active for more than 35 years. You can explore the rooms inside and picnic in a small area alongside the huge overshot wheel.

## Robert Louis Stevenson State Park

Between Calistoga and Middletown are about 3,000 acres of wild area on the eastern slopes and around the summit of Mt. St. Helena. A monument testifies that the author spent his honeymoon here. The site is undeveloped except for a fire trail leading to the remnants of his cabin and the old Silverado Mine. You can continue up to the lookout (about 4 miles) on top of this 4,344-foot peak that Stevenson called the "Mont Blanc of the Coast Range." Picnicking is permitted, but no fires.

## Conn Dam Recreation Area

Up off the valley floor in the east hills, this stopping-off spot offers cool Lake Hennessey for fishing, boating, and picnicking. The turnoff from the Silverado Trail is marked State 128-Conn Dam.

## Try Lake Berryessa for trout

Isolated in the dry, grassy hills that separate the Napa Valley from the Sacramento Valley, Lake Berryessa is principally a summer haunt of water-skiers and speed-minded boaters. But this popular, year-round fishing hole also has many quiet coves for hot-weather anglers.

All of the modest development is along 12 miles of the west shore, which falls into shadow while the east margin still bakes in the summer sun. A string of camper resorts can be reached by plainly marked stub roads leading away from State 128. Accommodations range from campsites to motels. Fairly extensive stretches of shoreline are open to bank fishing and rough picnicking. The east shore is closed to all use because fire hazard is extremely high in the grassy hills.

Berryessa was formed with the construction of Monticello Dam at its south tip. Much of the shoreline is steep and rugged. The gentlest stretches are at the northwest quarter where the drowning of Putah Creek formed a shallow arm.

Easiest access, especially for anyone trailering a boat or camper, is from Interstate 80. Turn north on Interstate 505 just beyond Vacaville to the Winters cutoff; then follow State 128 west to the dam at the south end of the lake. State 121 through Napa County is more scenic.

**Boating** is the best way to explore the lake. Launches are spaced at close intervals from Markley Canyon near the dam up to Putah Creek. (All are operated by resorts and charge fees, with the exception of one unimproved ramp east of the bridge across a narrow arm just south of Putah.)

**Fishing** is principally for trophy trout and bass in this sun-warmed lake. Shore fishing is best on points jutting into the lake. Anglers working from boats try for blue gill, crappie, catfish, Kokanee salmon, and trout.

## Clear Lake: California's largest

Local residents will tell you that Clear Lake is the largest lake entirely within California (Tahoe is bigger, but not wholly within the state). A natural, fairly shallow lake, it's about 19 miles long and up to 7½ miles wide, with a shore amply developed for recreation. In summer the water temperature reaches as high as 76°, ideal for water sports.

The direct route from the Bay Area to the southern tip of the lake (about 120 miles from San Francisco) is on State 29 through the Napa Valley. From the west, turn off from U.S. 101 at Hopland and follow State 175 to the lake and south through the Cobb Mountain resort area.

**Resorts** are largely concentrated a few miles north of Lower Lake. From this center, around Clearlake Highlands and Clearlake Park, you can continue north around the east side of the lake on State 53. This "inland" route takes you through sparse oak forest and grazing land, returning to the shore and State 20, which follows the shoreline north and around the "top" of the lake. Main resort centers are at Clearlake Oaks, Lucerne, and Nice.

On State 29, west-side resorts are around Konocti Bay, Soda Bay, and Lakeport. Konocti Harbor Inn has a "riverboat" for summer sightseeing.

Summer throngs begin arriving in May, and from then through September, resorts and roads near the lake are crowded. If you plan a visit then, be sure to make reservations ahead of time. For a free listing of places to stay, write the Lake County Chamber of Commerce, Lakeport, CA 95453.

Lakeport is one of the lake's boating centers. It has several of the county's public launching ramps, water ski ramp, public pier, and park with picnicking and swimming facilities. If you're interested in Lake County's history and the lore of the Pomo Indians, look into the museum on Third Street, near the County Courthouse.

**Anglers** flock to Clear Lake for some good bass fishing in spring and early summer. But October, with its balmy fall weather and scarcity of swimmers, speedboats, and water-skiers, offers the best fishing of the year-round season.

**Clear Lake State Park** (camping, picnicking) includes more than 2 miles of shoreline within its 500 acres. Most of the park is on a high, forested promontory overlooking Soda Bay.

**Fishing at Clear Lake** *is especially good during the spring and fall. Young angler has found his niche.*

# Into the Valley of the Moon

Historically, Sonoma is one of the most interesting towns in California. It's the site of Mission San Francisco Solano, last and northernmost of the 21 missions founded by the Franciscan fellows of Fra Junipero Serra. The Sonoma pueblo was headquarters for General Mariano Vallejo, the Mexican administrator at the time of the Bear Flag Revolt. It's where the Hungarian Agoston Haraszthy laid the groundwork for some premium California wines at his Buena Vista winery (see below). And Sonoma was the last home of author Jack London, who so romantically named the valley.

Sonoma lies 45 miles north of San Francisco. U.S. 101 across the Golden Gate is the main northward artery; then take State 37 east to an intersection with State 121, which heads north toward the town of Sonoma. One more turn, clearly marked, onto State 12 leads you right to the plaza.

The main approach from the north is State 12, cutting inland from U.S. 101 at Santa Rosa. Take the State 12 exit from the freeway. Coming from the east on Interstate 80, turn off onto State 37 at Vallejo and follow it along the north margin of the bay to its intersection with State 121.

The Sonoma Valley is also connected with other less hurried, more scenic roads. One back route leads through Vineburg, where you can pick up some fresh honey; another route (Oakville Trinity Road) crosses the Mayacamas ridge. You'll pass by the small Mayacamas winery.

## Touring the Wineries

Today, few wineries operate in or near Sonoma, although wine-growing north of San Francisco started here. Most of the cellars are open daily. Grand Cru Vineyards are open weekends only; advance appointments may be necessary. Here are some tasteful examples:

**Buena Vista,** started by Agoston Haraszthy in 1857, has had its ups and downs over the years, ranging from phylloxera (vine disease) to earthquake. Now a state historical landmark, the original stone buildings are restored, and picnic grounds adjoin the winery. Open daily from 9-5; tasting takes place in a tunnel carved into the sandstone hill.

**Hacienda Wine Cellars,** operated by Frank Bartholomew (the man who revived the Buena Vista in the 1940s) since 1973, is just a stone's throw away. Open daily 10-6; tours are by appointment.

**Sebastiani Vineyards,** right downtown, is also a state historical landmark. You'll see a crusher, basket press, barrels, and fermenting building. Open daily 10-5; tasting occurs at the front of the cellar.

## In and around Sonoma

The town of Sonoma embraces a spacious central plaza. Across from the northeast corner of the plaza stands the mission, founded July 4, 1823. Now a historical monument and museum, it contains historic church vestments, early photographs and documents, and 62 oil paintings of the missions. The chapel is preserved, although it is no longer used for religious services. Museum hours are 9 A.M. to 5 P.M. Two annual events are held around the plaza—the Ox Roast the first Sunday in June; Vintage Festival the last weekend in September.

**Sonoma State Historic Park** includes a number of buildings. The long, low adobe structure across Spain Street is the Blue Wing Inn, gambling room and saloon of the gold rush era. West on Spain from the mission, you pass Bear Flag National Historical Monument (in the northeast corner of the plaza park), Sonoma Barracks, Toscano Hotel, the servants' wing of Casa Grande (Vallejo's first home, most of which was destroyed by fire in 1867), Swiss Hotel (still in use as a restaurant), and the home of Salvador Vallejo, Mariano's brother.

For gastronomical rather than historical stops, try the French Bakery on the east side of the plaza or the Sonoma Cheese Factory on the north side.

**General Mariano Vallejo's home** is two blocks west and then north on Third Street West. Its name, Lachryma Montis ("mountain tear"), was suggested by the natural spring in the area. Adobe brick walls were covered by wood, so what looks like a Victorian Gothic house is surprisingly cool inside on a hot day. A section of wall near the porch entrance has been cut away and faced with glass to give visitors a better idea of construction. Also on the site is a handsome old warehouse built in 1852 of timber and bricks shipped around Cape

**Mariano Vallejo's home,** *Lachryma Montis, in Sonoma is open for touring; it's ½ mile from plaza.*

**Ruins** *of Jack London's Wolf House tower over young visitor. Author's wife built the nearby museum.*

Horn. Eventually converted to residential use, it became known as the Swiss Chalet. Today it serves as a museum and interpretive center for the Vallejo Home Historical Monument (open daily from 10 A.M. to 5 P.M.).

**Train Town,** a 10-acre park on State 12, is about a mile south of the plaza. For a small fee, you can ride the Sonoma Gaslight and Western Railroad into a miniature mining village. It's open daily.

**Jack London State Historic Park** is situated in the hills above the tiny community of Glen Ellen. The House of Happy Walls, built by London's wife, Charmian, after his death, is now a museum of the author's personal and professional life. The great rock walls and chimneys of Wolf House, which London planned but never occupied, are also in the park at the end of a ¾-mile trail beginning at the museum. London's grave, marked by a simply engraved lava boulder, is nearby.

To reach the park, turn off State 12 from Sonoma to Glen Ellen and continue uphill about a mile, following park signs. Hours are 10 A.M. to 5 P.M. daily except Thanksgiving, Christmas, and New Year's.

## Hiking and Camping Parks

Two fairly new parks make inviting camping and picnicking sites in the Valley of the Moon. Horsemen will find the parks particularly attractive because they can stay overnight in one and ride extensively in the other.

**Sugarloaf Ridge State Park** is a 2,000-acre preserve of forest, field, and stream that reaches up oak-covered hills to edge over the Sonoma-Napa county line. Warm in summer, pleasant in spring and fall, it's likely to be wet in winter. A group campground now invites equestrians to spend the night, ride over the meadowland, and view sites of old farm buildings. Stream fishing for trout is a good spring pastime.

You enter the park on Adobe Canyon Road, off State 12. The park gate is 2½ miles farther; the access road is not recommended for trailers.

**Annadel State Park** is for hikers, bikers, and riders —not auto explorers or campers. Keeping this in mind, you'll find plenty to enjoy in this almost 5,000-acre retreat of forest, lake, and meadow. Originally Pomo Indian land, it became part of a sprawling Spanish rancho and later a ranch called Annadel Farms. Rocky ledges around Lake Ilsanjo make welcoming picnic sites (bring your own water); no swimming, boating, or rafting allowed. Stocked in 1957, the lake still yields largemouth black bass and bluegill. Below Bennett Ridge, in the southeastern part of the park, is Ledsen Marsh —an ecological community of waterfowl and wildlife.

From Oakmont, take State 12 toward Santa Rosa; turn south on Los Alamos Road, which becomes Montgomery Drive. At Channel Drive turn left and follow signs to the parking lot. Here you can pick up a park folder and trail map.

# Russian River's Valleys

Early in the 1970s, the Russian River valleys began to emerge as a tourable wine district. The transformation from a region of bulk wineries into one of prestigious varietals has been accompanied by an architectural flowering.

Hub of the wine district is Healdsburg, although the valleys and their wineries sprawl north to Cloverdale, south to Santa Rosa, and west to Guerneville. The most impressive wine center is Alexander Valley, on State 128 east of Healdsburg; the most varied collection of orchards, vineyards, and resorts is on country roads west of Healdsburg. Healdsburg is about 1½ hours driving time north of San Francisco on U. S. 101.

## Touring the Wineries

A dozen wineries extend some sort of welcome to visitors. Housed in striking new buildings or occupying impressive traditional structures, most are near the freeway; none is a great distance away.

**Geyser Peak.** (U.S. 101 to Canyon Road) hides an old winery behind a striking new facade. Open 10-5 daily for tours, tasting, and visiting gift shop off dramatic interior hall.

**Italian Swiss Colony,** centered at Asti, was founded in the late 1800s as a communal refuge for out-of-work Italian Swiss. Tours (8-5) include movie; chalet-style tasting room.

**Korbel Champagne Cellars** (Guerneville), started in 1862 by the Korbel brothers and owned since 1954 by the Heck brothers, represents a mixture of tradition and progress. Tours (10:30, 1, and 2:30) start at depot out front. Refurbished brandy cellar is tasting room.

**Sonoma Vineyard's** new building in Windsor is a combination of cross and pyramid with a dramatic tasting room. Open 10-5 weekdays (10-6 weekends); lunches and dinners served from May through October in the Barrel Room by reservation. Summer outdoor concerts and theatrical performances.

**Souverain** (between Healdsburg and Geyserville) has a stark, highly visible new building patterned on lines of old hop barns. Overhead walkways give good tour views (10-4); restaurant open most months for lunch and dinner with reservations.

## In and around Santa Rosa

Sonoma County's largest city and the county seat, Santa Rosa was founded in 1833 by General Vallejo. Its Spanish, Mexican, and early American periods are still reflected in its architecture. The Marshall House, 835 Second Street (near the center of town), is one of the most charming and most accessible examples. Lunch is served daily (except Sunday) from 11:30 A.M. to 2:30 P.M. in elegant, spacious, high-ceilinged rooms with crystal chandeliers and other Victorian appointments. A second floor gift shop is open from 11 A.M. to 4 P.M.

Several good picnic spots include Spring Lake County Park (swimming, camping) on the east edge of town and Mt. Hood County Park (day use only) 5 miles northeast of Santa Rosa.

**Howarth Memorial Park** is Santa Rosa's biggest and most attractive. A 152-acre, tree-shaded retreat, it sits at the foot of the Coast Range. An imaginative, 20-acre children's area includes a pony ride, animal farm, merry-go-round, miniature train, and playground. Rides cost a minimal fee; other attractions are free.

A feature of the main park is a lovely 32-acre lake. Motorboats are prohibited, but you can rent sailboats, canoes, and rowboats for a modest hourly charge. The park also has picnic areas, several miles of hiking trails, tennis courts, and a softball field.

You enter on Summerfield Road between Sonoma Avenue and Montgomery Drive, about 5 minutes from the freeway. Howarth Park is open daily the year around; however, amusement rides and boat rentals are open daily in the summer but weekends only during spring and fall.

**The Luther Burbank Memorial Gardens,** now a city park, are a living testament to a great naturalist. Searching for the perfect climate and soil to start experimenting with plants, Burbank found what he needed in the Santa Rosa Valley. And it is here that he is buried, under a Cedar of Lebanon that he once planted. Examples of his work are shown in the gardens.

One block west is "The Church From One Tree," a chapel (complete with steeple) built from a single redwood; it's now the interesting Robert Ripley Museum.

**Highways and byways** lead north from Santa Rosa on U.S. 101, passing through Healdsburg, one of the few remaining areas still holding a spring blossom tour. As a wine center, it also hosts an October wine festival. At Geyserville, 7 miles north, you can turn off for Devil's Canyon Geysers, 22 miles east. Cloverdale, northernmost of the country's commercial citrus growing areas, has the state's oldest fair, dating back to 1892.

South of Santa Rosa is Petaluma, a dairy center and site of the world championship wrist-wrestling contest in October. Four miles east of town is Petaluma Adobe State Historic Park. Once General Vallejo's house and fort, it is now a museum furnished with period pieces and is one of the largest adobes still standing in California. Nine miles west of Petaluma on Red Hill Road is the over-century-old Rouge et Noir Cheese Factory. You can take a guided tour between 10 A.M. and 4 P.M., buy cheeses and other snacks, and have a picnic on the lawn overlooking the lake.

Sonoma County's back roads are good sources for fresh farm produce and handcrafts. For a free map and guide, write to Sonoma County Farm Trails, P. O. Box 6043, Santa Rosa, CA 95406.

# Along the Russian River

To summer visitors who have swarmed there since the early days of San Francisco, "The River" is the 12-mile cluster of resorts from Mirabel Park to Monte Rio. The most direct approach from the south is U.S. 101 to Cotati (48 miles from San Francisco) and then left on State 116 to Sebastopol and the river.

For a more leisurely approach, take either the Guerneville Road from Santa Rosa, the Fulton-Trenton Road (3½ miles north of Santa Rosa), the Eastside Road (3½ miles south of Healdsburg), or the Westside Road from Healdsburg to Hacienda. Other minor roads crisscross the area.

West and north on the river's great semicircle, the mountains rise to a seemingly inaccessible steepness. You can explore them on a drive up narrow Mill Creek Road that starts 1½ miles from Healdsburg on Westside Road. Its 4 miles of pavement take you up into the tangy air and forest stillness of Mill Creek Canyon.

## Guerneville and the riverside

All roads to the Russian River eventually lead to Guerneville. It's the center of the river resort area that extends as far east as Mirabel Park and west to Jenner, at the river's Pacific Ocean mouth.

You will find restaurants and places to stay overnight in Guerneville. During the summer season, this is the scene of bustling activity, with thousands of vacationers seeking a variety of ways to relax. (Make reservations well ahead of time if you plan to stay overnight.) The Pageant of Fire Mountain, an annual spectacular event, takes place over Labor Day weekend.

Farther upstream is good canoeing, where the Russian River flows through Alexander Valley. With a durable canoe or kayak, you can float between Asti and Healdsburg (where canoes can be rented) and Guerneville. River trips can last from 4 hours to 2 days. Be sure to include drinking water and a picnic and wear protective clothing against the hot summer sun.

Crowded and noisy during the summer, the river is quiet during the rest of the year until the steelhead and salmon fishermen begin to arrive in late fall. During steelhead season (November through February), resort owners and sporting goods stores keep track of steelhead runs from the time the fish cross the river bar until they pass Healdsburg upstream.

## Camping in the redwoods

Getting away from the river is easy if you visit either of the nearby parks. Choose between cool, dark, dense redwood groves or rolling coastal mountain country.

**Armstrong Redwoods State Reserve,** 2 miles north of Guerneville, has a driving loop through dimly-lit aisles of giant trees or hiking trails leading to park limits. Day-use picnic sites are among the trees or at the edge of a meadow. The large Red-

**Rafting** *down the Russian River appeals to this sly old dog. His companion is soaking up the summer sun.*

wood Forest Theatre has stage and musical productions during the summer and outdoor weddings the year around.

**Austin Creek State Recreation Area,** really an extension of Armstrong Redwoods, has more than 4,000 acres (compared to Armstrong's 700) and a complete change of terrain. Much of it is meadowland with madrone, Douglas fir, and alder in the canyons. Three creeks and about 100 springs run all year. Unlike Armstrong, it is warm in the winter. Equestrians use Horse Haven, a small, primitive camping area.

To reach Austin Creek, stay to the right after entering Armstrong until you reach the sign reading Redwood Lake Campground. From here, a narrow, steep, winding road (not recommended for trailers) runs 2½ miles to the top of a ridge, 2,000 feet above.

## Ukiah Valley - a Newcomer

For years Mendocino County vineyards have been quite anonymous—an appendage to Sonoma County. But in the early 1970s, large acreages of new plantings brought new wineries and more tourists.

**Places to pick** *your own berries are hard to find; a guide to Sonoma County's back roads tells you where.*

---

### Don't Miss

**Clear Lake** (Lake County, east of U.S. 101)—largest lake within state boundaries; in summer, a boating and water-skiing mecca; anglers arrive later for good fall fishing

**Jack London State Historic Park** (near Glen Ellen)—see House of Happy Walls (built by Jack London's wife) now used as a museum; the remains of Wolf House (mysteriously burned before they moved in); and London's simple grave

**Old Faithful Geyser** (Tubbs Lane, Calistoga)—one of three "faithful" geysers in the world; you'll watch and listen as 350° water rumbles, gurgles, and belches—finally gushing forth every 50 minutes

**Ripley Believe It or Not Museum** (Santa Rosa)—nestled in tall redwoods, a small church built from a single tree houses examples of Ripley's writings, as well as some of the oddities and curiosities he collected

**Silverado Museum** (St. Helena)—an inside look at a part of Robert Louis Stevenson's life in Napa Valley and additional mementos of later times in Samoa

**Sonoma Historic Park** (Sonoma)—not a formal park, this area encompasses the plaza and most of the buildings around it; visit the mission and museum, Blue Wing Inn, Sonoma Barracks, Toscano Hotel, and other remnants of the past

---

Lake Mendocino, alongside U.S. 101, is a cool spot for picnics after you tour local vineyards.

Probably the smallest area to cover geographically, the vineyards center around Ukiah, but new fields are being planted in the Redwood Valley and as far west as Boonville. These three are open regularly for tours and tasting:

**Parducci Wine Cellars** (Ukiah) is the valley's patriarch. Three generations have helped press the grapes. An informative tour (offered 9-6) tells their story. Out front, the tasting room is cheerful and usually crowded.

**Weibel Champagne Vineyards** (Redwood Valley), a long-established winery producing sparkling and other wines, built a new winery and tasting room in 1973. All their table wines will be made here. The tasting room (open 9-6), a reminder of the sparkling wines, resembles an inverted champagne coupe.

**Cresta Blanca's** building was originally designed as part of a co-op, but its equipment is decidedly up to date. You'll recognize the name; it's been around since the late 1800s. From U.S. 101 take the Lake Mendocino exit 1 mile. Tour and taste daily from 10-5.

# The Sierra's Gold: Yosemite to Tahoe

 Described as a "Range of Light" by the great naturalist John Muir, the Sierra Nevada is the largest single mountain range in the country. Rising gradually from the floor of the Central Valley, these mighty mountains ascend to a jagged crest that runs from 7,000 to 14,000 feet in altitude and then plunge almost vertically to desertlike Owens Valley to the east.

Examples of glacial action are visible in many areas. Nearly every deep-cut valley owes its present configuration to glacial abrasion. The best-known evidence of glacial power is Yosemite Valley, formed by the cutting action of slow-moving ice during the Ice Age.

Higher elevations of the Sierra offer fishing in clear mountain lakes and streams, boating and water-skiing on large and lovely Lake Tahoe, and hiking trails into wilderness areas. In winter, skiers flock to its many snow-clad slopes. Awe-inspiring scenery attracts many visitors to Yosemite National Park, at its most dramatic in spring when waterfalls leap over valley walls to splash against rocks 1,000 feet below.

Along the Sierra foothills between Yosemite and Tahoe are reminders of bustling Gold Rush days. Small mining operations continue, and every spring gold-seekers patiently pan for "color" alongside rushing streams. The old towns are well worth visiting. Many verge on ghost town status; some are covered by a facade of modernity. A few have been preserved in a state of arrested decay as state historic parks. One (Columbia State Historic Park) is being restored as a model of early days in California history when every would-be prospector's dream was "going to see the elephant" (anticipating experiences in the gold fields).

**Horseback** *is one way to view Yosemite's scenic grandeur. Packers also provide guides and food for high-country trips.*

# Yosemite – in This Park, Nature Shows Off

By any standard one of the most spectacular national parks, Yosemite has beauty of form in graceful domes and towering cliffs, beauty of motion in plunging waterfalls and rippling rivers, and beauty of color—from the red snow plant to the purple glow of sunset on canyon walls.

Only 7 of Yosemite's approximately 1,200 square miles are occupied by its famous valley. But here most visitors concentrate, missing other beauties and wonders—glaciers, giant sequoias, Alpine meadows, and 13,000-foot Sierra Nevada peaks. Although the valley is a logical place to begin a visit, one should go to Yosemite with the knowledge that not all is found here.

A very popular vacation destination, Yosemite National Park offers an exceptionally wide variety of things to do and places to stay.

To reach Yosemite take State Highway 120 from Manteca or Modesto or State 140 from Merced. From Southern California, take State 41 from Fresno. During the summer when the road is clear of snow, you can enter from the east side of the park (via U.S. 395) over Tioga Pass on State 120. U.S. 395, State 120, and State 89 provide a scenic back road link between Yosemite and Lake Tahoe —particularly lovely in autumn.

Yosemite Transportation Company provides connecting bus service to Yosemite from Merced (the year around) and Fresno (summer). For information and reservations, write Yosemite Park and Curry Co., Yosemite National Park, CA 95389, or call toll free in California to (800) 692-5811.

## Timing your visit

June, July, and August are the valley's busiest months; campers fill the park nightly. Camping restrictions help somewhat to relieve the congestion. You can escape crowds by getting up into the high country.

In the "off season" (before Memorial Day and after Labor Day), you can revel in the joys of virtual isolation, gazing at views unobscured by fellow visitors. Spring is beautiful. Waterfalls splash through misty rainbows to the valley floor. In autumn, when falls dwindle to a trickle, polychromatic leaves adequately compensate.

Winter gives Yosemite a fragile, fairyland look. Frosty weather makes difficult hiking but signals the beginning of snow fun. Major valley roads from the west are kept open (State 140 has first priority for snow removal); be sure to carry chains.

## Lodging—luxury hotel to canvas tent

Yosemite offers a wide choice of accommodations. To avoid valley summer crowds, don't overlook the advantages of staying at Wawona, Tuolumne Meadows, and White Wolf.

For cabin or hotel reservations (always advisable, and required during the summer) write to the Yosemite Park and Curry Co. Reservations are no longer accepted for valley campgrounds; it's first come, first served.

**In Yosemite Valley** the Ahwahnee Hotel offers luxurious accommodations. Open the year around, except for a short time in December, the Ahwahnee has a gift shop, lounge, and exquisite dining room. Golfers enjoy the 9-hole "pitch and putt" course.

Popular Yosemite Lodge, with Yosemite Falls as a backdrop, is within walking distance of the village. Open all year, the lodge offers sleeping accommodations that range from attractive hotel rooms to redwood cabins with or without bath, to tent cabins (summer only) and cottage housekeeping units. Lodge buildings contain a lounge, shops, cafeteria, dining room, and coffee shop.

Curry Village, rustic and informal, has cabins, tent cabins (summer only), and some hotel-type rooms. Cabins come with or without bath; without-bath cabins are available all year.

**At Wawona** the hotel is informal but gracious. It has a dining room, swimming pool, 9-hole golf course, and tennis court, and it is near stables. This area is popular because of its tree-fringed setting.

**Above the valley floor,** Tuolumne Meadows Lodge has simple tent cabins and a central dining hall where meals are served family style. White Wolf Lodge has both cabins and tents. Both Tuolumne Meadows and White Wolf are reached along the Tioga Pass Road; Tuolumne, near the park's east entrance, is 60 miles from the valley, and White Wolf, near the Middle Fork of the Tuolumne River, is 31 miles away.

**Campgrounds** maintained throughout the valley are open from mid-May to mid-September (it's possible to camp the year around); campgrounds in the high country have a shorter season, depending on the snow. To control the camping population in the valley, the total number is restricted to 5,000 persons, and a 7-day camping limit is enforced from June 1 to September 15 (30-day limit thereafter). Trailers are accommodated in most campgrounds, but no utility hookups are provided except at a private camp at Wawona. Some campgrounds have sanitary stations. Pets are allowed only in specified campgrounds and must be kept on leash and off trails.

## Getting to Know the Park

During summer months, an active naturalist program is carried on in the park, with campfire talks, nature walks, lectures, and field trips. You may obtain a free park newspaper, *The Yosemite Guide,* at entrance stations or at visitor centers. Make the visitor center at Yosemite Village your first stop. Not only do rangers mount excellent exhibits explaining the how and why of Yosemite in graphic detail, but they also supply brochures on open-air tram car valley tours, hiking and saddle trips, as well as park maps.

More than 700 miles of trails in the park offer every kind of hiking possibility—from leisurely walks of an hour or so to trips of a week or longer.

### Highlights of the valley

Moving around the valley is easy. Park your car and ride the free shuttlebus to all the highlights. Another way to see the valley is on bicycle—the roads are mostly level and the distances easily pedaled. During spring and fall, you'll have the roads practically to yourself. You can rent bikes at Yosemite Lodge and Curry Village (summer only).

Saddle and pack animals are available at Yosemite Valley stables (outside the valley at Tuolumne Meadows, Wawona, and White Wolf).

The 7-square-mile Yosemite Valley is neither the deepest nor the longest phenomenon of its kind in the Sierra, but of all the glacial gorges it exhibits the sheerest walls, the most distinctive monoliths, the flattest floor, the widest meadows, and the finest array of waterfalls.

The floor of the valley is a level meadow threaded by a dashing mountain river (the Merced) and diversified with groves of pines and oaks, thickets of shrubbery, and beautiful varieties of flowers, ferns, and grasses.

**The valley walls** rise, almost vertically, to a height of 2,000 to 4,000 feet above the meadow. Great domes and pinnacles stand out against the sky. Most conspicuous are El Capitan, Cathedral Rocks, Three Brothers, Sentinel Rock, and Half Dome.

**Yosemite** *offers waterfalls to please all. Women* **(above)** *gaze at powerful Yosemite Falls tumbling from valley walls; hikers* **(right)** *follow the Mist Trail from Vernal Falls.*

**Biking** *is one of the best ways to see Yosemite Valley highlights.*

**Fertile clouds** *and swirling mist partially obscure Yosemite Valley's towering mountain walls and snow-clad peaks. To left in photo stands majestic El Capitan; the waterfall is graceful Bridalveil.*

**Rushing waterfalls** tumble from the cliffs, each with its own particular beauty. A ¼-mile walk to the rustic bridge over Yosemite Creek gives you an idea of Yosemite Falls' awesome power and volume. Bridalveil impresses, not because of its size but because of its sheer, lacy beauty.

**Yosemite Indian Garden,** behind the visitor center, is an addition to the wildflower garden originally laid out in the 1920s. Here, during the summer, Miwok Indians demonstrate ancient techniques of grinding acorns, weaving baskets, and making arrowheads. Occasionally, Indians will dance in the round house.

**Happy Isles Trail Center** is another valley museum. Ranger naturalists interpret park features and satisfy visitor curiosity. Ask them questions any time. The center is also a trailhead for the John Muir Trail, Vernal and Nevada Falls (the Mist Trail), and the high country. Happy Isles itself is delightful, especially in early morning and evening —here, the Merced River breaks up into fingers and flows around several tiny islands. Nearby are the Indian Caves and natural Mirror Lake, worthy attractions in the upper valley.

**The Yosemite Travel Museum,** at the Arch Rock entrance from Merced (State 140), displays old rail cars, engines, a train station from Bagby—even an antique snow plow.

## Sequoia-surrounded Wawona

Known for its grove of giant sequoias, the Wawona region, near the south entrance (State 41) at about the same altitude as the valley (4,000 feet), is a popular place to stay.

**The Mariposa Grove,** part of President Lincoln's original grant for preservation, is an outstanding feature. You may have heard about this grove because of its famous "tree you can drive through." A tunnel was cut in 1881 to permit passage of horse-drawn stagecoaches. Although the tree fell in the winter of 1969, you can still view the stump.

In the Mariposa Grove are over 200 trees that measure 10 feet or more in diameter, and thousands of smaller ones. The largest tree in Yosemite, and probably the oldest, is the Grizzly Giant, which approaches the size of the largest tree in the world (the General Sherman of Sequoia National Park).

Park private vehicles at the edge of the grove; free trams transport visitors through the trees, where the Sequoia story is presented by park interpreters. Trams leave every 15 minutes during the summer, hourly during the spring and fall.

Wandering through the groves gives one a serene feeling and a sense of reverence for these long living giants of nature. At Wawona Pt. beautiful panoramas unfold.

**Pioneer Yosemite History Center,** at Wawona, tells of man's life in the park. You'll see some of the first buildings, horse-drawn vehicles, and "living history" demonstrations. To get to the history center, you cross a covered bridge, built in 1858.

## Why climb to Glacier Point?

The view is the thing at Glacier Pt.—a tremendous sweep of the length of the valley in both directions.

Half Dome is at your front door; Vernal Fall is prominent; Nevada Fall's roar deafens; and beyond rise the snowclad peaks of Yosemite's back country. You look down into a world of miniature people, cars, and buildings. The Merced River is a tiny creek, and the roads are a network of dark ribbons. Temporary structures at the precipitous point include a snack stand, restrooms, and a gift shop.

The road to Glacier Pt. (closed in winter beyond Badger Pass Ski Area) winds through the forest and around lush meadow. After getting a ride to Glacier Pt., you can hike down along one of several fine trails to the valley floor:

**Four-Mile Trail** zigzags down the canyon wall to the valley floor about 2.2 miles west of Curry Village. Short and steep, it's really about 4.6 miles.

**Panorama Trail** drops down into Illilouette Canyon and beyond, ending eventually at Happy Isles. Varied terrain makes all of this 8-mile route interesting—from infrequently seen Illilouette waterfall across thundering Nevada Fall (a great picnic spot) and down the stone steps of Mist Trail, wet from Vernal Fall.

**Pohono Trail** follows the rim for almost the full length of the valley, descending near the Wawona Tunnel (13 miles), and arriving on the valley floor in the vicinity of Bridalveil Fall. It's particularly lovely when the wildflowers bloom in June and early July.

## The high country: Yosemite's back door

A circle of six High Sierra camps is maintained by Yosemite Park and Curry Co. for hikers and saddle parties who wish to enjoy this country with maximum convenience and minimum expense. The camps, about 10 miles apart, consist of dormitory tents grouped near a large central dining tent in which you eat family style. Advance reservations are required.

Tuolumne Meadows, gateway to the high country, makes an ideal headquarters for exploring. Other camps are at Merced Lake, Vogelsang, Sunrise, Glen Aulin, and May Lake. Fees include breakfast and dinner; box lunches may be purchased separately.

Several days a week during the summer, a 6-day guided saddle trip leaves Yosemite Valley and makes a circuit of the High Sierra camps, stopping one night in each camp. A 4-day saddle trip leaves Tuolumne Meadows with overnight stops at Glen Aulin, May Lake, and Sunrise camps. Anglers may enjoy the 3-day trip to Merced Lake from Yosemite Valley. An experienced fishing guide escorts the party; you must have a California fishing license.

If you prefer to hike, there are guided 7-day trips

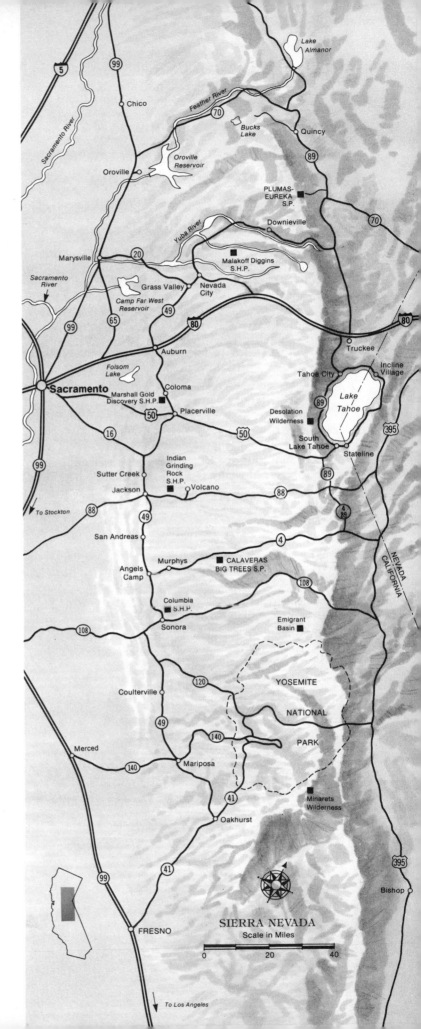

SIERRA NEVADA
Scale in Miles

leaving Tuolumne Meadows each Monday during the summer. Reservations must be made at least 6 months in advance for either saddle or hiking trips. For rates and information, write to Yosemite Park and Curry Co.

## Yosemite in Winter

Yosemite Valley is unusually splendid when snow fills it and drapes the surrounding cliffs and sentinel peaks.

To prevent overcrowding of the back country, travelers need wilderness permits for day use or overnight stays. These may be obtained free at ranger stations or visitor centers or by writing Box 577, Yosemite, CA 95389. Individuals may obtain permits on the day of the trip; parties of over 14 must apply for permits 2 weeks in advance. In this picture-book setting, you can enjoy sledding, ski-touring, and other winter activities against a backdrop of white-etched canyon walls and waterfall courses frosted by frozen mist.

You can rent sleds and snow saucers at Curry Village. The ice skating rink is open daily; rental skates are available.

Ski facilities are at Badger Pass, a 20-mile drive from the valley floor. Facilities include a double chair lift, T-bar, day lodge, snack bar, and child care center at the Ski Tots Playhouse.

Cross-country skiing lessons are directed by the Mountain Shop in the valley.

Ski season usually extends from mid-December to early April. From the valley you can get a free bus ride to the Badger Pass Ski Area; first preference goes to guests at Yosemite Lodge.

## Wilderness North and South of Yosemite

Massive granite peaks along the Sierra's backbone tower above pine forests, green meadows, and alpine lakes of the wild areas on both sides of the national park. Isolated in winter, except for skiing on the eastern side near June and Mammoth lakes, the peaks are penetrated during the summer by hikers, backpackers, and mountain climbers following well-marked trails.

### Emigrant Wilderness

Emigrant Basin Primitive Area became Emigrant Wilderness in early 1975. Located just north of Yosemite National Park, it covers 105,000 acres—all within the Stanislaus National Forest. Elevations range from 5,200 feet near Cherry Lake at the south to 11,570 feet at Leavitt Peak at the northeast corner. Snow blankets the area from mid-October until June, covering some sections the year around. Summer temperatures fluctuate—from 90° during the day to below freezing at night.

The basin was named for a party of emigrants seeking a shortcut over the Sierra Nevada; a head-

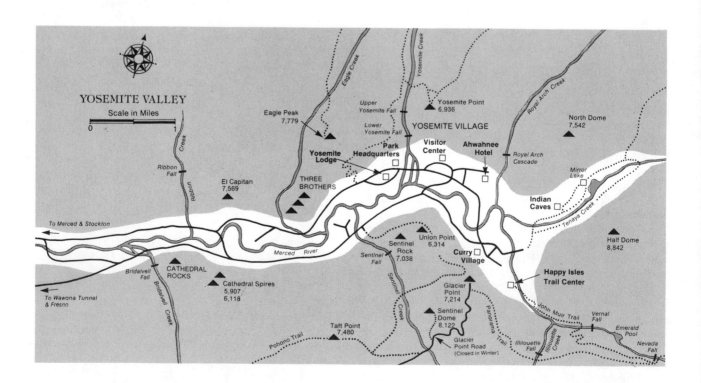

**Waiting for breakfast** *call at Vogelsang.*
*Even the dining room is in a tent.*

**Cross-country skier** *slides along Yosemite Valley*
*floor past well-known Half Dome.*

**Ranger describes** *flora and fauna of*
*Yosemite's high country at Tuolumne Meadows.*

stone marks the grave of one pioneer who died in 1853 near Summit Creek.

About 100 lakes in Emigrant Basin offer trout fishing; some of the larger lakes (Huckleberry, Emigrant, and Long) stretch over more than 100 acres. Nearest main highway is State 108, from which short stub roads lead to trail heads. Lakes, streams, and campsites are connected by 142 miles of trails. Though there are no improved campgrounds, some of the heavily used sites, such as Emigrant Lakes, Cow Meadow, and Bucks Lake, have log tables and sanitation facilities. In most of the basin, you'll find plenty of wood and water.

## Minarets Wilderness

From Yosemite the John Muir Trail enters the Minarets Wilderness at Donohue Pass (11,100 feet). The trail leaves the wilderness 4 miles northwest of the Devil's Post Pile National Monument. Elevations vary from 7,600 to 13,157 feet. Mt. Dana, jewel of the north corner, stands over 13,000 feet, towering above its sister peaks—Mt. Gibbs, Mt. Lewis, and nearly a dozen more—all over 12,000 feet. Glaciers and barren peaks offer excellent opportunities for experienced mountaineers.

Backpacking and camping traffic is heavy during the summer; along the more heavily traveled trails, it's a little hard to find the wilderness experience.

Garnet Lake, Thousand Island Lake, and Shadow Lake are among the numerous lakes and large streams forming the headwaters of the Middle and North Forks of the San Joaquin River. Trout fishing is excellent in these 109,500 acres.

Access to the Minarets is from State 120 on the north, from State 203 through Mammoth Lakes on the east, and from Clover Meadow from the town of North Fork on the west. Commercial packers operate from Agnew Meadow and Reds Meadow on the east and from Clover Meadow on the west.

# Gold Country:
# A Historical Reflection

James Marshall changed the course of California history in January 1848 when he discovered gold in the millrace of Sutter's sawmill in Coloma. Within a year, California was known worldwide, and fortune-seeking miners started the migration that would open the West.

Remnants of these tumultuous times still exist in the Gold Rush Country of the Sierra Nevada foothills. Appropriately numbered State 49 runs through the heart of this rolling grassland and fir-clad hills, staying around 2,000 feet except where it dips into deep river canyons and climbs mountains above Downieville.

**When to go?** Every season has its advantages. Summer (between Memorial Day and Labor Day) is the most popular tourist time. This is when theatrical groups perform and when many of the colorful local events take place. Shops, museums, and other historical attractions are more likely to be open, but the weather is apt to be hot in the lower elevations, and back roads tend to be dusty.

Spring brings wildflower weather. In the valleys, spring arrives in February and March. As late as April and May, some mountain towns may still have snow; back roads may be deep with mud. Gold panning is best in the spring when the snow melts in the higher mountains and fills dry stream beds; but if you're planning on swimming in some of those deep rivers, wait until the summer sun warms their icy depths.

When fall arrives, rains settle summer dust and wash the oaks, poplars, locusts, and eastern maples, brightening the old towns with yellow and vermilion. In winter, snow covers the higher altitudes, but touring can be fun because many an old ruin looks better when dampened than it does under the hot summer sun.

**Accommodations** are plentiful in the larger towns, although reservations are advisable during the summer. The Gold Country has comfortable, up-to-date hotels and motels and a few charming old inns (see Special Feature on page 114). Camping is impractical in summer at lower elevations unless you're around a lake to cool off. But heading east from State 49, you can reach campgrounds at higher, cooler levels.

On the following pages are described some of the main points of interest in and around major towns along State 49—in the Southern Mines, the central Mother Lode, and the Northern Mines areas. For more detailed description of the Gold Country and for some of its rich history and lore, refer to the *Sunset* book *Gold Rush Country*.

## Scouting the Southern Mines

The placer and quartz veins in the Southern Mines never rivaled those to the north. At the southern tip near Yosemite, the country was better known to Mexican ranchers and Indian traders than to gold seekers. Tourists arrived almost as soon as the prospectors did.

This section contains a large, active town, a few smaller communities, and isolated hamlets bordering on ghost-town status. Lively Oakhurst, Mariposa, and Sonora make good bases for exploring the surrounding countryside; elsewhere, facilities are limited.

### Back roads from Oakhurst

The southern terminus of the Mother Lode Highway (State 49), Oakhurst—called Fresno Flats in its heyday—today shows little evidence of once-hectic mining activity. The original jail, refurbished inside, is now one of the unique shops at the Holiday Village center. About a block down the street, the "Little Church on the Hill" was built in Fresno Flats in 1891.

During the summer, Oakhurst presents melodramas Friday and Saturday evenings in an 1800s-period theater (see Special Feature on page 114).

Coarsegold—8 miles south of Oakhurst on State 41—still survives. A single nugget worth $15,000 started the mining claim called Texas Flats—one of the oldest, deepest, and most extensively worked mines in this area. Rubble remains. One reminder of the past is a pump, dated 1852, that served a well dug in the middle of the main street.

A series of back roads northeast of Coarsegold leads through Knowles, with its landscape of granite, and Raymond, an early stage stop for Yosemite-bound travelers. Along Ben Hur Road, you'll pass crumbling remains of an early Chinese "stone wall"; workers received 25 cents for laying 25 feet of this wall daily.

**Horses roam** *on gently rolling hillside along the Ben Hur Road near Mariposa.*

**Would-be miner** *patiently tries his luck at gold panning while friends picnic.*

**Because too-hard ground** *discouraged gravedigging, people of Hornitos entombed banditos' dead bodies in these macabre "little ovens."*

## Mariposa—a key to the past

Far from being a ghost town, Mariposa gets a sizable amount of traffic because of its convenient location halfway between Merced and Yosemite. Scattered along the sides of the valley enfolding Mariposa Creek, buildings are a blend of old and new. One of the Gold Country's choicest bits of architecture, the two-story courthouse at the north end of town has been in use continuously since it was erected in 1854; its tower clock has dutifully rung the hours since it was installed in 1866. An excellent historical center and museum on Jessie Street depicts life over a century ago. Open daily May through October, it's closed in January and open weekends only the rest of the year.

**North of Mariposa,** watch for Mt. Bullion, where more than $4 million in gold came from the now-vanished Princeton Mine. Mt. Ophir, up the road, had California's first private mint which supposedly produced $50 hexagonal gold slugs (none have been found).

**A side trip to Hornitos** can be made from Mt. Bullion (13 miles) or from Bear Valley (11 miles). A small, lazy town, Hornitos has many charming old buildings framing its Mexican-style plaza. At High Street and Bear Valley Road is the entrance to an escape tunnel through which the Mother Lode's most famous badman, Joaquin Murieta, retreated from the fandango hall when things got too hot upstairs. Interesting remains include a grim little jail, now a museum; ruins of the Ghirardelli Store operated by San Francisco's chocolate king; St. Catherine's Church and the boot hill below; and the school, built in the early 1860s.

**At Bear Valley,** ruins still sitting along the highway include the Bon Ton Saloon (a cafe), a boarding house, Trabucco's store, and the I.O.O.F. Hall which houses the Oso Museum. Nothing remains of John C. Fremont's "White House," from where he conducted the business of his vast Mariposa Grant.

About 2 miles north of Bear Valley, a turnout off State 49 affords excellent views of the Merced River gorge below and the sinuous, 1,000-foot descent into Hell's Hollow. At the bottom are Lake McClure and the Bagby Recreation Area.

**Coulterville** is enriched by the presence of the old Jeffrey Hotel built in 1851 of rock and adobe. The walls of this old hotel are 3 feet thick. Adjoining it is the Magnolia Saloon, displaying a fine collection of firearms, minerals, coins, and other memorabilia. Across the street are the remains of the Coulter Hotel and the Wells Fargo building, once operated by Buffalo Bill's brother. In front of these buildings in the small plaza are the local "hangin' tree" and a small steam engine once used to haul ore from the Mary Harrison Mine north of town. One Chinese adobe, the Sun Sun Wo store, is all that remains of a once sizable Chinese population.

**Chinese Camp** lies 21 miles north of Coulterville along State 49. Driving north, watch for the Moccasin Creek Power Plant where State 120 intersects with State 49. A marker near the bridge tells of Jacksonville, a once important gold town now inundated by the Don Pedro Reservoir.

Notice the "trees of heaven" in picturesque Chinese Camp. No one really knows just where the Chinese who settled here came from, but there were at least 5,000 mining the area in the early 1850s, and a full scale war once took place between two tongs. It's a popular place to explore; you'll find good ruins and a few homes along the tranquil streets.

## History lives around Sonora

Sonora is as bustling today as it was a century ago. The county seat of Tuolumne and a trading center for the surrounding cattle and lumber country, Sonora has layered modern facades over the aged buildings lining Washington Street. Traffic moves slowly along the crowded thoroughfare, but a drive

**St. James Episcopal Church** *graces Sonora's Washington Street. Elegant building is over 100 years old.*

half a block off the main street takes you back to Gold Rush days. Sonora's outstanding piece of old architecture is St. James Episcopal Church—on Washington Street at the north end of town. Built in 1860, the graceful structure is said to be the Gold Country's most beautiful frame building. At the century-old jail on West Bradford Street, you can pick up a walking map of heritage homes, including the Gunn House, now an inn (see Special Feature on page 114).

**Jamestown,** south of Sonora, tries valiantly to retain its antiquity. Some of the best wood-frame structures were destroyed by a fire in the 1960s, but a few proud buildings still remain: a fancy gingerbread and brick emporium on Main Street, the Community Methodist Church, and the restored Willows Hotel (bar and restaurant). At Rail Town 1897 you can tour the old Sierra Railroad yards and take a ride on Hooterville Cannonball of *Petticoat Junction* fame. Prices are moderate for the tour and 18-mile ride. For a full schedule of excursions (including 82-mile Saturday night dinner trips), write Sierra Railroad, Drawer 515, Jamestown, CA 95327. Rail Town is open daily in the summer from 9:30 A.M. to 5:30 P.M., weekends from April to June, and Saturdays from Labor Day to November 1.

**Columbia State Historic Park,** no dry, dusty collection of buildings, is a lively town geared to visitors. An ideal starting point for any Gold Country touring, Columbia will provide you with a sizable fund of knowledge about mining and miners' habits that will help you figure out other, more confusing ruins and deserted mining camps.

Everything in Columbia is clearly labeled, and an abundance of maps and guidebooks explain attractions in detail. Though it may seem a little commercial, Columbia offers much to see and do in one place. Children enjoy panning for "color" in Matelot Gulch, riding the jouncing stagecoach, sipping sarsaparilla at the Stage Driver's Retreat saloon, or even getting a haircut at the state's oldest barbershop. Fallon House is still the setting for summer theatricals (see Special Feature on page 114), and Columbia House Restaurant serves Hangtown Fry.

Once called the "Gem of the Southern Mines" for its gold output, Columbia (4 miles north of Sonora) deserves high billing today for its unparalleled collection of reconstructed buildings and mining artifacts.

**Jackass Hill and Tuttletown,** north of Columbia, acquired most of their fame from their early residents. Mark Twain's cabin is reconstructed on its original site on Jackass Hill. Ruins remain of Swerer's store in Tuttletown, where Bret Harte was once a clerk and Twain a customer.

# Central Mother Lode – Heart of the Gold Country

Much of California's Gold Country was called the Mother Lode, but the section between Melones to the south and Auburn to the north contained the primary gold vein that gave the area its name. The most-visited part of the Gold Country, the Mother Lode contains most of the interesting, attractive historical towns that are relatively intact. Colorful annual events include the crowd-drawing Jumping Frog Contest. Family recreational activities, such as fishing, boating, swimming, and skiing, abound.

## Angels Camp to San Andreas: from frogs to fandangos

Thanks to Mark Twain, Angels Camp is probably better noted for its frog-jumping contest in May than for its important Gold Rush background. In Angels Camp you'll find a few remembrances of the past—the Angels Hotel and jailhouse behind, foundations of the Angels mine (one of the best in the area), and a museum with a good collection of minerals and early-day artifacts scattered inside and outside a building at the north end of town.

At Carson Hill, south of town, a nugget weighing 195 pounds came from this richest of all Mother Lode camps. Fifteen miles of tunnels honeycomb the hill; they extend down as far as 5,000 feet.

**Detour to Murphys** (on State 4), and you'll feel as if the clock stopped almost a half-century ago. Gingerbread Victorians peek shyly from behind white picket fences and tall locust trees lining the main streets. It's a good town for strolling; tourists are treated like guests. Settled in 1848 by the Murphy brothers, Murphys claimed a population of 5,000 at its rollicking peak. The Murphys Hotel, opened in 1856 by James Sperry and John Perry, has an illustrious register of temporary residents —U. S. Grant, Thomas Lipton, Horatio Alger, "Charles Bolton" (better known as Black Bart, the notorious stagecoach robber), and many others. The Black Bart Players hold performances during the summer (see Special Feature on page 114).

Other buildings of interest include the Peter Traver building, housing the Old Timers Museum; the ever-present I.O.O.F. Hall; St. Patrick's Catholic Church; and the one-room jail.

Many caverns are found around Murphys. Mercer Caves (1 mile north) and Moaning Cave (on the Murphys-Vallecito Road) welcome amateur underground spelunkers for a modest fee.

**Calaveras Big Trees State Park,** about 15 miles northeast of Murphys on State 4, has the only groves of *Sequoiadendron giganteum* (the huge

*(Continued on page 116)*

**Shotgun seats** *cost extra aboard stagecoach in old Columbia, one attraction in restored gold town.*

**Steaming** *through the gold country, you're aboard the Sierra Railroad; tour yard at Jamestown depot.*

# Inns and Entertainment

## ENTERTAINMENT

Old Gold Rush towns come alive during the summer. Your trip will be enhanced by a visit to one of the melodramas, comedies, and dramas in the theaters listed below. And in most areas, you'll find old-fashioned inns nearby. Below is a listing (from south to north) of some "play groups" and the closest hostelries.

**Oakhurst.** The Golden Chain Theatre presents old-time melodrama beginning around July 1. Performances are Friday and Saturday nights through mid-September; curtain time is 8:15. For information and tickets, write the Golden Chain Theatre, Box 604, Oakhurst, CA 93644.

**Mariposa.** The open-air amphitheater in Mariposa City Park is the setting for productions on Friday and Saturday nights from July through Labor Day. Plays start around dark. For information on the rotating schedule, write or phone the Department of Parks and Recreation, Box 732, Mariposa, CA 95338; phone (209) 966-2498.

**Columbia.** The Fallon House Tneatre is the setting for the University of the Pacific Reperctory Theatre's summer season. Beginning the first weekend in July, performances are held Tuesday through Saturday nights (along with a few matinees) at 8:30. For program information write Drama Department, University of the Pacific, Stockton, CA 95211, or call (209) 946-2116; for reservations write to Fallon House Theatre, Columbia State Park, CA 95310, after the third weekend in June.

**Murphys.** Though there are no performances during the summer, the Black Bart Players offer farces and comedy on Saturday evenings in April and November. For information, write Black Bart Players, Box 104, Murphys, CA 95247, or call (209) 728-3379, Saturdays only.

**Volcano.** In the tiny Cobblestone Gallery, the Volcano Pioneer Players carry on a fine tradition —Volcano had the first theater in California. You can watch thespians performing Friday and Saturday night at 8:15 from the middle of May through the middle of October. For information and tickets (seating is at a premium), write Box 222, Volcano, CA 95689, or call (209) 296-4696.

**Drytown.** The Claypipers, one of the oldest performing groups in the Gold Country, offer polished melodrama and olio productions each Saturday night from mid-May through September. (On holiday weekends they include a few Friday and Sunday performances.) Advance reservations are always required; for tickets, write to Mrs. Cleo Nokes, Drytown Club, Drytown, CA 95699, or call (209) 245-3812.

**Coloma.** The Coloma Crescent Players present melodrama every weekend from July 4 through Labor Day. At present they perform in the state park. For information and reservations, write the El Dorado Chamber of Commerce, 542 Main St., Placerville, CA 95667, or call (916) 626-2344.

**Folsom.** The Sutter Gaslighters perform each weekend; shows change every 4 months. Performances start at 8:30 P.M. Fridays and Saturdays. For information and reservations, write to The Sutter Club, 720 Sutter St., Folsom, CA 95630.

**Nevada City.** Over the years the venerable theater in Nevada City has featured such well-known personalities as Mark Twain and Lola Montez. Now a State Historical Landmark, the century-old building boasts a facade restored to former elegance. For year-round program information, write Old Nevada Theater, Box 1066, Nevada City, CA 95959, or call (916) 265-6161.

## INNS

**Coulterville.** Jeffery Hotel, Coulterville, CA 95311; (209) 878-3400: Originally a store with fandango hall upstairs; 7 rustic rooms; main attraction is Magnolia Room museum and bar adjoining lobby—fine display of all types of currency, rocks, guns, and "sayings."

**Sonora.** Gunn House, Sonora, CA 95370; (209) 532-3421: Priceless antiques combine with modern conveniences in 1851 adobe hotel, once a private residence; 27 large rooms with private baths.

**Columbia.** The City Hotel was operating in the late 1800s. Nine rooms, furnished in the period, have wash basins and stools; showers are down the hall. Dining room serves meals. For reservations, write Columbia State Park, Columbia, CA 95310, or call (209) 532-5415.

**Murphys.** Murphys Hotel, Box 329, Murphys, CA 95247; (209) 728-3454: Two-story, 1860-era hotel; 12 rooms upstairs with 2 modern baths; 20 motel units with private baths; dining room open daily; historic guest ledger.

**Mokelumne Hill.** Hotel Leger, Mokelumne Hill, CA 95245; (209) 286-1312: Handsome Victorian hotel; spacious rooms, 7 with private baths; pool; dining room open daily.

**Jackson.** National Hotel, 2 Water St., Jackson, CA 95642; (209) 223-0500: Old-fashioned saloon entrance, 50 rooms upstairs, over half with private baths; Louisiana House, on lower level, serves dinner Wednesday through Sunday, breakfast on Sunday; antique auctions held every three months.

**Volcano.** St. George Hotel, Volcano, CA 95685; (209) 296-4458: Venerable, three-story building; simple, comfortable furnishings in rooms, with nearby bathrooms; dining room serves meals to those with advance reservations.

**Sutter Creek.** Sutter Creek Inn, 75 Main St., Sutter Creek, CA 95685; (209) 267-5606: Eighteen rooms in this converted old home and outbuildings; intimate comfort is keynote; some rooms with fireplaces; some have private baths, others share; for fun, try the swinging beds; breakfast in kitchen included in price; no children.

Bellotti Inn, 53 Main St., Sutter Creek, CA 95685; (209) 267-5211: Three-story, unpretentious hostelry over a century old; 28 rooms, 15 with private baths; restaurant open daily for lunch and dinner.

**Amador City.** The Mine House, Box 226, Amador City, CA 95601; (209) 267-5900: Formerly Keystone Mine offices; each of 8 rooms (with baths) named for original use—Vault, Retort, Assay, Stores, Grinding, Directors, Bookkeeping, and Keystone; morning coffee and juice brought to room; pool.

**Coloma.** Sierra Nevada House III, Box 268, Coloma, CA 95613; (916) 622-5856: Well-appointed replica of an old-timer; private baths; old soda parlor serves meals, and dining also available (with reservations) in Gold Rush and Victorian rooms; price of room includes breakfast.

**Georgetown.** Georgetown Hotel, Georgetown, CA 95634; (916) 333-4373: Simple Victorian-style rooms; no private baths, but 7-foot claw-leg tub is worth the walk; dining room serves meals.

Woodside Mine, Georgetown, CA 95634; (916) 333-4499: Restored Victorian hotel opens about mid-1976; 7 rooms, some with private bath; no children; exotic gardens; price of room includes breakfast.

**Nevada City.** National Hotel, Nevada City, CA 95959; (916) 265-4551: Gold Rush exterior remains intact, and the interior furnishings are Victorian; private baths; dining room serves lunch and dinner; pool.

Red Castle, 109 Prospect St., Nevada City, CA 95959; (916) 265-5135: Restored, 1860-era private residence overlooks city; lovely antiques; suites have private bath; continental breakfast included; no children.

**Musicians tune up** *outside Columbia's Fallon House Theatre; repertory starts in July.*

**Gingerbread** *Red Castle atop Nevada City's Prospect Hill offers rooms with view.*

**Flittering fireflies** *provide olio entertainment at Drytown melodramas.*

Tiny *St. Sava's Serbian Orthodox Church in Jackson is the mother church for North American continent.*

**How do you start** *a frog jumping? This entrant at Angels Camp contest believes a sharp thump helps.*

*. . . Calaveras Big Trees State Park (cont'd.)*

cousin of the coast redwoods) in a state park. By following the nature trail, you can climb a stairway to the top of a 24-foot-wide stump for a special look at these giants. Year-round camping allows for snow bunny fun in winter and water play in summer on the North Fork of the Stanislaus River, which runs through the park. Both the river and Beaver Creek offer trout fishing. Two campgrounds provide 129 improved campsites; reservations are required during busy months.

**Bear Valley,** further up the road, is not to be confused with the ghost town to the south. This is an all-year recreation area where you can ski Mt. Reba's trails in winter or enjoy riding, swimming, and tennis when the snow melts. Lodging ranges from a hotel room to a mountain cabin. In August, Bear Valley presents classical music concerts. For information, write P. O. Box 8, Bear Valley, CA 95223.

**San Andreas,** 12 miles from Angels Camp on State 49, can be reached by a series of interesting side roads east of the main highway. One leads through the little mountain towns of Sheepranch (where George Hearst, father of William Randolph, ran the profit-making Sheepranch Mine, which helped enhance the great family fortune) and Mountain

Ranch, where a former dance hall now respectably houses memorabilia.

Another interesting approach is the road paralleling State 49 between Altaville and San Andreas. You pass through sites of former mining camps of Dogtown, Scratch Gulch, and Brandy Flat. At Calaveritas you'll see the only tangible evidence of a once-flourishing gold area. Supposedly Joaquin Murieta was a frequent visitor to the fandango halls; the old Costa store stands as mute testimony to these turbulent times.

Little of San Andreas shows its past. But the county museum, housed in the courthouse one block off Main Street, is worth a stop. Behind it is the old jail where Black Bart was held for trial. West of town is the Pioneer Cemetery, dating back at least to 1851. You'll find some intriguing inscriptions on the headstones still standing.

## Cuisine and culture around Jackson

Jackson, a town that has kept up with progress, is also trying to preserve its 19th-century heritage. Modern facades have transformed many of the old buildings along the main street, but a walk along side streets reveals some of the flavor of the past.

One of the most interesting buildings in town is the Brown House, built in the 1860s on a hill about 2 blocks east of the main part of town. Today it serves as the county museum. On the narrow main street are the Odd Fellows Hall and the restored National Hotel (see Special Feature on page 114). St. Sava's Serbian Orthodox Church may be tiny— but it's the mother church of the entire western hemisphere. Built in 1894, it's a few blocks off the main street.

For many decades two great hard-rock mines— the Kennedy and the Argonaut—were very important to Jackson's economy, but neither has been worked in many years. The huge tailing wheels built to carry waste from the mines to a settling pond on the other side of the hills are still there (two in pieces); they can be seen from State 49. For a closer view, drive the Jackson Gate road northeast from town and hike the well-marked trails. Along this road you'll find some good Italian restaurants.

In what used to be the main building of the Argonaut Mine (on Vogan Toll Road) is a restaurant and art center. You'll see art students capturing vistas of surrounding hills, and you can view their finished work in the gallery. If you stay for dinner (reservations only), you may see them serving.

At the Chamber of Commerce office (junction of State 88 and State 49), you can pick up walking tours of Amador County towns, as well as a well-done area map. Bikers will want a copy of a 27-mile bike route. Though the chamber office is closed weekends, printed material is also available at the museum.

State 88 (now open all year) heads east from Jackson over Carson Pass past several good summer trout lakes (Bear Reservoir, Silver Lake, and Caples Lake) and a couple of winter ski areas—the newest and largest is Kirkwood at 7,800 feet.

**Mokelumne Hill,** 7 miles south of Jackson on State 49, has many buildings constructed of light brown stone (rhyolite tuff), a material common to much of the Mother Lode. The I.O.O.F. hall was the first three-story building in the Gold Country. Once a tough, wild town, "Mok Hill" has had two racial strifes—the Chilean War, at nearby Chili Gulch, and the French War, on a hill overlooking town. A murder a week was not uncommon during the early days—hard to believe when you stroll through this most peaceful community.

Interesting buildings include the remains of the Mayer store, the beautiful wooden Congregational Church (oldest in California), and famous old Hotel Leger (still operating as an inn; see Special Feature on page 114), which incorporates the building that was once the county courthouse.

**Volcano,** a side trip of about 12 miles east from Jackson off State 88 on Volcano Road, has many remains of the early town—the St. George Hotel, the old jail, a brewery built in 1856, the Odd Fellows-Masonic Hall, the Adams Express Office, and the assay office. Don't miss Old Abe, a Civil War cannon. On summer weekends in the Cobblestone Gallery, the Volcano Pioneer Players perform (see Special Feature on page 114).

Near Volcano are the Indian Grinding Rock State Historic Park (camping, huge limestone outcropping, and reconstructed Miwok village); the Masonic Cave, where meetings were held in 1854; and Daffodil Hill, where you'll see a springtime explosion of color.

**Sutter Creek, Amador City, and Drytown** (north of Jackson) are meccas for antiquers. In addition to shops on tiny main streets, you'll usually find a flea market somewhere. Craft stores sell everything from hand-loomed skirts to nugget jewelry.

Sutter Creek and Amador City were important quartz mining centers; headframes attest to onetime mining activities. Both towns have interesting inns, and Drytown offers the famed Claypipers during the summer (see Special Feature on pages 114 and 115).

## Poking around Placerville

Placerville, county seat of El Dorado County, was one of the great camps of the Gold Country. Founded in 1848, it was originally called Dry Diggin's because the miners had to cart the dry soil down to running water to wash out the gold. The next year some grisly lynchings gave the town a new name—Hangtown. In 1854 it became Placerville, a bow to self-conscious pride, but movement is afoot by some citizens to revive its previous foreboding name, even though Hangman's Tree is today marked only by a plaque.

The Old City Hall (built in 1857) and its next-door neighbor have been refurbished in 49er style and still serve as city offices. The Odd Fellows have been using their hall since 1859. The County Museum in the fairgrounds houses memorabilia of some of the men who began their careers here—Studebaker, Armour, and Stanford.

In Bedford Park, 1 mile north of town, you can don a hard hat and visit the old Gold Bug Mine, check out a gold pan and sift the sands of Little Big Creek, and drive up the hill to view the stamp press mill. The park is a good spot for hiking or picnicking.

**Headframe** *of Keystone Mine in Amador City still stands. Picturesque town is antiquers' delight.*

# Apples, Wine, and Christmas Trees

Fresh-picked apples, apple pies, cakes, strudels, and cider tempt visitors to Apple Hill, that fabulously fertile stretch of land from Camino to Placerville off U.S. 50. October is harvest month, but new attractions extend the season into December.

Although the emphasis is still on apples, many ranches have added other products for sale: pear juice, buckwheat honey, vinegar, pumpkins, gourds, and decorative Indian corn.

Several farms provide the opportunity for you to come to Apple Hill in December, cut your own Christmas tree, and enjoy apple goodies at the same time. Visitors find displays of handcrafted holiday season decorations.

Boeger Winery, just reopened on Apple Hill, has a history of more than 100 years. The first wines were produced in the old winery building (now the tasting room) in 1872. If you look up at the ceiling, you'll see the original chutes which dropped the grape juice into barrels. The distillery up the hill remains as a museum piece.

Four turnoffs from U.S. 50 at Camino provide access to Apple Hill; once you're off the freeway, roads are well-marked. You can pick up bro-

**It's first come,** *first served at Apple Hill's peak season; you'll also find pies and cider.*

chures containing detailed maps at any stand or barn along the way. Pack a lunch to enjoy with your apples and wine at one of the many picnic grounds.

---

**Coloma,** north of Placerville on State 49, is the birthplace of California's golden history. Now a state park, Coloma is one of the most important stops in the Mother Lode. Here James Marshall first discovered gold on John Sutter's land; here you will see Sutter's Mill reconstructed exactly to match the original. On the hill behind town is a bronze statue of Marshall, and down the road from the statue is the cabin in which he lived after the gold discovery.

About 70 percent of the town of Coloma is within the park. Buildings are marked for easy identification, and rangers in the museum provide detailed maps, showing the points of interest. Parades, dancing, melodramas and examples of mining highlight January's Gold Discovery Days. The Coloma Crescent Players present melodrama during the summer (see Special Feature pages 114 and 115).

Private campgrounds are scattered around the area of the American River, and you'll find two hotels: the Sierra Nevada House III (well-appointed replica of an old-timer) in Coloma and the western-style hotel north of town at Gold Rush Resort (to be completed in 1976).

**Auburn,** farther north at the junction of State 49 and Interstate Highway 80, is modern at the top of the hill and traditional below and west of the imposing county courthouse. To see the brick and stone structures built in the 1850s and 1860s, walk along Lincoln Way and Court and Commercial streets. You can pick up a complimentary "Guide to Auburn's Old Town" from the Chamber of Commerce at 1101 High St. Look for the round-fronted brick Union Bar; the little frame Joss House, distinguished only by the plank with foot-high, incised Chinese characters above the door; the square, four-story firehouse; the Wells Fargo Office, now a gift shop; and the post office.

## The Northern Mines

Deep-quartz mining was first developed in the Northern Mines; it's also the birthplace of highly destructive hydraulic mining, a process in which entire mountain ridges were washed away. Summertime is the best time to visit this area because most of your wanderings will be on side roads, often impassable for winter snows and spring run-off. Accommodations are primarily limited to the Grass Valley-Nevada City area. Check fuel and supplies for a day's outing. Scenery is spectacular. Plan a picnic beside a waterfall on a back road to Alleghany or sift sands along a rushing river near Downieville.

## Grass Valley and west

A disastrous fire in 1855 destroyed the early community of Grass Valley, leaving little to recall the town's mining camp days. But it still has narrow streets and a few old structures, such as the cottage of Lola Montez (corner of Mill and Walsh streets), whose daring behavior made her the talk of Europe and America. Once a year the Grass Valley-Nevada City Kiwanis Club offers a tour of quartz mines in the area. The tour, which takes a good part of the day, includes visits to several mines and a stop at the best mining museum in the Gold Country—the Nevada County Historical Mining Museum in Boston Ravine (Lower Mill Street), open daily from 11 A.M. to 5 P.M. in summer. Even the most sophisticated tourist is impressed by the vast display of mining equipment.

West of Grass Valley on State 20 are a few hamlets worth a slight detour. Rough and Ready seceded from the Union in 1850 and did not legally return until 1948. Three of the oldest landmarks are the schoolhouse, the I.O.O.F. Hall, and the blacksmith shop. The Old Toll House now extracts revenues from the sale of antiques. Smartville, Timbuctoo, and Browns Valley were once prosperous mining towns, but only a few structures and some ruins remain. Two miles southwest of French Corral, across the South Fork of the Yuba River, stands the Bridgeport Bridge, longest (230 feet) remaining single-span covered bridge in the entire West.

## Nevada City through Sierra City

Nevada City has acquired a well-deserved reputation for beautiful homes, interesting shops, and carefully preserved antiquity. It's a good base from which to explore side roads east of State 49, and it's only a few miles to Malakoff Diggins State Historic Park, site of an impressive example of hydraulic mining.

Residential sections of town contain many gabled frame houses, and the downtown area has a number of historical buildings: the Ott Assay Office, where ore from the Comstock Lode was first analyzed and found rich in silver; the National Hotel, whose balconies and balustrades reach out over the sidewalk; and the red brick Firehouse No. 2, now a museum with a collection of Gold Rush remnants.

For further exploration follow some of the side roads. You can reach the old high-country camps of Goodyears Bar, Forest, and Alleghany by turning south off State 49 on the Mountain House Road 3 miles west of Downieville.

Fire and flood have done their best to destroy the mountain settlement of Downieville, but it is still one of the most entrancing of the remaining

**Malakoff Diggins'** *scars from huge hydraulic mining operation are gradually softening with time.*

**Replica of Sutter's sawmill** *stands near the American River in Coloma; this was site of gold discovery.*

gold towns. The old stone, brick, and frame buildings—many of which were built in the 1860s or earlier—face on quiet, crooked streets and cling to the mountainsides above the Yuba River.

The towering, jagged Sierra Buttes, visible for many miles in all directions, overshadow the half-ghost town of Sierra City. Between 1850 and 1852, Sierra City miners tunneled through these dramatic granite peaks in their search for gold-bearing rock. In Sierra City are several structures of an early vintage—the largest is Busch Building, two stories of brick and a third of lumber, built in 1871.

# Exploring Feather River Country

Rich in scenery and history, the Feather River Country presents a varied topography—rocky canyons, fern-filled ravines, high mountains, leaf-covered foothills and chaparral slopes, second-growth pine and fir forests. Through all this flows the Feather River.

Three major waterways form the Feather River: North Fork, Middle Fork, and South Fork. A lesser one flowing into the North Fork is the West Branch. State 70 follows the North Fork of the Feather and affords panoramic views of canyon country. The Middle Fork, the most rugged, offers some of the finest trout fishing in California. The site of early placer mining locations, the South Fork has many swimming holes and hiking trails. Along its stretches are seven reservoirs—the highest at 5,000 feet is 500-acre Grass Valley Lake.

Spanish explorer Don Luis Arguello named the river in 1820. He reached its lower end during the band-tailed pigeon migration and dubbed it "El Rio de las Plumas" for the feathers floating in it.

The Maidu Indians inhabited the area, hunting deer with bow and arrow, spearing salmon and steelhead, and searching the hillsides for acorns, roots, and herbs. But because the Feather River was the site of major gold strikes (Bidwell Bar, a gold discovery site, is now under 450 feet of water), by 1860 the Indian way of life was destroyed by the hordes of gold seekers from the East.

The Feather River Highway, State 70, connects the Central Valley and the Sierra. Following the deep canyon of the North Fork, it touches the edges of the upper Middle Fork, crosses nine bridges and tunnels through three outcroppings of solid granite.

Along most of this route are a number of Forest Service campgrounds, major resorts, and cabin settlements. Most stretches along the way are heavily fished. Stub roads lead off to old mining settlements, to little pocket valleys that have been cultivated since 1850, and to trout-filled lakes beneath granite domes. Trails take off where roads end. Here you'll find a back pack handy.

## Sights around Oroville

Oroville, 70 miles north of Sacramento on State 70, is the gateway to the Feather River Country. Today a lumber processing center and olive-growing area, Oroville first sprang up as Ophir City—a boisterous tent town of Gold Rush days. In the 1870s, when thousands of Chinese worked the diggings in the area, Oroville's Chinatown was the largest in California.

## Temple, white frame house, and diamonds

The richest reminder of Oroville's past is the Chinese Temple, built in 1863 and now a museum of Oriental artifacts, at Broderick Street behind the levee of the Feather River. A more recent addition, Tapestry Hall, is connected to the temple by an open courtyard and garden with a graceful copper pagoda and small reflecting pool surrounded by Chinese plantings. At the entrance to the temple is a 2-ton brass incense burner said to have been the gift of the Emperor Quong She of the Ching Dynasty. You can visit the temple from 10 A.M. to 12 noon, 1 to 4 P.M. Friday through Tuesday, 1 to 5 P.M. Wednesday and Thursday.

Another Oroville landmark is the Judge C. F. Lott Memorial Home in Sank Park. Completed in 1856, the white frame dwelling is furnished with period pieces and sits among landscaped gardens. The house is open Wednesday through Sunday from 10:30 A.M. to 4 P.M., Monday and Tuesday by appointment; June 1 to October 15 daily. From December 1 to January 15 the house is closed. A broad patio, added recently, is the site of afternoon programs during spring and summer months.

North of Oroville, in the tiny town of Cherokee, you'll see a few more remnants of gold mining days—ruins of the Spring Valley Assay Office and an old hotel converted into a museum. The first diamonds discovered in the United States were picked out of a sluice box here in 1866, but no extensive diamond mining was ever done.

## Superlatives apply to Lake Oroville

With a surface area of about 15,800 acres and about 167 miles of shoreline, Lake Oroville was created by the Oroville Dam, 5½ miles northeast of Oroville. Towering 770 feet above metropolitan Oroville, it is the highest dam in the United States and the highest earth fill dam in the world.

**Quiet stretch** *of the Feather River makes fishing a pleasure; other parts of river have rushing water.*

**Oroville's Chinese Temple** *on Broderick Street is all that remains of a once-sizable Chinese community.*

Much of the water stored in the lake is diverted into a system of aqueducts, tunnels, and basins that extends the length of California. Adjoining the dam in the Feather River Canyon wall is a power-house that can generate enough electricity to supply a city of a million people. The dam offers a large measure of protection against river floods.

The lake, now designated a state recreation area, affords a variety of outdoor activities. Most popular are boating, water-skiing, swimming, fishing, and sailing. Picnicking and camping facilities are available, and there are reserved areas for boat-in camping and houseboat mooring.

At the park's visitor center are interpretive displays and information on the dam and lake. An observation area affords a panoramic view of Lake Oroville on one side and Oroville and the remainder of the vast water project on the other side. For information about recreational activities, write to Lake Oroville State Recreation Area, 400 Glen Drive, Oroville, CA 95965.

Across the Middle Fork arm of Lake Oroville is the Bidwell Bar Bridge. The suspension bridge, 627 feet above the river bed before the lake was full, now is only 47 feet above water.

# If Forest Recreation Attracts You...

Thousands of acres of forested land in the Plumas and Tahoe national forests offer trout fishing or swimming in mountain streams, camping in secluded spots, hiking or horseback riding, hunting, and skiing. Interstate 70 and 80 and State 49 and 89 are the main forest land routes. Much of the Plumas National Forest is in Feather River country; Tahoe National Forest extends south and east to the Nevada border. For a detailed map of roads, trails, campsites, and lakes, write to either Plumas National Forest, Quincy, CA 95971, or Tahoe National Forest, Nevada City, CA 95959.

## Feather Falls—a picturesque leap

The Feather Falls Scenic Area is a 14,890-acre preserve of forested canyons, soaring granite domes, and plunging waterfalls in a remote section of Plumas National Forest just north and slightly east of Lake Oroville. Set aside by the Forest Service to preserve the special qualities of this segment of the Feather River drainage, the scenic area includes Feather Falls and Bald Rock Canyon.

Feather Falls, a plumelike cascade of the Fall River plunging 640 feet in a single leap, lends its name to the scenic area. In the spring and early summer, you can see the falls by boating to the end of the Middle Fork arm of Lake Oroville and then climbing a hazardous half-mile trail. For an eagle's-eye overlook, follow a 3½-mile trail from a road turning off at Feather Falls Village.

Along the Bald Rock Dome canyon rim, you'll catch some scenic views, but the canyon floor is primitive and inaccessible. Though the Milsap Bar

Road crosses the Middle Fork at the upper end of the canyon, not even a foot trail descends to its inner depths.

To reach the Milsap Bar Bridge from Lake Oroville, follow the Oroville-Quincy Highway north for about 16 miles (along Berry Creek) to the Brush Creek Ranger Station. Then head east on the Milsap Bar Road about 7 miles to the river crossing.

## Drop your line in Bucks Lake

Formed in 1929 when Bucks Creek was dammed, the lake is nestled in the Feather River country at a mile-high elevation. To reach the lake, follow the Feather River Highway (State 70) to Quincy and then turn west on the paved, 17-mile road to Bucks Lake. The lake can also be approached from Oroville on the Oroville-Quincy and Spanish Ranch roads.

Boating (rentals available), swimming, waterskiing, and fishing are prime attractions at the south shore resort area. Here, too, you'll find Forest Service and private campgrounds. For wilderness camping, cross the lake to the roadless north shore, where you'll find a number of excellent camping and fishing spots.

Hikers and horsemen can reach 10 other lakes and numerous streams scattered through the back country. Good fishing destinations are Bear Creek, Grizzly Creek, and the Middle Fork of the Feather, reached on foot, by horseback, or by jeep.

At nearby Lower Bucks Lake, fishing is good for rainbows and browns. Undeveloped campsites are on the north side of this lake, too. Access is over a dirt road from the Bucks Lake south shore.

## Plumas-Eureka State Park

On the slopes of Eureka Peak, surrounded by Plumas forest land, is the nearly 5,000-acre Plumas-Eureka State Park. Park headquarters are at Johnsville (a partially state-owned ghost town), 6 miles west from the intersection of State 70 and 89 near Blairsden. Hiking trails (many of them leftover roads from mining days) take you up Eureka Peak, Mt. Elwell, and Mt. Washington to the south. Picnic facilities are available, and there is a campground on Upper Jamison Creek. Trout fishing is excellent at Eureka and Madora lakes and in the numerous mountain streams.

The old mining town of Johnsville and the Plumas-Eureka stamp mill within the park recall gold mining days. The museum and hard-rock mining exhibit at park headquarters will interest California history buffs. Open from 9 A.M. to 5 P.M., the park charges a day-use fee.

After October 1 the campground closes, but the park is open all year. Heavy snowfall encourages skiing—even the miners of the 1850s raced down slopes. Eureka Bowl is open during the winter. Facilities include a rope tow and an equipment rental concession.

**Johnsville,** *center of Plumas-Eureka State Park, has many collapsed and decaying buildings like those above.*

**Judge Lott's** *home in Oroville is a memento of the past —both inside and out. It's open for tours.*

# Lake Tahoe: California's Playground

Between the two main emigrant routes of California's early settlers (now U.S. Highway 50 and Interstate 80) lies Lake Tahoe. Surrounded by the heavily timbered Sierra Nevada, beautiful, unbelievably blue Lake Tahoe blossomed as a resort area in the 1870s when Lucky Baldwin built a large lodge and took guests out on the lake in his 168-foot steamer. Fifty years later when skiing became popular, roads were kept open in the winter, and the lake became an all-year playground.

Boating, swimming (the water is cold), and water-skiing are the main summer activities; skiing is the prime winter attraction. Since Lake Tahoe never freezes over, you can fish the year around.

Many people prefer to visit the lake in the spring or fall before the seasonal crowds arrive. However, during the off-season the weather is unpredictable. Snow can fall from October to June. If you visit Tahoe during the winter, you should carry tire chains. Check weather conditions that can make mountain driving hazardous.

Tahoe offers a variety of accommodations. You have a choice of resorts, motels, campgrounds (most open in summer only), or private cabins. For information concerning south shore accommodations and recreational facilities, write to South Lake Tahoe Chamber of Commerce, Box 15090, South Lake Tahoe, CA 95702. For north shore information, write to the Greater North Lake Tahoe Chamber of Commerce, Box 884, Tahoe City, CA 95730. Reservations in season are advisable.

Part of Lake Tahoe is in Nevada. On the Nevada side are gambling establishments that operate around the clock. Principal gaming areas are at Stateline at the south shore and Crystal Bay at the north shore.

## Circling the Lake

Lake Tahoe is 22 miles long and 8 to 12 miles wide. You can drive around the lake on a 71-mile shoreline road offering excellent views of the lake, its many coves, and the sheer mountain sides that plummet into the water. Occasionally winter snows may close a section of U.S. 89 between Tahoe City and Tahoe Valley.

## The lively south shore

Lake Tahoe's south shore is more heavily populated than the north shore. Resorts, motels, and private cabins are plentiful, there are a number of public beaches, and Nevada's Stateline offers gambling and nightclub entertainment in such luxurious high-rise hotels as Harrah's, Harvey's, and Sahara Tahoe. South Lake Tahoe, sprawling against the California-Nevada border, is the major city in the area.

Visitors to the area can get a quick introduction to its colorful historic past by browsing about the Lake Tahoe Historical Society's quaint Log Cabin Museum, behind the Al Tahoe fire station.

To reach the south shore, take State 50 from Sacramento or State 88 and 89 from Stockton. Scheduled (PSA and Air California) and charter airlines fly into Tahoe from California cities. Buses make daily runs.

**Emerald Bay,** at the southwestern tip of the lake, is Tahoe's famed scenic attraction. The bay is entirely within Bliss and Emerald Bay state parks, and its waters surround Tahoe's only island, Emerald Isle. The road around Emerald Bay is high

**Emerald Bay,** *bounded by two state parks, is most scenic inlet at Lake Tahoe. High road around the southwest shore provides good views of the lake.*

above the water, and the view is unparalleled anywhere else on the lake.

Unseen from the road, at the southern tip of the bay, is a 38-room mansion, called "Vikingsholm," once a summer residence. A striking example of Scandinavian architecture, Vikingsholm was patterned after a Norse fortress of 800 A.D. During summer the house is open to visitors daily. Park your car at Inspiration Point and then hike about a mile to the house. Daily excursion boats from South Lake Tahoe cross the lake, entering the bay.

At the head of the bay is a parking area for a short hike up to Eagle Falls. Picnic facilities are nearby, and camping units are located in both parks.

**Sugar Pine Pt. State Park,** up the road, is set in a dense grove of the trees for which it was named. Similar to other mountain parks in the vicinity, it is somewhat more protected from the heavy winter snows. Open all year, the park offers winter camping, cross-country skiing, and snowshoeing, in addition to its summer activities. The Ehrman mansion, acquired by the state with the property, is now an interpretive center and museum.

**South of Emerald Bay,** you'll find several Forest Service beaches. The El Dorado National Forest Visitors Center, on State 89 north of Camp Richardson, offers slide presentations, group campfires at the Lake of the Sky Amphitheater, guided half-day walks into the Desolation Wilderness, lecture

**Vikingsholm,** *hidden at southern tip of Emerald Bay, is an exact replica of 800 A.D. Norseman fortress. Park and walk down to water's edge to tour.*

**LAKE TAHOE**

Scale in Miles

0       2       4

**Nevada's** *beach park, popular with campers, provides sheltered picnic tables, drinking water, views.*

**Sunbathers, paddlers, and sailors** *share the placid lakefront beach at south end of Lake Tahoe.*

programs at Angora Ridge fire lookout station, boat tours of Echo Lake, and short walks through surrounding meadows.

A stream profile chamber allows you and the fish to exchange glances along an artificially created bypass of Taylor Creek, a natural trout and salmon spawning stream flowing from Fallen Leaf Lake to Lake Tahoe. The visitors center is open from 9 A.M. to 6 P.M. daily June 21 to September 21.

**The South Lake Tahoe City Beach,** on Lakeshore Boulevard, offers water-skiing and swimming. Picnic fires and overnight camping are prohibited on the beach, but approximately 150 campsites are within walking distance at the South Lake Tahoe El Dorado Recreational Area.

**Nevada Beach Recreational Area,** on the eastern side of the lake, serves day-use visitors in addition to providing campsites for tents or trailers.

Pocket resorts, such as Zephyr Cove and Glenbrook, also provide beach and boat access for guests.

## What the north shore offers

The Crystal Bay area is a center of activity for the north shore. Here, motels, lodges, condominiums, cabins, and gambling casinos crowd State 28 on either side. Once you cross into California, the casinos disappear, but the towns of Brockway, Kings Beach, and Tahoe Vista are fused to form a solid resort area.

A pine-forested area between Carnelian Bay and Tahoe City is relatively undeveloped. Tahoe City, closest town to Squaw Valley, Alpine Meadows, and other ski areas on the lake's west shore, offers winter and summer entertainment. You'll find a golf course, public beach, and state recreation area.

**Nevada's Incline Village** complex, east of Crystal Bay on State 28, has a good family ski area. In summer you'll find golf (two 18-hole courses), tennis courts, riding trails, and bowling. Location scenes for TV's "Bonanza" series were filmed at the Ponderosa Ranch nearby.

**Lake Tahoe Nevada State Park,** south of Incline, makes up part of the northeastern shore, encompassing rocky points (good for fishing), sandy beaches, launching facilities, and picnic grounds.

## Summer fun on the lake

Lake Tahoe is a mecca for boaters and water-skiers. There's plenty of room for everyone, and the many coves and harbors along the lake's shore are appealing. Many places around the lake rent boats; if you have your own boat, you'll find plenty of launching ramps. But during the heavy summer season, you may have trouble finding a mooring. If a summer thunderstorm appears imminent, do not venture too far from shore, for the lake can become very rough.

**Swimmers** unaffected by the cold water will find plenty of public beaches. At the south end of the lake are three Forest Service beaches (Pope, Baldwin, and Kiva). You can also swim at D. L. Bliss and Emerald Bay state parks, Sugar Pine Pt. State Park, and South Lake Tahoe Recreation Area. North shore offers public beaches at Tahoe City and Kings Beach. On the Nevada side, try Sand Harbor Beach State Recreation Area and Nevada Beach Campground. Many boat harbors also have beaches.

**Fishing** is good for rainbow, Mackinaw, silver, brown, eastern brook, and cutthroat trout. Local fishermen report the waters from the mouth of Emerald Bay south toward Baldwin Beach are excellent for Kokanee salmon, introduced into the lake in 1940. California and Nevada fishing licenses are valid anywhere on the lake, but you must depart from and return to the state that issues the license. In the many lakes and streams close to Tahoe, you can trout fish from May to October.

**Hiking and riding trails** around Tahoe are excellent. The Forest Service publishes hikers' maps. Inquire locally for other trips. You'll be able to rent horses at several spots around the lake.

## Skiing—choose your slope

The Lake Tahoe Basin is one of the most compactly developed ski regions in the world. You can ski at

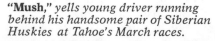

*Tahoe's snow-clad slopes excite winter skiers. Almost 20 resorts offer runs for snow bunnies and pros.*

**"Mush,"** *yells young driver running behind his handsome pair of Siberian Huskies at Tahoe's March races.*

any of 20 ski areas in and around Tahoe. For skiing information write to the South Lake Tahoe and Greater North Lake Tahoe chambers of commerce.

**South shore's** major ski area is Heavenly Valley; you turn at Ski Run Boulevard. The tram operates all year, offering grand summer views of the lake.

**North Shore** ski areas range from four in Nevada to a cluster of resorts north and west on the California side of the lake.

**Squaw Valley,** locale of the 1960 Winter Olympics, is 8 miles south of Truckee. You turn off on a 2-mile side road from State 89; you turn on when you catch your first glimpse of the greatly refurbished resort. Squaw has had its ups and downs, but it has always had big-league skiing.

You'll find an ice-skating rink, a heated all-year swimming pool, and spectator centers from which you can watch the activity on the slopes.

For information on accommodations and skiing, write Squaw Valley USA, Box 2407, Olympic Valley, CA 95730.

# Branching Out from the Lake

Two popular destinations lie at either end of Lake Tahoe. Donner Lake, off Interstate 80, is surrounded by summer cabins. Desolation Wilderness, west of State 50, is not populated at all—except in summer when backpackers penetrate its heart.

## Donner Lake

Just 2 miles west of Truckee along Interstate 80, Donner Memorial State Park is a popular recreation area alongside Donner Lake. The park stands as a memorial to the members of the ill-fated Donner Party who camped here during the winter of 1846-47. Almost half of the 89 persons in the party perished in the severe Sierra winter cold and heavy snows. A monument stands in the park on the site of the Brien family shack. Its stone base is 22 feet high—the depth of snow during that fateful winter.

The Emigrant Trail Museum in the park displays Indian and Donner Party relics. On display near the museum is a steam trailer that once hauled cut lumber on the eastern slope of the Sierra. Most of the park trails begin at the museum.

## Tired of Crowds? Try Desolation Wilderness

Just over the ridge along Lake Tahoe's southwest shore is Desolation Wilderness, a favorite of Sierra connoisseurs. The best time of year here is between

## Don't Miss

**Columbia State Historic Park** (State 49 north of Sonora)—good starting point for Gold Rush browsing; in restored period buildings, old-time activities continue

**Feather River Canyon** (along State 70 in Butte and Plumas counties)—one of Northern California's most beautiful canyons and scenic rivers; favorite trout fishing and camping destination

**Lake Tahoe** (California-Nevada border)—second-highest lake in the world; all-year playground with California's finest winter skiing and summer boating

**Marshall Gold Discovery State Historic Park** (State 49 at Coloma)—site of the state's first gold discovery; see restoration of Sutter's sawmill, Marshall's cabin, and replica of first gold nugget

**Nevada County Historical Mining Museum** (in Grass Valley's Boston Ravine)—the Gold Rush country's finest collection of mining artifacts, from pick and shovel to Pelton wheel

**Oroville Dam** (Oroville Reservoir)—towering earth fill dam (770 feet above town) is the world's highest; backs up large water recreational area

**Plumas-Eureka State Park** (south of Quincy off State 70)—5,000-acre park in northern Sierra Nevada surrounds ghost town of Johnsville; mine chain buckets were 1800s ski lift

**Yosemite National Park** (east from Merced)—showcase of nature's talents on a grand scale; spectacular waterfalls, massive granite domes, far-reaching meadows, and groves of sequoias

July 15 and October 1. September is a good month—crowds have thinned out and the air is autumn crisp. Snow usually begins to fall in November, making the wilderness inaccessible.

As its name implies, the area is wild and lonely, glistening with glacier-polished granite slopes and huge boulders, and nearly devoid of trees. But there are also forests of fir, pine, hemlock, juniper, and aspens. In the spring, colorful wildflowers brighten Sierra meadows. The wilderness contains about 70 named lakes, all good for trout fishing but too cold for swimming.

Within Desolation Wilderness's 63,469 acres, you can hike about 50 miles of trails with five major trail entrances to choose from. The Tahoe-Yosemite trail is much used and connects many lakes. Backpack trips are extremely popular. Or, if you prefer, try a stock trip, using animals to carry supplies.

For information on backpacking or wilderness trips, write to District Ranger, U.S. Forest Service, P.O. Box 8465, South Lake Tahoe, CA 95705, or write the service at Pollock Pines, CA 95726.

# Into the Northern Wonderland

 Splashing streams, towering snow-covered peaks, snug valleys encircled by forested slopes, miles of deep blue waters, and some of nature's most unusual attractions make up the northern wonderland, an area stretching from the Coast Range east to Nevada and from the upper Sacramento Valley to the Oregon border.

Outdoor recreation is unlimited. You can fish the Klamath, water-ski on Whiskeytown Lake, houseboat on Shasta and Trinity lakes, hike magnificent wilderness, sail at Eagle Lake, or camp along clear mountain streams. At Lava Beds National Monument and Lassen Volcanic National Park, you can see unusual land formations caused by volcanic action.

Snow activities in winter center around Lassen Park and the Shasta Recreation Area. Try skiing, snowshoeing, or cross-country treks.

Interstate Highway 5 is the main north-south route through the northern mountains, and State Highway 299, the main east-west route. The highways join at Redding, hub of this outdoor playland, 234 miles north of San Francisco and 173 miles north of Sacramento. U.S. Highway 395 provides easy access to the northeastern part of the state.

For maps, brochures, and detailed information on this area, write to Shasta-Cascade Wonderland Association, P.O. Box 1988, Redding, CA 96001, or stop by their offices at So. Market and Parkview streets.

Bring a tent or trailer for freedom in this mountain country. A back pack and sleeping bag allow you to go deep into wilderness areas for delightful solitude. Accommodations are available throughout most of this region, but it's advisable to plan ahead.

*__Arms of Trinity Lake__ are easily explored by houseboat. Rentals, resorts, and roads are all on the lake's west side.*

# A Water World

Boating is popular in the northland. Most of the activity centers around the lakes closest to Redding—Shasta, Whiskeytown, and Trinity. You can rent power boats, sailboats, or houseboats (Shasta and Trinity) and get water-skiing instruction at Shasta. Islands, inlets, and sandy beaches make picnicking popular. Campgrounds and marinas are plentiful and boat access is good.

Other good boating lakes are north and east of Redding. Most of them are noted primarily for fishing; several have good campgrounds and marinas. All are easily reached on good roads.

It's a fisherman's paradise. Mountain lakes and streams offer good catches all year. This is salmon and steelhead country; Chinook can weigh up to 55 pounds. Limits vary according to area. In some trophy waters, the limit is two trout. Anyone wishing to fish these waters should read the angling regulations and restrictions on limits, size of hooks, type of lure, and stream closures.

## A Trio of Lakes

Established in 1965 as part of the Federal Bureau of Reclamation's Central Valley Project, the Whiskeytown-Shasta-Trinity National Recreation Area consists of three units—Whiskeytown Lake, Shasta Lake, and Claire Engle (Trinity)-Lewiston lakes. All are popular summer destinations with boaters, campers, water-skiers, and picnickers. For detailed

**Young angler** *brings in his first fish with the aid of an old pro. Fall fishing is good at Whiskeytown Reservoir, though the weather may turn cold.*

information on the recreation area, write to Shasta-Trinity National Forest, 1615 Continental St., Redding, CA 96001, or to Shasta-Cascade Wonderland Association, P. O. Box 1988, Redding, CA 96001.

## Whiskeytown Lake—try trout trolling

Eight miles west of Redding on State 299 is the Whiskeytown Reservoir, created when the Whiskeytown Dam was constructed to divert water from the Trinity River into the Central Valley. The lake is good for trout and Kokanee fishing from either boat or shore. Best time to fish is in fall or early spring. Water-skiing, scuba diving, swimming, and boating are popular because of the 37-mile shoreline with its large and small coves. Whiskeytown offers some of the top sailing waters in the northern mountains.

Two marinas—Oak Bottom and Brandy Creek—provide all services; boats launch from Whiskey Creek picnic area north of the highway. Other picnic and camping areas (some close to the beach) are designated. No fires are allowed on the beaches.

Some of Northern California's most beautiful scenery surrounds Whiskeytown Lake. A number of hiking and riding trails cross streams, climbing high enough to afford sweeping views of the lake's blue waters dotted with wooded islands.

Blacktail deer is the important game animal, though there are seasons on pigeon, quail, grouse, and even bear. No hunting is permitted in areas of concentrated use.

The National Park Service maintains a Visitor Center just off State 299 on the east side of the lake. On the shore of the lake is the Kennedy Memorial, which commemorates President Kennedy's dedication of the dam and lake in 1963.

Below the dam, Clear Creek (once a major gold and silver producing stream) winds through steep gorges and rocky hills. About 5 miles of the creek's waters are open to trout fishing.

## The choices at Shasta Lake

Nine miles north of Redding is Shasta, California's second highest dam, serving as the great barrier between the mountains and the valley. Behind it stretches Shasta Lake, the largest unit of the three-lake National Recreation Area. Everything about

**Placid waters** *of Lake Shasta sparkle behind Shasta Dam, the second highest in California. Part of the three-lake National Recreation Area, Shasta is a favorite with swimmers, boaters, and fishermen.*

Shasta Lake is on a grand scale. This great, four-fingered reservoir, the largest manmade lake in California, covers 30,000 acres and has 370 miles of shoreline. Shasta's many arms reach back into the canyons of the Sacramento, McCloud, and Pit rivers and Squaw Creek.

Shasta Lake is wide and unusually serene. Resorts on the lake (most clustered around Interstate 5) offer swimming, fishing, water sports, and boating (by the hour or day). Craft range from canoes to paddlewheelers. Houseboats offer all the conveniences of a small housekeeping cabin with the added advantages of providing movable scenery. Boat and hiking tours and interpretive programs are offered during the summer season.

If you have your own boat, you'll find ramps at resorts and at several campsites along Shasta's shores. The Forest Service maintains a number of campgrounds around the lake. A few can be reached by boat only, and you may have to get your water from a spring or the lake itself.

Shasta Lake is particularly inviting in the spring when the redbuds bloom and in the early autumn when the oaks change color. Summer is the heavy-use season: be sure to make houseboat, resort, or private campground reservations well in advance.

**Lake fishing** takes place the year around for 17 varieties of game fish, including German brown, rainbow and Kamloops trout, black bass, Kokanee, and crappie. Since fish move frequently from one section to another, there's no "best place" for angling. Trout feed near the surface except during the summer, when they're found down about 50 to 150 feet. For crappie and bass, try angling around rocky points or where streams enter the lake. Limit on trout and salmon is five.

**Shasta Dam,** the key structure in the Central Valley Project, is 602 feet high and two-thirds of a mile long at its crest. It's open daily. Tours are self-guided; a model and film explain how the dam works. You'll get a good view of Mt. Shasta looming in the distance.

**Shasta Caverns,** a deep, complex series of limestone caves overlooking the McCloud River arm of Shasta Lake, are fun to explore, but just getting there is an adventure. You travel first by boat and then by bus up a steep, 800-foot rise to the cavern entrance—a deceptively normal-looking door in the mountainside that leads to geological formations possibly a million years old.

Multicolored fluted columns, 60-foot-high stone draperies in symmetrical folds, and crystalline stalactite and stalagmite formations are featured on the 2-hour tour (including the cross-water trip). Knowledgeable guides take you through well lighted tunnels and up stairs (over 100 at one point). Take a sweater, for the temperature is a constant 58°. The caverns are open daily the year around. From May 1 to September 30, tours start at 8 A.M.; service is reduced to three daily trips (10

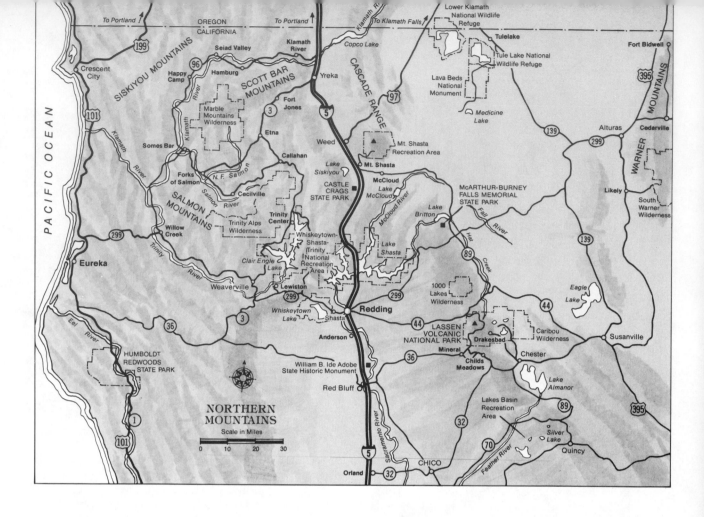

NORTHERN
MOUNTAINS

Scale in Miles

0    10    20    30

A.M., noon, and 2 P.M.) from October 1 through April 30, weather permitting. Admission charges are moderate.

To reach the caverns, take the O'Brien-Shasta Caverns offramp from Interstate 5 about 16 miles north of Redding. Follow the signs for about 2 miles to the Visitor Center. If you're boating, you can dock at the caverns landing on the east side of the McCloud arm.

## Clair Engle (Trinity)-Lewiston Lakes

Although Clair Engle Lake is the official name on most maps, residents of Trinity County still call this 16,500-acre impoundage Trinity Lake. By either name, it's the focal point of the Trinity National Recreation Area, a sparsely populated expanse of lake and forest. It offers excellent fishing for trout and smallmouth trophy bass, large and small campgrounds (some with sandy swimming beaches), marinas and launching ramps, swimming and sailing, water-skiing, and houseboat rentals (Cedar Stock Resort, Estrellita, and Trinity Center). All facilities are on the west side of the lake within the shadow of the rugged Trinity Alps.

A new visitor center is open on the highway near the Tannery Gulch arm of the lake, and another visitor center is located 2 miles above

Trinity Dam on Buckeye Road. Tours, self-guided trails, and amphitheater programs are available during the summer. For additional information write to the District Ranger, U.S. Forest Service, Weaverville, CA 96093, or to Shasta-Cascade.

Lewiston Reservoir, downstream from Trinity Dam, is at an elevation of about 1,900 feet. Seven miles long, very narrow, and resembling a slow-moving river more than a lake, Lewiston offers good trout fishing. Trailer parks, campgrounds, boat rentals, and public boat-launching ramps sit on the west side of the lake. For noncampers, the Trinity country offers a selection of nearby resorts and overnight accommodations in Weaverville, Lewiston, and Douglas City.

To reach Trinity Lake, drive 49 miles west from Redding to Weaverville on State 299; then follow State 3 about 10 miles. Turn off at the Buckeye Creek Road to reach the northern end of Lewiston Reservoir or approach the south end from State 299 at the Lewiston turnoff; it's about 6 miles.

## A Lake Loop

Boaters, campers, and anglers all have their "favorite" lake. Here, singled out from the multitude of lakes in the north country, are some of the most

**Sail raised,** *small boat is readied for launch at Eagle Lake's Gallatin Beach. Low hills overlook lake in rear.*

popular, as well as a couple of the lesser known. Lodging is nearby; see the *Sunset* publication *Western Campsites* for campgrounds.

**Lake Siskiyou,** a 430-acre impoundment of the Sacramento River in Box Canyon, was constructed solely for recreation purposes. Shoreline facilities include picnic and camp sites, boat rentals, a ramp and wharf, and a spacious, sandy beach. Besides swimming and boating, the lake offers year-round trout fishing. To reach the lake, take the Central Mt. Shasta offramp from Interstate 5 just west of the city of Mt. Shasta.

**Lake McCloud** is a little off the beaten track, but this is part of its charm. Tarantula Gulch provides boating access for year-round trout fishing or just cruising in crystal clear, blue water. From Interstate 5, take State 89 to the town of McCloud (9 miles) and follow a signed road heading south from town for about 12 miles. Watch for lumber trucks in summer; the road could be closed in winter. On the way you'll pass a public, 9-hole golf course; it offers no sand traps but challenging water hazards.

The quaint, gas-lighted town of McCloud nestled at the foot of majestic Mt. Shasta was first built as a lumber town. Don't miss the local emporium containing everything from hardware to jewelry.

**Medicine Lake,** about 500 years old, lies in what was once a volcanic crater. Burnt Lava Flow, to the south, has some of the most awesome lava formations in Northern California. A high mountain lake, Medicine opens around July 1. Nights are chilly even in midsummer. Cold, clear, and deep, the lake is a popular fishing and boating area and even gets some hardy water skiers. The Forest Service recently completed a boat dock, ramp, and picnic area. The enclosed swimming area has a beautiful, sandy beach. From the south you can reach Medicine Lake by following State 89 east from McCloud to Bartle and turning north on a good (but not too well-marked) road for 32 miles. From the north, take the marked road from Lava Beds National Monument or take State 139 west from Perez.

**Eagle Lake,** in Lassen County, is one of California's largest natural lakes—and also one of its cleanest and least crowded. Here are plenty of spacious, tree-sheltered campgrounds and 27,000 acres of clear, blue water for excellent sailing. The lake also serves as a feeding ground for a rare breeding colony of osprey. Fishing is good for the large Eagle Lake trophy trout, a natural hybrid that is the only game fish adapted to the unusually alkaline water. The limit is three and catches up to 7 pounds are not uncommon.

Gallatin Beach, at the southern end of the lake, is a recreation center with store, marina, boat rentals, ramp, sandy beach, and shady picnic area.

From Interstate 5 take the Lassen Park turnoff from either Redding (State 44) or Red Bluff (State 36). The highways skirt the park on either side and join west of Susanville, closest town to the lake. The main beach and campground are reached on Eagle Lake Road. State 139 runs along the eastern shore.

**Lake Almanor,** 52 square miles of azure water mirroring snow-capped Mt. Lassen and rimmed with evergreen forest, is in Plumas County, 80 miles east of Red Bluff on State 36. Almanor, created by a dam on the Feather River, is also easily accessible from U.S. 395 and State 70. Summer lake surface temperatures of 75° make it ideal for swimming, water-skiing, and boating. Many resorts around the lake offer rentals, docking, and launching areas. A free public boat ramp is located west of the dam.

Fishing is excellent for trophy rainbow and brown trout, Kokanee, bass, catfish, and perch. Gould Swamp is a "hot spot" in spring, and summer night fishing near the shore is productive. During spring and fall, trolling for trout and Kokanee pays off. In addition to Almanor, there are some 50 lakes in the area and 500 miles of streams.

Additional recreational activities include a 9-hole golf course at Lake Almanor Country Club, holiday sailboat races, hunting, and rock collecting. Several nearby family ski areas (Stover Mountain, Lassen Park, Coopervale, and Eagle's Peak) operate during the winter. Slopes around the lake offer good tobogganing, sledding, and other snow fun.

**Lakes Basin Recreational Area,** almost on the border of Sierra and Plumas counties, is roughly halfway between Lassen Park and Lake Tahoe. A collection of small lakes conveniently located close to the road makes this a good family fishing and hiking outing. A 23-site campground serves as a convenient base camp. Grassy Lake, the closest, is often overfished; nearby Big Bear and Little Bear lakes hold rainbow; in Cub and Silver lakes, look for brook trout; and at Long Lake, the largest, you can rent boats. Distances between lakes are short; you can hike, fish, and return to your car in the same day. There's trailside camping at Silver Lake; from there, it's an easy walk to less-fished lakes.

From State 89 turn off at Graeagle and follow Gold Lake Road south. From Lakes Basin you can continue south to Sierra City and State 49.

# Rivers for All Fishermen

Among the many rivers of the northern part of the state, a few stand out because of size, beauty, and accessibility but primarily because of the fishing. Here you'll encounter the salmon and the steelhead (seagoing rainbow; see page 135), a challenge for any angler.

To see salmon spawn artificially, visit the Coleman National Fish Culture Station, the world's largest salmon hatchery, 6 miles off Interstate 5 at Anderson above Red Bluff (or visit the new spawning channel at Red Bluff). Spawning salmon provide a spectacular show during the fall and winter run. You can also get a good look at salmon in Redding's Caldwell Park, where manmade falls on the Sacramento River are lighted during spring and summer nights. Falls are dismantled in winter.

But the rivers are where you catch fish, and below we have listed the major streams. For angling information, check with the Shasta-Cascade Wonderland Association in Redding.

## Fishing the Klamath

Although not a long river, the Klamath is an impressive stream within cliffed canyons. It offers some of the state's best steelhead fishing. The Klamath River winds through the mountains from Oregon and heads west to the California coast. Most of its course is paralleled by State 96.

Along the highway, river communities offer lodges and resorts. Several Forest Service campgrounds spread out beside the river's banks. Try Happy Camp, Seiad Valley, Klamath River, Hornbrook, and Yreka for accommodations.

The most sought-after fish in the Klamath is the steelhead; next in popularity are the Chinook and silver salmon. Fishing is best from late summer to early spring for anadromous fish (fish going from the sea up rivers to spawn), mainly steelhead. Above Copco Lake the Klamath is a trophy fishing water with a five-trout limit.

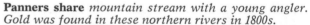
**Panners share** *mountain stream with a young angler. Gold was found in these northern rivers in 1800s.*

**Wooded campgrounds** *along State Highway 299 are a cool retreat for Trinity River fishermen.*

# What Is a Steelhead?

Why do you find fishermen wading waist deep in bone-chilling waters or huddled in drifting dories with numbed fingers, fumbling to refasten snagged rig or bait? They're out to catch the elusive steelhead coming in from the sea to begin their remarkable winter journey back to their birthplace. This is a fish with a single purpose—to make its way up the river to spawn.

The steelhead, which many consider the most spirited fish in the West, is nothing more than a seagoing rainbow trout. Like any other wild rainbow, the steelhead begins life in the clear running water of a mountain stream. Completely indistinguishable from its stay-at-home neighbor, it shares the same coloring and scientific name *(Salmo gairdnerii)*.

But, after a couple of years, the young steelhead yields to some primeval urge to migrate. Drifting downstream on the first leg of a long trek to the Pacific Ocean, it pauses at the river mouth just long enough to undergo a remarkable transformation: the blue green of its back turns steely blue, the spots disappear from body and fins, and its lateral red line fades to silver. The rainbow has become a salt-water steelhead.

Little is known about how the steelhead spends its life at sea for the next couple of years, but a larger, stronger, and wiser fish returns from the ocean depths and, once again changing its markings back to those of a typical-looking rainbow, is off on its difficult trek back to the ancestral spawning ground.

Arriving at last (unless interfered with by some wily angler), the steelhead spawns. Unlike the Pacific salmon that spawn only to die, though, the steelhead may spawn and return again to sea. Steelhead rarely live longer than 8 years, but some manage as many as five complete spawning migrations during their life span. This is a truly remarkable fish.

Only along the coast of the Pacific Northwest do factors of topography and climate permit a public fishery for large migrations of these anadromous trout through the winter season.

## Along the Trinity

The Trinity River also offers good steelhead fishing, particularly during the fall and winter. Fishing for salmon is at its best in late spring and early fall. Much of the Trinity follows State 299; accommodations are available at small towns along the highway. Campgrounds are scattered along the river.

## Check the action in Salmon River

The Salmon River, in the mountains west of Scott Valley, has its main salmon run in late July, August, and September. Steelhead start moving in just behind the salmon. Check angling regulations; there are special closures on this river. Seemingly unknown Forest Service campgrounds are found in some of the most beautiful mountainous terrain. Resorts offer guide service and small towns in the Scott Valley have limited accommodations.

## The mighty Sacramento

The Sacramento River starts in the Trinity Divide country and ends up all the way down in the Sacramento Valley. This is California's major navigable recreational river. You'll see tremendous wildlife, including some endangered bird species.

Anadromous fishing (below the dams) is excellent; several good salmon runs start around the latter part of August. This is when the big ones (up to 55 pounds) are caught. Spring runs begin the latter part of January and continue through March. Steelhead fishing is at its finest from mid-September into November.

## Favorite trout streams

It would be impossible to list all the good fishing streams in this great northern outdoorland. Anglers can always find a place to wet their lines, usually with good results. The season begins on the Sunday closest to May 1 and ends November 15. Here are listed, by county, a few of the favorites:

**Lassen:** Willow Creek and the Susan River.

**Modoc:** South Fork of the Pit River, East Creek, Mill Creek, Parsnip Creek.

**Plumas:** Middle Fork of Feather River, Nelson Creek, Yellow Creek upstream to Cottonwood.

**Shasta:** Fall River (some trophy waters), Spring Creek, Hat Creek from Lake Britton upstream, upper Sacramento River including Castle Creek.

**Siskiyou:** Scott River, McCloud River, Beaver Creek, Indian Creek, Canyon Creek.

**Tehama:** Deer Creek, Mill Creek, Battle Creek, Beegum Creek, South Fork of Cottonwood Creek.

**Trinity:** Blue Tent Creek, Coffee Creek, Canyon Creek.

# Into the Mountains

Few roads lead into the heart of the northern mountains. Three large mountain ranges—Klamath-Scott (including the Trinity, Salmon, and Marble mountains), Cascades, and Warner mountains—contain beckoning wilderness areas accessible only to packers and campers. You can sample the fringes by car. Resorts offer lodging, meals, and guides into the interior. Remember, you will need a permit to enter any wilderness area.

## A Wilderness Experience

Only a handful of towns in this region offer tourist lodging. But take heart: these mountains can be more inviting than the towering Sierra range to the southeast. They are less crowded, generally not so rugged, and more compact. Rivers and mountain streams offer excellent fishing; the national forests invite camping and packing.

Snow melts around the lakes by the middle of June, sometimes not until the first of July. July through September is the best time for the trails.

Packers and hikers use these points: Happy Camp, Seiad Valley, and Hamburg on the Klamath; Somesbar at the confluence of the Klamath and Salmon; Forks of Salmon and Sawyers Bar on the Salmon River; and Etna, Greenview, Ft. Jones, and Scott Bar along the Scott River.

### Trinity Alps—hidden high country

The unexpectedly high and rugged Trinity Alps are well screened by lower mountains; you scarcely notice them driving Interstate 5. An easy approach on cross-mountain State 299 has never brought them heavy traffic.

The Trinity Alps have some striking resemblances to the Sierra. Massive granite peaks sweep up from an alpine highland. Dozens of lakes pocketed in glacial basins feed the outlet creeks and rivers. But the Trinity Alps are much more compact than the Sierra (trails to the high mountains are shorter) and, being closer to coastal moisture, Trinity has proportionately more and fuller streams, greener and thicker underbrush.

Trinity splits the difference between the dry heat of the upper Sacramento Valley and the damp coolness of the Humboldt coast. It has two zones—a low, warmer canyon country and a cool, high mountain wilderness.

The Trinity Alps are a small Mother Lode. Three main roads form a circle around the Alps and link old gold towns. The principal road, State 299, parallels the Trinity Trail, famous as an Indian path, pioneer trail, and Gold Rush wagon road. The second, State 3, was once part of the main route —the old California-Oregon Wagon Road—north from Shasta to Callahan and Yreka. The third, a dirt road, taps the Salmon River settlement and the north and west slopes.

### Marble Mountains Wilderness

Winding up the Scott River from Hamburg to Ft. Jones and Etna and down the North Fork of the Salmon River to Sawyers Bar, Forks of Salmon, and Somesbar, the loop road encircles the Marble Mountains—more than 200,000 acres of isolation.

**Meals taste better** *in the open. Guests at Trinity Alps resort help prepare breakfast on pack trip.*

**Pack trips** *into the wilderness areas of the Trinity, Scott, and Marble mountains are the only way to view scenic attractions. Packers supply provisions and equipment and act as guides to best fishing spots.*

The Marble Mountains are walking mountains, easier to get around in than the Trinity Alps to the south. You have to fight brush along the streams, and the trails are precipitous in places but, for the most part, scenic and easy to follow.

Almost in the exact center of the wilderness area are the Sky High Lakes, a hub from which main and spur trails go in all directions. Most of the trails wind through forests of red and white fir, mountain hemlock, western white pine, Douglas fir, black oak, and rare weeping spruce.

## The Wild Cascades

Extending all the way from British Columbia through Washington and Oregon, the Cascade Range ends at Lassen Volcanic National Park. Mt. Shasta and Lassen Peak are the two outstanding mountains in Northern California.

Around Lassen are two wilderness areas popular with backpackers and fishermen because of the number of small lakes.

### It's uphill to Thousand Lakes

Four major trails enter the Thousand Lakes Wilderness, about 12 miles north of Lassen Park. Because all trails are uphill, back packs can get uncommonly heavy. But the pleasure of camping beneath lodgepole pines and the number of lakes in this valley compensate for the rigors of the hike.

Three-mile Cyprus Camp Trail, beginning at Cyprus Campground at the northwest end of the wilderness, is the easiest trail, climbing about 1,000 feet to Lake Eiler, the largest lake. At least six of the lakes provide good rainbow trout action almost any time of the day. Another campground (Bunchgrass) is south of the wilderness. You can drive to the wilderness on several unimproved roads from State 89; check with the ranger at Hat Creek.

### Caribou Peak Wilderness

Because of its easy access from Silver Lake in Lassen County, Caribou Peak is a popular, but still isolated, wild area. Just east of Lassen Park, Caribou contains a series of lakes along gradually sloping trails. Fishing for brook and rainbow is good.

As with Thousand Lakes, Caribou Peak is at its best from the latter part of June through the summer months. Several campgrounds are located close to Silver Lake.

## Wandering into the Warners

If the Warner Mountains were near a large city, they would be famed for their scenery and aswarm with visitors. But because they are in Modoc County, in the northeastern part of the state, and reached by little-traveled highways, they are still somewhat of a discovery.

# Bigfoot – Man or Myth?

Leaving all the rest of California's scenic splendors behind, many people head for vacation spots among the relatively unspoiled wooded areas along the Trinity and Klamath River valleys near the state's northern border. Here, civilization encroaches slowly; much of the land is protected as a national forest and as a mecca for fishing, hunting, camping, or just getting away from it all. Yet there is one disconcerting, mysterious note in this idyllic scene—the occasional unexplainable footprints of Bigfoot!

Reported sightings of Bigfoot, supposedly a creature from 7 to 14 feet in height and weighing from 300 to 800 pounds, have spanned a century. The creature is said to be totally covered with hair except for its face, palms, and soles. Facial features are said to be more humanoid than those of apes or gorillas, with flat nose and broad nostrils, short ears, and dark, leathery skin. Photographs show that Bigfoot walks upright with an erect stance and human stride ranging from 4 to 10 feet long.

Nevertheless, the giant footprints are the only tangible evidence of this "monster" (perhaps a relative of the Abominable Snowman of the Himalayas). You can buy footprint castings in Willow Creek, Weaverville, and on the Hoopa Valley Indian Reservation. Over Labor Day, Willow Creek, gateway to Bigfoot country, has an annual festival (as do Happy Camp and Weaverville)—Bigfoot Daze—during which spectators are invited

**Bigfoot's footprints,** *cast in plaster, intrigue guests and perpetuate legend.*

to compare their foot sizes with those of Bigfoot. Skeptics and believers are about evenly divided as to the creature's actual existence, but at least it's cause for a celebration.

---

The topography may bring to mind parts of the Rockies — where unmodified rock strata slant steadily up to a summit ridge and break away abruptly on the other side. The long western slopes are carpeted in a random patchwork of pine, aspen, fir, juniper, sage, and grasses.

You won't find any resorts or lodges in the Warners. You can take one-day outings into the high country from Alturas, but if you want to remain in the mountains, you must camp out. Packers operate from Alturas.

The only paved road across the Warners is the Cedar Pass route, which descends into Surprise Valley, a ranching area. If you take this road to Cedarville (on State 299), you can return to U.S. 395 through Fandango Pass on a maintained gravel road. Cedarville's most historic building is the Bonner Trading Post, a log cabin built in 1865 as a trading post for early immigrants and settlers. At the valley's northern tip is Ft. Bidwell, an army outpost from 1866 to 1892 and school for Paiute Indians from 1892 to 1930.

The highest part of the Warner Mountains is preserved as a 70,000-acre wilderness where no motor vehicles are permitted and the only signs of civilization are grazing sheep and cattle. Traversing the wilderness is the 24-mile-long Summit Trail, hugging the top of the range with views of Mt. Shasta and Lassen Peak to the west and, to the east, Surprise Valley 4,000 feet below and into Nevada. The trail skirts the three highest peaks—Squaw, Warren, and Eagle. All are climbable.

It takes 2 or 3 days to hike the entire trail; side trails lead to secondary roadheads that can shorten your trip. Side trails also lead to some fine trout fishing, especially in Pine, Mill, and East creeks and South Emerson Lake. Blue Lake (actually in Lassen County) is reached more easily on the road that goes from Likely toward Jess Valley, one of the prettiest spots you'll encounter.

From the south the Summit Trail starts at the Patterson ranger station, 42 miles by car from Alturas; it ends at Pepperdines Camp, 20 miles east of Alturas.

# Nature's Wonders

In California's far north you can discover some of nature's finest handiwork. Awe-inspiring Shasta's icy slopes still tempt the intrepid climber. Mt. Lassen's snow-capped peak looms over a valley of bubbling sulphur pools, vestiges of volcanic activity of the not-too-distant past. Craters, chimneys, and cones of Lava Beds National Monument in the state's northeastern corner were the setting for California's only major Indian war. Not far away is the resting place for waterfowl that travel the Pacific Flyway.

It's a land of contrasts. You can climb the cluster of domes and spires that make up Castle Crags; hike down to Burney Falls, a scenic waterfall (familiar to many because it adorned a beer can); or take a lantern and clamber through Subway Cave, a lava formation set incongruously adjacent to Hot Creek just north of Lassen Park.

## Mighty Mt. Shasta

Lore and legend surround majestic Mt. Shasta. This immense mountain, rising to 14,161 feet, dominates the landscape for more than one hundred miles. Volcanic in origin, it is composed of two cones: Shasta itself, and Shastina, a small cone that rises from the western flank. Five glaciers mantle the eastern and northeastern flanks above the 10,000-foot level.

Mt. Shasta City, on the west side of Strawberry Valley and right at the base of the mountain, was settled in the 1850s. When the Shasta route of the Southern Pacific Railroad reached the settlement in 1886, a townsite was laid out along the railroad. In 1924 the town took the name of the mountain that towers above it. Mt. Shasta is considered a sacred mountain by many people; over a dozen cults flourish in the tiny town.

### Climbing the sleeping giant

Perpetual glaciers, white water in deep canyons, little jewels of lakes, dense forests and open valleys, and wildflowers in spring tempt climbers. Even though the angle of climb is rarely greater than 35 degrees, the ascent taxes most climbers.

August is considered the best month to make a climb. Snow and ice are minimal then and weather conditions most stable. Special Forest Service brochures show recommended routes of ascent. Climbers are asked to check in and out at Mt. Shasta City Police Department. Hiking equipment can be rented, and maps are available.

### Skiing Shasta

Because Mt. Shasta normally gets a heavy snow pack, skiing often lasts well into spring and, in some years, into summer. The slopes of the ski bowl range from a 35 percent drop in the upper area to a 10 percent drop in the lower.

Two double chairlifts take you to above timberline; there are also a T-bar and a rope tow. The lodge has a cafeteria, cocktail lounge, and ski school but no overnight accommodations. Lodging and restaurants are available at Mt. Shasta, Weed, and Dunsmuir. You'll find ski rentals on the road.

To reach the bowl, leave Interstate 5 at Mt. Shasta City, about 60 miles north of Redding, and drive about 15 miles east on the Everitt Memorial Highway.

## Lassen – a Volcanic Park

Until May 30, 1914, Lassen Peak's claim to fame was as a landmark for pioneer Peter Lassen, who guided emigrant parties over the mountains and into the Sacramento Valley. Then began the year-long eruptions of smoke, stones, steam, gases, and ashes that culminated in the spectacular events of May 19, 1915. On that day a red-glowing column of lava rose in the crater and spilled over the sides, melting the snow on the mountain's northeast flank and sending 20-ton boulders and devastating floods of warm mud 18 miles down into the valleys of Lost Creek and Hat Creek.

Three days later, Lassen literally "blew its top." A column of vapor and ashes rose 30,000 feet into the sky. A terrific blast of steam and hot gases ripped out the side of the mountain and rushed northeast, killing all vegetation in its path for mile after mile. As far away as Reno, streets were buried under several inches of ash. Declining eruptions continued into 1917. On a visit to Lassen today, you will see striking examples of past volcanic activity, as well as evidence of present action.

Though much of the Lassen country is accessible only by trail, no point in the park's 163 square miles is more than a day's hike from the road. A brochure available at the park entrance shows the self-guiding nature trails and key points of interest.

## Lassen Peak

The Lassen Peak road, linked at both ends to State 89, traverses the western part of the park between West Sulphur Creek and Manzanita Lake. It crosses a shoulder of the volcano at 8,512 feet. Winding around three sides of the peak, the road affords stunning views of the volcano, examples of its destructive action, and vistas of woods and meadows, streams and lakes. After the first snowstorm, the road is closed until late spring, except for the section leading to the Lassen Park ski area.

A good trail takes you to the top of Lassen Peak. The hike is not difficult; it takes about 2 hours to climb from the highway—an ascent of 2,000 feet. From the highest point you will see not only the clear-cut evidences of the 1914-17 activity but also the distant Sierra Nevada in the vicinity of Tahoe, the Coast Range ascending northward to the Trinity Alps, and the icy cone of Mt. Shasta.

## The "hot spots"

Sulphur Works Thermal Area, near the park's south boundary, is the most accessible of the hydrothermal regions. North of here you pass Brokeoff Mountain, Mt. Diller, Mt. Connard, and Pilot Pinnacle—peripheral remnants of the much higher Mt. Tehama, a huge strato-volcano that collapsed perhaps as recently as 10,000 to 11,000 years ago.

Well-marked interpretive trails wind among the park's hissing steam vents and bubbling mudpots. A steaming stream borders the road's edge.

Biggest and showiest of the thermal areas is Bumpass Hell. You'll first notice a vague smell of sulphur as you descend into a natural bowl eaten out of a hard lava rock by hot acids. The barren landscape is violently roaring hot springs, boiling muddy pools, crystallized "solfataras," gurgling mud volcanoes, "morning glory" pools, deep turquoise waters over layers of fool's gold, and a mineralized "River Styx."

## The eastern side

From the town of Chester on State 36, two roads enter the eastern section of Lassen. On one road you drive 16 miles to Drakesbad, an old but comfortable spa that is open in summer. The road is paved, except for the last few miles. At Drakesbad, gateway to the Lassen wilderness, is a 2-mile, sign-guided trail around Boiling Springs Lake.

A second road from Chester leads to Juniper and Horseshoe lakes. Paved for the first 7 miles, it is then unsurfaced and difficult for large trailers. Horseshoe is a good base camp for hikes to Snag and Jakey lakes.

Accommodations at present are limited to Drakesbad in the southern part of the park. Drakesbad Guest Ranch (open from July 1 to Labor Day) can accommodate 50 in the main building and surrounding cabins. Saddle and pack trips can be arranged with guides. Facilities at Manzanita Lake (in the northwest section) were closed in 1974 because of geologic hazard in the Chaos Crags area.

**Steam rises** *from Boiling Springs Lake in Lassen Park's Drakesbad area.*

**Snow on Mt. Shasta** *lasts long into summer. Mt. Shasta City is skiers' closest lodging.*

# A Historical Sampler

Turn back the clock in the north country by sampling a few of the remnants of yesteryear. A drive through now-quiet villages still shows evidence of the raucous 19th century when gold fever reigned. Visit the home of California's only president; photograph the roofless, grass-filled buildings of the one-time "Queen City" of the northern mines; tour a temple of Chinese worship; or wander around some of the gingerbread houses of early pioneers.

## The Ide Adobe

Along the west bank of the Sacramento River, near Red Bluff, stands the William B. Ide Adobe State Historical Monument, a travelers' oasis. Picnic on verdant grounds overlooking the river, have a refreshing drink of cool water, or just stretch your legs by wandering through the shady 4-acre park, a landmark to the short-lived Bear Flag Party and California's president. The adobe ranch house is now a museum; a restored carriage house, smokehouse, and corral suggest ranch life in the 1850s. The park is open daily from 8 A.M. to 5 P.M.; there's no admission charge. From Interstate 5, take State 36 through Red Bluff; turn right at Adobe Road. Mooring facilities for boaters are near the old ferry site.

## Red Bluff Victorians

Of a later vintage are the grand Victorian homes of Red Bluff. The Kelly-Griggs House Museum (311 Washington Street) is a classic. Nearly 100 years old, it's open to the public Thursday through Sunday from 2 to 5 P.M. At the museum you can buy a Victorian "windshield tour" of central Red Bluff, including the cottage of Mrs. John Brown (widow of the celebrated abolitionist of Harper's Ferry).

## Gold Country

Northern California's gold rush was never as well chronicled as mining in the Sierra Nevada. Yet many millions in gold were extracted by miners who thronged north in the 1850s. The La Grange Mine, started in 1851, was for years the largest operating hydraulic mine in the world. Two sample drives plunge you into Gold Country: one follows along State 299 within an hour's drive west of Redding; the other meanders through scenic Scott Valley at the foot of the Marble and Trinity mountains.

**The Trinity Trail.** Shasta, 6 miles west of Redding, is a mere ghost of its former lusty self. Today, shells and facades of "the longest row of brick buildings in California" speak for its prosperous past. Visit the Shasta County Courthouse (now a museum) to learn about Shasta's rise and fall.

**William B. Ide Adobe** *ranch house stands on banks of the Sacramento River near Red Bluff.*

Two tiny towns to poke around in are French Gulch and Lewiston. Both have historic hotels, picturesque churches, and one-room schoolhouses. Signs direct you to turn-offs from State 299.

Weaverville seems enchanted with its past. A hundred years have brought little change in its frontier-Victorian aspect except for the honey locusts grown tall and the trim lawns, flowers, and picket fences. At the J. J. "Jake" Jackson Memorial Museum, open daily from May through November, you'll learn Trinity history amid nostalgic surroundings. Next door, across a pleasant park furnished with mining equipment, is the exotic Joss House, evoking memories of the important role of Chinese gold miners in California's history. Now it's a State Historic Park, where rangers conduct guided temple tours daily.

**Into Scott Valley.** From Weaverville, State 3 roams along the edge of Trinity Lake, through the mountains, and into peaceful Scott Valley. At Trinity Center the Scott Museum (open most of the year) gives you an idea of how it was to live during the days of the gold boom.

At the southern edge of agricultural Scott Valley, Callahan was a trading center for miners and ranchers. No traffic crowds the block-long main street. Several century-old buildings line the boardwalks. Plan to spend some time if you enter the Callahan Emporium, "Biggest Little Store in the World." Some of its wide variety of merchandise has been there for years.

Etna appears to be almost a metropolis if you see it after you visit Callahan. You'll enjoy many fine old buildings. A museum is usually open summer afternoons.

Ft. Jones, up the road, was the site of an army outpost on the old stage road. You'll find an exceptionally fine Indian museum. Up the McAdam Creek Road are the remains of a couple of bullet-riddled cabins of Deadwood, where Lotta Crabtree danced and Joaquin Miller cooked.

**Spires and domes** *in Castle Crags State Park are easily seen from Interstate 5. Trails lead from park to top.*

**Light your lantern** *before descending into the depths of Lava Beds, Skull Ice Cave.*

You'll find three campgrounds (Summit Lakes, Sulphur Works, and Crags) located along the Lassen Park road. Other campgrounds are at Warner Valley and Juniper and Butte lakes.

Winter sports center around the southwest entrance. Food and ski rentals are available. Tows for both beginners and advanced skiers operate on weekends. Overnight lodging is available at Mineral, Chester, Childs Meadows. Terrain and snow conditions favor cross-country skiing (also very popular in the Manzanita Lake areas); check first with the park ranger.

For more detailed information, write to Lassen Volcanic National Park headquarters at Mineral, CA 96063. Permits are required to get into Lassen's back country.

## California's Lonely Corner

Centuries ago, flaming volcanoes in northeastern California erupted masses of molten basaltic lava that spread over the more level land below in rivers of liquid rock. Upon cooling, they formed one of California's most fascinating landscapes. It's a rugged terrain with yawning chasms, cinder cones, and craters scattered over the surface. The official name is Lava Beds National Monument.

Adjoining the monument on the north are Tule Lake and Lower Klamath National Wildlife Refuges, administered by the Fish and Wildlife Service, U.S. Department of the Interior. At these havens for millions of migratory birds, some 200 species have been sighted during flight season each spring and autumn.

## Lava Beds National Monument

"Nobody will ever want these rocks. Give me a home here." That last, desperate plea of Modoc Indian Chief Captain Jack was never fulfilled. In 1872 Captain Jack lost the battle for his homeland —the volcanic plains and caves that are now California's Lava Beds National Monument.

During a day's visit, you can explore some of the 300 caves and other striking volcanic features of the monument and reconstruct the last stand of the Modocs by roaming through complex trenches and natural fortifications.

Just off State 139, almost to the Oregon border, these 72 square miles contain 1,500-year-old lava flows, high cinder buttes, pictographs and petroglyphs, and what is probably the world's outstanding exhibit of lava tubes. Lanterns are provided for self-guided explorations. The largest concentration of caverns is along Cave Loop Road near the monument's headquarters.

If you park off the road and search with binoculars, you may see some California bighorn sheep in a large enclosure along Gillem's Bluff. In the southern section of the park is a campground near monument headquarters. Look for other lodging, food, gasoline, and auto repair shops in nearby Tulelake.

## Tule Lake and Lower Klamath

North of Lava Beds are two of the wildlife refuges that make up the Klamath Basin (in northern California and southeastern Oregon), a "stop off" for the largest annual concentration of waterfowl on the North American continent. A large portion of the Pacific Flyway population gathers here every spring and fall. It's a photographer's paradise.

Hunting is permitted in certain designated areas during regular waterfowl and state pheasant seasons. Lodging is available at Tulelake, Newell, and Dorris; in addition, two campgrounds are located between the refuge areas. Maps and regulations are given out at the Tule Lake National Wildlife Refuge Headquarters at the north end of the refuge.

## Two Great State Parks

Although not as outstanding or as well known as Lassen or Lava Beds, Castle Crags and Burney Falls are two gems that shouldn't be missed. Camp settings are particularly attractive, and there's plenty to see and do.

## Castle Crags State Park

A cluster of gray white granite domes and spires rising out of the evergreen forest 48 miles north of Redding marks the site of Castle Crags State Park, a 3,447-acre reserve straddling Interstate 5 and the Sacramento River.

Long, warm summers and easy access make this park a popular place to camp or picnic from about the first of April to the end of October. Most popular activities are swimming and fishing in the river, hiking in the park or into the back country, and rock climbing in the Crags.

The principal trail takes you up a prominent cluster of rock castles west of the highway. You can drive up Kettlebelly Road to its end (about a mile) and then follow the trail, which climbs about 2,000 feet in 2.7 miles to the foot of the Dome. At Indian Springs, a little off the main trail and about a mile from the top, water trickles out of fern-covered rocks. In 1855 an Indian war was fought among these jumbled crags. Joaquin Miller, "the poet of the Sierras," wrote some heroic accounts of the battle in which he claimed to have been wounded by an arrow.

Though no hookups are provided, many campsites are large enough to accommodate trailers. Rest rooms, hot showers, and washtubs are nearby.

## McArthur-Burney Falls

Burney Falls, one of the most beautiful natural phenomena in California, is the chief attraction in

# Don't Miss

**Burney Falls** (McArthur-Burney Falls Memorial State Park)—twin falls stream over 129-foot cliffs to splash into emerald pool below; a walk down the trail into the canyon allows views of misty rainbows

**Chinese Joss House** (Weaverville)—oldest and most authentic Chinese temple in California; beautiful blend of architecture and color; still used as a place of worship

**Lassen Volcanic National Park**—steaming streams, bubbling mudpots, sulphur smells, and hissing vents against a backdrop of forested slopes, clear lakes, and steep peaks make Lassen one of the country's showiest thermal areas

**McCloud** (near junction of Interstate 5 and State 89)—quaint wooden village sitting at Shasta's feet; wander the gas-lighted street for a turn-of-the-century feeling

**Shasta Caverns** (Shasta Lake)—series of limestone caverns atop bluffs overlooking lake; getting there is part of the fun—by boat, bus, and a series of steps

**Subway Cave** (off State 89 north of Lassen)—an easy, 1/3-mile hike from a parking lot takes you through the underground world of a lava tube; Stubtoe Hall and Windtunnel are reminders to bring a flashlight and a jacket

**William B. Ide Adobe** (on Sacramento River north of Red Bluff)—simple adobe house and outbuildings of leader of Bear Flag Party, now a historical museum; river setting is an ideal stopping-off place for a picnic

the McArthur Memorial Park, near the intersection of State 299 and 89. Burney Creek, welling up out of a subterranean source, divides into two fairly equal flows of water and goes streaming over a 129-foot-high cliff into an emerald pool. On sunlit mornings a little rainbow can be seen in the mist blowing down the canyon at the foot of the falls.

The 565-acre park (open the year around) includes nearly 2 miles of frontage along Burney Creek, along with a bit of shoreline on Lake Britton, a 9-mile-long, manmade lake popular with swimmers, fishers, boaters, and water-skiers. Scattered throughout the forest are campsites (no trailer hookups) and a grocery store, snack bar, and gift shop open from mid-April to mid-October.

Trails wander through the park; you descend through the mist to the foot of Burney Falls and continue down the canyon to the lake. Fishing for bass, pike, and trout is good in Burney Creek and Lake Britton.

# Sacramento & the Big Valley

The flat Central Valley provides a strong contrast to the surrounding mountainous lands. On the east are the Sierra Nevada Mountains, on the west the Coast Range. To the south rise the Tehachapis, and to the north the foothills of the southern Cascades and the northern Coast Range meet.

The Central Valley extends 465 miles from north to south and is 30 to 60 miles wide. The big valley actually includes two valleys —the Sacramento through which the Sacramento River flows, and the San Joaquin, named for the river that runs part way through it.

Agriculture is its mainstay. Orchards, vineyards, and such staple crops as onions, sweet potatoes, and grain are the area's economic base. These lands are grazing grounds for dairy cattle and livestock. Two inland ports—at Sacramento and Stockton—open up the landlocked valley, providing access to the sea.

Interstate Highway 5, on the valley's western side, is fast becoming the most traveled route between Southern and Northern California, although at present a short stretch between Stockton and Sacramento is not yet completed. A swift but lonely, monotonous road, it bypasses the towns that grew up along State Highway 99, which runs right through the valley. Feeder roads connect the two highways along their routes, leading through small agricultural communities.

Although the San Joaquin Valley extends south below Bakersfield, the section identified with Northern California ends at Fresno. For a description of the southern part of the valley, see the *Sunset* book *Travel Guide to Southern California.*

The Delta—a vast inland sea—offers miles of good boating and fishing. It's the Central Valley's greatest recreation asset.

**Winding Sacramento River** *slices upper part of state's Central Valley. Flat, fertile farmland lies beside.*

# The Sacramento Valley – from Gold to Grain

The Sacramento Valley grew up during the Gold Rush days when river steamers and sailing schooners on the Sacramento and Feather rivers connected such communities as Marysville and Red Bluff to Sacramento. After gold panned out, agriculture developed. Grain ranches were built close to the Sacramento River, and grain soon became the valley's chief product.

These large grain fields were subsequently subdivided. Smaller, irrigated ranches became orchards, citrus groves, vineyards; alfalfa, vegetables, and some newcomers—cotton, rice, and sugar beets—were also planted. These crops remain the heart of the valley's agriculture.

The city of Sacramento, once a lusty boom town with its roots deep in the Gold Rush, soon emerged as an agricultural center and merchandising outlet for the rich valley. Some of its past still peeks out amidst the tremendous growth of its present.

## California's Capital City

Most of the major highway routes through central California pass through or around Sacramento, the state capital. To the east, Interstate 80 and U.S. Highway 50 lead into the Sierra, to Lake Tahoe, and on to Nevada. For southern travel, State 99 and Interstate 5 are the main arteries. To the north, these highways, uniting at Red Bluff, lead into the northern mountains. The main route to the San Francisco Bay area is Interstate 80.

Happily situated at the confluence of the American and Sacramento rivers, the city (whose summer temperatures soar into the 90s) offers water enthusiasts a wide choice of skin diving, water-skiing, swimming, and all types of boating. You'll find public boat launches at Miller Park, Discovery Park, and Elkhorn Bridge, 10 miles north. For specific visitor information, stop by the Community/Convention Center (1100 14th St.) or the Morse Building in Old Sacramento.

### In and around the state capitol

Dominating the city, the domed capitol building (9th Street between L and N streets), surrounded by its well-groomed park, has an impressive approach—across the Sacramento River on ornate Tower Bridge and east up well-landscaped Capitol Mall.

**Touring the capitol** (completed in 1874) and its newer East Wing annex is worthwhile, although at present the main building is excluded from the tour as an earthquake safety precaution. (Individuals may enter at their own risk.) Public tours (weekdays at 10:30 A.M. and 1:30 P.M.) start inside the east entrance. A series of 58 exhibits—one for each California county—displays the state's commercial, scenic, and recreational assets.

View the Senate and Assembly chambers from the third floor visitors' galleries. If a bill is up for vote when the legislature is in session (generally January to June) you can see government in action. When a measure comes up for a vote, the legislator

**Sacramento's state capitol** *is outstanding landmark in downtown area. Visitors can tour interior daily.*

pushes a button on his or her desk, flashing colors on a board—red for "no," green for "yes."

**Capitol Park,** an oasis on hot valley days, has 40 acres of more than 40,000 trees, shrubs, and plants. You'll see plants and trees from all over the world, including a collection of trees brought from Civil War battlefields. Among some 2,200 plantings, more than 800 varieties of camellias bloom; peak season is February and March. The park includes a trout pond, several monuments, and lots of squirrels. You can pick up a booklet suggesting three walking tours at the State Police Office on the ground floor of the capitol.

**The State Library** (open Monday through Friday from 8 A.M. to 5 P.M.), housed in a handsome granite building adjoining the capitol, is worth a visit, especially for history buffs. The general reading room, adorned with a Maynard Dixon mural depicting California's growth, maintains an excellent file of present and past California newspapers.

**The City and County Historical Museum** (1009 7th Street) is housed in Pioneer Hall, a building constructed by the California Society of Pioneers in 1868. Exhibits and artifacts of early Indian life, Gold Rush days, and Old Sacramento are on dis-

play weekdays from 10 A.M. to 5 P.M. (weekends to 4 P.M.); admission is free.

**The Governor's Mansion** (16th and H streets) stands empty today. Built in 1877, it was acquired by the state in 1903 for Governor George Pardee. Home to 13 governors, the 15-room Victorian-Gothic structure, now a state historical landmark, is open for public tours daily from 10 A.M. to 5 P.M. (except Thanksgiving, Christmas, and New Year's Day). There's a slight admission charge for adults.

## Historic Sacramento

Sacramento's story began with the splash of an anchor in the American River in 1839. Captain John A. Sutter had navigated a little fleet up the Sacramento River from San Francisco en route to the land grant he obtained from the Mexican government. On a small knoll not far from the anchorage, he built a fort, established an embarcadero, and started farming the area he called New Helvetia.

**Sutter's Fort** (2701 L Street) is the reconstructed site of the settlement founded by Sutter. The town of Sacramento sprang up around the fort after James Marshall discovered gold at nearby Coloma

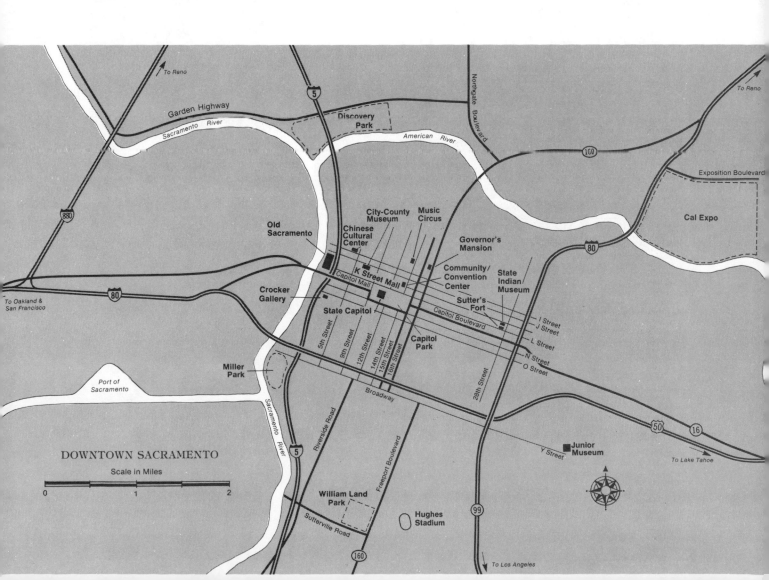

in 1848. Now the fort stands in the center of the city, housing a collection of historical mementos.

Sutter built the fort to protect his land grant of some 76 square miles. Here in 1844 he entertained the United States exploring party led by John C. Fremont and his guide, Kit Carson. During the Bear Flag Revolt of 1846, General Vallejo was detained here. After gold was discovered, Sutter lost his land to newcomers and later went east. Between 1891-93 the state of California restored the fort, following sketches and plans from Sutter's day.

Exhibits include carpenter, cooper, and blacksmith shops, prison, and living quarters. Headsets allow visitors to tour at their own speed. The fort is open daily from 10 A.M. to 5 P.M. (except for holidays); admission, including headsets, is 50 cents for adults, half price for children.

**The State Indian Museum,** adjacent to Sutter's Fort, interprets the Indian way of life in California through the use of frequently changing exhibits ranging from archeology to mythology. Hours are the same as for Sutter's Fort. Admission is 25 cents for adults; children are free.

**The E. B. Crocker Art Gallery** (216 O Street), a stately Victorian mansion built by Judge Crocker in 1873 for his private art collection, is the oldest art museum in the West. The building's elegant interior—sweeping staircases, parquetry floors, repoussé ceilings, and grand ballroom—makes a perfect setting for the collection of paintings, drawings, decorative arts, and sculpture. Of particular interest are the Oriental and contemporary American art collections. A new wing increases exhibition space by nearly half. The gallery is open to the public Tuesday from 2 to 10 P.M. and Wednesday through Sunday from 10 A.M. to 5 P.M.

**Old Sacramento,** after years of deterioration and neglect, has begun its comeback. Imaginative individuals are restoring a 28-acre section of the waterfront to recreate the colorful atmosphere of Sacramento in the 1850s and 1860s. One of the 41 historical buildings being restored and reconstructed is the Big Four Building—one-time headquarters for the Central Pacific Railroad financed by Huntington, Hopkins, Crocker, and Stanford. Erected in 1852, it is now relocated on I Street between Front and 2nd streets. Another restored structure is the John F. Morse Building, 2nd and K streets, built in 1865 for Dr. Morse, Sacramento's first physician and first editor of the *Sacramento Union.* Other structures demolished for Interstate 5 are being recreated in this new location. A railroad museum and park are on the drawing boards.

Wagons, carriages, stagecoaches, wooden signs, painted awnings, and plank sidewalks give Old Sacramento the look of its golden ages. Happily, it

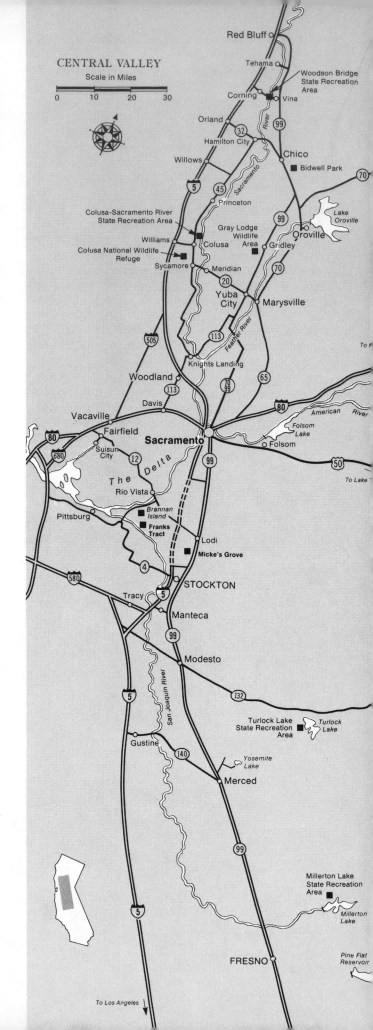

is not a museum. It's a living, self-sustaining business district with some of the city's most unique restaurants and "watering holes," gift stores, and antique shops—all geared to recreate the city that was, a century and a quarter ago.

Old Sacramento is on the eastern bank of the Sacramento River between Capitol Mall and I Street, west of Interstate 5.

**The Chinese Cultural Center,** east of Old Sacramento between 4th and 5th and I and J streets, features buildings of Oriental design, a mall with a Chinese garden, residences, stores, offices, and restaurants—a developing Chinatown set around the Confucius Temple at 4th and I streets.

## Family fun

With a variety of activities to choose from, outdoor family outings are popular. Biking, hiking, boating, and picnicking are all within minutes from downtown Sacramento.

**William Land Park** on Freeport Boulevard (State 160 and Sutterville Road) in the southern part of the city is so vast it seldom seems crowded. It has pools, gardens, a 9-hole golf course, ball diamonds, picnic grounds, and a grove of Japanese flowering cherry trees among its 236 landscaped acres. Children's favorites include the large zoo, Fairytale Town (with child-size reproductions of fairy tale themes), kiddie rides in the amusement area, and pony rides nearby.

**Gibson Ranch County Park,** just north of Sacramento, is a child's delight. Youngsters can see domestic animals, peacocks, and pheasants or watch milking demonstrations. An 8-acre lake stocked with fish (children under 16 need no fishing license) makes a natural habitat for ducks, mudhens, geese, and muskrats.

One of the ranch buildings houses a historical museum displaying western objects. You can watch horses being shod in a blacksmith shop. Stables rent horses and ponies, offer hayrides, and provide riding lessons. On the 245 acres, you'll find many hiking trails and picnic spots. To reach the park, follow Watt Avenue north to Elverta Road. Turn left onto Elverta and follow this road to the entrance. Gibson Ranch is open daily from 7 A.M. to dusk. There's no admission charge for your children to meet the animals.

**The Junior Museum** (4900 Y Street at the old State Fair Grounds) contains many interesting displays of California natural history and has an excellent collection of live animals native to the area. Children find it hard to resist the unusual library that lends not books but animals. Open daily Tuesday through Saturday from 9:30 A.M. to 5 P.M. (Sunday, noon to 3 P.M.); there's a slight admission fee.

**Outdoor restaurants** *are part of new look in Old Sacramento. Shops, Eagle Theater are also being restored.*

**Parkway** *along Sacramento's American River has biking, hiking, bridle trails, boating, picnicking.*

*Along the Sacramento, boaters feel far removed from city's bustle. Solitary bird perched on a stump (left) or pastoral blend of boat and landing (below) are common.*

**Riders and horses** *find a pleasant way to cool off along the shallow edge of the river.*

**The American River Parkway,** an irregular, 23-mile-long strip of green, stretches along the banks of the American River from Nimbus Dam to the stream's junction with the Sacramento River. Along the parkway are several county parks: C. M. Goethe County Park offers hiking and riding trails; Discovery Park, at the confluence of the rivers, has boat launching facilities; and Ancil Hoffman County Park has an 18-hole golf course. Picnicking sites are plentiful. Fishing the American River produces catches of shad, steelhead, or salmon. Group float trips are popular with kayakers and rafters.

Winding its way along the river bank is the American River Bicycle Trail, which eventually will run the entire 35-plus miles from Discovery Park to the city of Folsom. For now, more than 20 paved miles are open, with picnic tables, restrooms, and other facilities along the way.

**Folsom is fun.** Shops on gas-lighted Sutter Street intrigue visitors. The structures are a mixture of old and new, set in western surroundings. Tourists flock to the Flea Fair in April and Peddlers' Fair in October. In addition, famous Folsom Prison has a craft shop you may visit. Free area tourist guides are available in the old Southern Pacific Depot. Folsom is 15 miles northeast of Sacramento, off U.S. 50.

Up the road 2 miles, popular Folsom Lake State Recreation Area offers a chance to cool off during the summer heat. You'll find plentiful camping along both the main reservoir and the Lake Natoma arm. In addition to other water-oriented activities, sailboating is popular. Fishermen try for trout, bass, perch, catfish, and Kokanee salmon.

**Nuts** are the theme for two family fun destinations. At the California Almond Growers Exchange (18th and C streets), you can tour and taste in the world's largest almond "factory." Open weekdays from 8 A.M. to 5:30 P.M., Saturday from 10 A.M. to 4 P.M. Plant tours start at 10 A.M. and 2 P.M. On Saturdays, tours begin at 9:10 A.M. and 4 P.M.

Thirty miles west of Sacramento is the Nut Tree,

a restaurant *cum* amusement park, complete with train and airport—a popular fly-in destination for pilots. It all started with a single black walnut tree planted in 1860 to shade passers-by on the Emigrant Trail.

## North of Sacramento

The major highways running north of Sacramento are Interstate 5 and State 99. Both leave from Sacramento, with Interstate 5 taking a more westerly course. In Red Bluff the highways converge, and Interstate 5 continues into Oregon. The Sacramento River runs between the two highways; the Feather closely parallels State 99.

## Along the back roads

The quiet towns and countryside along the banks of the Sacramento River seem to have changed little since the early 1900s. To discover the surrounding area, you'll have to stray slightly from Interstate 5.

Spring is a good time to drive State 45—a two-lane, lightly traveled back road that follows the Sacramento's meanderings. The tall cottonwoods

## Boating-Up the Sacramento

Sometimes called the Nile of the West, the Sacramento River, born in the Klamath Mountains, meanders along on its way south to San Francisco Bay in a combination of placid pools and turbulent waters.

During Gold Rush days, hydraulic mining destroyed what was once a prosperous freight and passenger service on the Sacramento as far north as Red Bluff. Shoals formed, navigation channels were lost, and silt was dumped into the river bed. The last of the passenger boats disappeared in 1941.

But you can still boat up the Sacramento, a voyage of quiet solitude, white water, and an ever-changing panorama of shoreside attractions. As you head farther north, you'll see deer along the banks and waterfowl winging low over the river. Drift fishing and back-trolling for shad, trout, bass, and catfish make pleasant summer activities.

Along the way you'll find sandy beaches to pull in for sunbathing and picnicking and some lovely, verdant parks where you may be the only visitor —Woodson Bridge, Los Molinos, and Anderson River. Some have overnight camping. You'll pass underneath some of the most picturesque bridges spanning any river.

Breaking up the trip into three days, you can make a leisurely run of 87 miles from Sacramento's Miller Park (a good launching spot) to Colusa. At the Cruise 'n Tarry Marina, you can dock and arrange for a ride into town or ask for the nearest camping spots. These marinas are good places to check the water ahead.

From Colusa to Red Bluff it's 101 miles. No navigational charts mark these waters. You'll find your first riffles, strong current, and lower water. Watch for snags and floating debris. At the Red Bluff Diversion Dam, you must take your boat around Red Bluff Lake to continue upstream.

**Cruising upstream** *beyond Colusa's deep channel and against the river's current is a challenge.*

Redding is only 53 miles away, but this can be the most treacherous part of the trip because the water level may be quite low, depending on the flow from Keswick Dam below Shasta. More water is released for irrigation from May to September—your best time for navigation.

To simplify your voyage, you might plan ahead and have someone drive a vehicle from Sacramento, meeting you at Red Bluff and Redding. Don't attempt this trip except in a jet boat or an outboard with a shallow draw. Safety precautions might include an extra prop and a few simple tools. It's wise to carry extra gas and oil in case the next marina is closed.

It's not an easy voyage up the Sacramento, but it is a real adventure in boating—one you'll want to repeat.

Wildfowl preen *and wade in shallow resting ponds at Gray Lodge Wildlife Area.*

Tourists admire *gigantic Hooker Oak in Chico's Bidwell Park. Tree has 150-foot spread.*

Children *with raft enjoy a little water sport in a tree-shaded spot on Big Chico Creek.*

along the river have leafed out, fruit orchards are in bloom, crops have been planted, and summer's heat hasn't yet descended on the valley.

To reach State 45 if you're coming from San Francisco on Interstate 80, turn north at Davis on State 113 and drive 22 miles to Knight's Landing. From Sacramento, take Interstate 5 to Woodland (home of some turn-of-the-century architectural gems) and then head north on State 113.

In Knight's Landing—a small river community somewhat reminiscent of towns along Mark Twain's Mississippi—turn left on Fourth Street, a narrow levee road running along the south bank of the river. Fourth Street soon joins State 45, which angles northwest across open farmland. Notice the rice "checks"—flooded areas of land surrounded by low levees.

Past Sycamore, turn east on State 20, across a narrow swing bridge, to visit Meridian. Poke around the quiet, shaded streets. Near the river there's a small grocery store with ancient floors that creak, a lazy paddle fan above the door, and a selection of ice cream bars for a hot day. After you cross back over the river, Colusa is 5 miles north. State 45 continues as far as Hamilton City (between Chico and Orland); State 20 joins Interstate 5.

The only cable ferry left on the Sacramento River operates at Princeton, north of Colusa on State 45. Here you and your car can be transported across the river on a ferry pulled from bank to bank by a cable.

**Colusa National Wildlife Refuge,** 3 miles southwest of Colusa on State 20, is one of four Sacramento Valley refuges providing a winter home for millions of migratory wildfowl. You can pick up guide-yourself tour booklets at refuge headquarters. The area is open from dawn to dusk.

**Gray Lodge Wildlife Area,** just west of Gridley and 65 miles north of Sacramento near State 99, is one of the best places to watch the massive late autumn and winter migrations of ducks and geese from the Yukon, Saskatchewan, and British

Columbia breeding grounds. Aquatic plants and cereal crops are grown on the 6,800-acre state reserve to entice wildfowl away from feasting in surrounding private fields. One portion of the reserve is a wildlife sanctuary; on a larger section, hunting is permitted during the season. You must obtain a pass before driving through on hunting days.

More than 200 species of birds frequent the reserve. The wildlife area is open daily during daylight hours. At the area headquarters is a small museum with bird specimens.

## Up the Sacramento River

Upstream from Sacramento as far as Colusa, the Sacramento is a river of commerce, although the commercial traffic it bears today (mostly tugs and oil barges) is insignificant compared to that of the past. Remnants of yesteryear are visible along the river: occasionally you'll see half-rotting wharves through the cottonwoods and willows that mark the sites of forgotten towns. The tall piers where steamers tied up have been replaced by long floats for pleasure boating and fishing.

Swimming and water-skiing are possible anywhere along the Sacramento—the farther you are from Shasta Dam, the warmer the water. Colusa is a popular water-skiing center, with public floats and a jumping ramp.

**The Colusa-Sacramento River State Recreation Area,** a delightful, 67-acre oasis on the west shore, has a launching ramp, picnic sites, sandy beach, and unimproved campsites. In summer, a 140-foot floating dock makes boat tie-up easy.

Most of the towns and fishing resorts along the river have launching facilities for trailered boats. Motorless boats are suitable only for downstream trips. Rowing or paddling against the strong current is always difficult—at some points, impossible. Life jackets should always be worn while boating the upper Sacramento and also while fishing along steep, slippery banks. Below Colusa tie up where barges won't swing close to shore and strike your boat or bounce it around in their wakes.

Fishing for salmon begins in June. The fall run, perhaps the most important, starts in late September and overlaps the steelhead migration that comes in October and November. Though most fishing is done from boats in the main current, bank fishing is perfectly practical. Cast far out, let your lure glide downstream, and then retrieve it against the current.

To fish from a boat, it's a good idea to hire a guide at one of the resorts for your first time out. He can show you where the best spots are and how to handle tackle for the best results. If you take your own boat, be sure to have a good anchor to hold you against the current. Then the flow of the river will do your "trolling" for you.

**Woodson Bridge State Recreation Area,** bisected by the Sacramento River, is just 3 miles west of State 99 at Vina or 6 miles east of Interstate 5 at Corning. The park is an almost unspoiled example of riverbottom lands. Part of it is covered with oaks; a flood plain section is densely wooded with willows, cottonwoods, and sycamores. In the park you can swim, boat, hike, and camp. Fishing is excellent. Adjoining Tehama County Park has a small picnic area, playground, and concessions.

## Chico

Here is the most impressive and unexpected park in the whole valley. The green excitement starts downtown with the campus of Chico State College and the grounds of the colonial mansion of town founder John Bidwell. Then Bidwell Park winds up Chico Creek, 10 miles into the foothills. Swimming, golf, and picnicking are popular. Gigantic Hooker Oak, with a spread of 150 feet, is a landmark.

**Mountain climbing** *beckons among heights in Chico's Bidwell Park. Swimming, golf, picnics are popular.*

# The Delightful Delta

One of the most startling experiences for new visitors in the Delta region is to look across an island field of softly swaying grain and see the profile of a freighter moving silently along the levee top. Yet this is one of the Delta's most characteristic sights. Here, too, pleasure craft throw sudsy wakes across narrow sloughs and find hidden anchorages under bowing trees, where shipboard anglers throw out lines to hook lurking fish.

What is the Delta? The Sacramento-San Joaquin Delta is an irregularly bounded area of almost 740,000 acres that extends from Sacramento south a little beyond Tracy and from Pittsburg east to Stockton. About 50,000 of its acres are water, strung out in more than 700 miles of meandering channels bearing such astonishing names as Hog, Little Potato, Lost Whiskey, Little Conception, and Lookout Slough.

Once a great inland everglade densely forested with stands of valley oak and bull pine, the area was devoured by the furnaces of old river boats. Denuded expanses of mud that remained were later transformed into levee-rimmed islands (many still called tracts) that produced fortunes in asparagus and fruits for Delta farmers.

The first "resorts" in this area were farmhouses that just happened to have a boat or two for rent. After reports of the excellent fishing began to spread, small, makeshift fishing camps sprang up along levee roads. Recreational fishing and boating became big business, and resort marinas replaced small fishing camps.

As you drive between Sacramento and Manteca on State 99, you're never more than 10 or 15 miles east of the Delta region, but you hardly know it's there. Until now, major highways have circumvented it entirely; however, when Interstate 5 is completed, it will cross the heart of the Delta.

## Boating is big business

You don't have to be a boat owner to enjoy cruising the Delta. Here, more than a hundred marinas, resorts, harbors, and fishing camps rent boats. Most are 12 to 14-foot fishing skiffs and houseboats. The "floating motels" of the Delta range from small, nonpowered barges ($10 to $12 a day) to luxurious, well-appointed floating homes (with electricity, running water, complete kitchens, and, in some cases, complete bathrooms) that sleep six or more people. Rental for one of these large, better-appointed houseboats runs about $50 to $75 a day or $300 to $450 a week. Rates vary according to the number of persons aboard and the season.

The remainder of the Delta rental fleet is a mixed assortment of cruisers, ski boats, small sailboats, and miscellaneous small craft.

There's not much chance of getting seriously lost in the Delta, but it is easy to become temporarily confused about your exact whereabouts. A good map, marine chart, or guide book is essential for the newcomer. The basic guide to navigation in the Delta region is Chart 5527SC (San Joaquin River). Send $3.25 to the Distribution Division (C44), National Ocean Survey, Riverdale, MD 20840. Chart 5528SC is a navigation guide to the Sacramento River from Andrus Island to Sacramento, including the northern reaches of the Delta. These charts indicate channel depths, bridge and overhead cable clearances, channel markers, and various hazards to navigation.

Although commercial traffic is found throughout the Delta, there are only two main deep-water channels. Pleasure craft are required to yield the right of way to ships navigating within these confined channels. For free pamphlets on California boating regulations and water safety, write to Department of Navigation and Ocean Development, 1416 Ninth St., Sacramento, CA 95814, or contact the Coast Guard District Office at 630 Sansome St., San Francisco, CA 94126.

## Swimming and water-skiing

Although the waterways of the Delta are not the most inviting place for swimming and water-skiing, both are popular, despite the rather sluggish nature of the water. Considerate water-skiers avoid quiet anchorages in respect to fishermen.

## Fishing—bass is best

Fishing is an all-year activity in the Delta, but spring is a peak season for one of the Delta's most sought-after game fish—the striped bass. Salmon and steelhead pass through the Delta on their fall migration up the Sacramento River, but the Delta itself seldom presents the ideal water conditions for trout fishing.

**Locke's** *two-story buildings rise only one story above the levee. This Delta town is a picturesque Chinese community.*

**Boating** *is the Delta's most popular water sport; skiing is good in wide, straight channels.*

**Cruising** *along the Delta, you'll pass by river towns unseen from highways to the east.*

Most of the resort operators in the Delta have been there a long time and can guide you to the best fishing holes.

## Accommodations

Ideally, your boat will be your home on the Delta's waterways. In the cities you'll find modern motels that lie along the edge of the Delta, and an occasional old charmer of a hotel can be discovered in the river towns along the Sacramento. But adequate accommodations in the Delta proper are scarce. A few of the resort marinas offer house-keeping cabins or small campgrounds. Brannan Island State Recreation Area (the only developed public campground in the Delta) has a 100-unit campground with room for trailers. Franks Tract Recreation Area, reached only by boat, is mostly underwater, with facilities limited to a small dock, two picnic tables, and pit toilets.

Most of the larger resorts operate snack bars, and you'll find a few isolated cafes; if you're after a full-scale dinner, plan on one of the larger towns on the outskirts. The seasoned Delta sailor, though, brings along his own provisions because stores are spaced far apart and are difficult to find.

# San Joaquin Valley

South of Sacramento the Central Valley follows the course of the San Joaquin River, which flows northward to meet the Sacramento. Agricultural development came later in this part of the valley. State 99 and Interstate 5 are the main routes south of Sacramento.

The Lodi and Fresno areas are famed for their sweet appetizer and dessert wines. Long, warm summers give grapes their maximum sugar content. About a half-dozen wineries and tasting rooms are open to visitors in the Lodi area, home of the table wine pressed from the Tokay grape. Fresno, hub of the other wine district, also has wineries welcoming visitors. For a listing of wineries open for touring, write the Wine Institute, 717 Market St., San Francisco, CA 94103, or consult the *Sunset* book *California Wine Country*.

## Two Large Towns

Though Stockton was a booming mining town in the 1850s, almost nothing existed south of here until the post-World War II boom. Now, Stockton and Fresno are among the largest valley cities along State 99. Both offer some welcome "cooling off" spots.

## Strolling in Stockton

Connected by a 76-mile channel, the Port of Stockton delivers agricultural and manufactured goods to the San Francisco Bay area. Docks on the immediate west edge of downtown Stockton serve around 700 cargo vessels a year.

The campus of the University of the Pacific, at Pacific Avenue and Stadium Drive, has ivy-covered Gothic buildings surrounded by expansive lawns and tall shade trees.

**Victory Park,** at North Pershing Avenue and Acacia Street, offers picnic tables under lofty trees, playground equipment, a duck pond, open spaces, and a museum. In the Pioneer Museum and Haggin Galleries, you'll find an art collection strong in 19th-century French and American paintings and usually a traveling or local art show. Several rooms depict Indian and pioneer life in the valley. Admission is free; hours are 1:30 to 5 P.M. Tuesday through Sunday.

**Pixie Woods,** in Louis Park 2 miles west of Stockton, is a children's fantasyland playground with dragons to climb on and a giraffe to slide down. Hours from mid-June to mid-September are noon to 8 P.M. daily except Monday and Tuesday. The park closes earlier the rest of the year.

**Large freighters** *venture down the San Joaquin as far as the port at Stockton, delivering manufactured goods and picking up farm produce.*

**Fresno's Roeding Park** *is cool oasis for valley travelers. Paddle boating is only one of large park's attractions.*

## Fresno's fresh face

Downtown Fresno radiates a parklike atmosphere. In the central business district—Fulton Street from Inyo to Tuolumne streets—you can stroll through a mall embellished with trees, flowers, pools, fountains, and modern sculpture.

A pioneer nurseryman planted verdant Roeding Park with hundreds of trees, including many picturesque eucalyptus. A 157-acre oasis, it's a great place for a picnic; children can enjoy a zoo, amusement area, boat rides, and playgrounds.

Seven miles west of Fresno, at 7160 West Eucalyptus Avenue, is the Edwardian mansion and estate of wealthy land developer M. Theo Kearney; it's open to afternoon tours Thursday through Sunday. Take Kearney Boulevard from Fresno.

## Stops along the Way

Often it's much easier, especially with children, to pack a picnic lunch on a long, hot trip. Even a stop to stretch your legs will be more pleasant if you know where to go. Here is a list of parks or stops to enrich your trip:

**Lodi Lake,** once a swamp overflow from the Mokelumne River, is now a big, tree-lined recreation spot offering boating, swimming, and picnicking on the north side of Lodi.

**Micke's Grove,** 5 miles south of Lodi and a mile west of State 99 by way of Armstrong Road, is now a San Joaquin county park containing one of the few remaining large stands of native valley oaks. It has a small garden zoo where flowers bloom all year under the oak trees and in planters that serve the unusual purpose of separating animals' cages.

**Caswell Memorial State Park,** 16 miles south of Stockton and about 5 miles west of State 99, provides a cool place to picnic in a 258-acre park, 90 acres of which remain a primitive area. Walk the mile-long trail under a ceiling of arched branches.

**Miller Ranch** has an impressive collection of antique vehicles (farm machinery, horse-drawn vehicles, bicycles, tractors, and automobiles). The privately owned ranch, 10 miles east of Modesto at 9425 Yosemite Boulevard, also has antique household items, a general store, blacksmith shop, and old-time barbershop.

**Turlock Lake State Recreation Area** campsites are along the Tuolumne River; picnicking is on the lake. Fishing is good in the river, and you can also swim there during low-water season. On the lake side are swimming beaches, a water-ski beach, a boat harbor, and launching ramps. Groceries and fishing supplies are available at this park, 23 miles east of Modesto on State 132.

**Three state parks** around Merced offer picnicking, swimming, and fishing alongside rivers. The first two have campsites: McConnel Park (a few miles east of State 99 on the south shore of the Merced River); George J. Hatfield Park (5 miles east of Newman on the San Joaquin River); and Fremont Ford Park (between Merced and Gustine on State 140).

Seven miles northeast of Merced, just up into the hills, 400-acre Yosemite Lake is popular for boating and shoreline picnicking. Sloping shores make ideal family swimming.

**Millerton Lake,** 22 miles north of Fresno, has campgrounds at the north shore (7 miles north of Friant) and a boat and motor rental concession on the south bay. Boat launching ramps are located at both areas. The lake, about 16 miles long, offers boating, good fishing, and swimming. A boat access camp is 16 miles upstream at Temperance Flat.

**Pine Flat Reservoir,** 32 miles east of Fresno, offers a variety of water sports. Popular with campers, the 20-mile-long lake also makes a good picnic spot. It's located in the scenic Sierra Nevada foothills where steep ridges form the entrance to Kings Canyon National Park.

# Index

## Photographers

**Ansel Adams:** 106. **John D. Anderson:** 98 (top), 119 (bottom). **John Arms:** 16 (left, top right), 17 (bottom), 40, 73 (top left).
**Robert G. Bander:** 11 (right), 29 (right), 50 (left), 51, 63, 64 (all), 77 (top left). **Barbara J. Braasch:** 43 (left), 45, 47 (bottom left), 50 (right), 130, 138, 151. **California Wine Institute:** 93 (left). **Clyde Childress:** 67. **Glenn M. Christiansen:** 6 (right), 17 (top), 19 (left), 32 (right), 34 (right), 44 (right), 59, 60, 113 (top), 117, 119 (top), 126 (right), 146. **Claypipers:** 115 (left)
**Kenneth Cooperrider:** 109 (top right). **John B. Cowan:** 152 (top left). **Richard Dawson:** 6 (left), 37, 131, 145. **East Bay Regional Park District:** 48 (right). **El Dorado County Chamber of Commerce:** 118. **Hans Engh:** 122 (left). **Roger Flanagan:** 16 (bottom right), 22, 25. **Michael Fong:** 121 (left). **Lee Foster:** 23 (right), 31, 34 (bottom left), 93 (right), 95, 142 (left), 155 (bottom left). **Gerald R. Fredrick:** 12, 19 (right), 24 (left), 32 (left), 43 (right), 47 (right), 54 (right), 61 (left, top right), 73 (bottom right, bottom left), 109 (left), 113 (bottom), 142 (right), 150 (all), 152 (top right, bottom left), back cover.
**Mike Hayden:** 134 (left). **Cecil Helms:** 87, 111 (left), 112, 125 (all), 149 (top). **Forrest Jackson:** 103. **Phil Kipper:** 74.
**John Litton:** 56 (right). **Martin Litton:** 88. **Osmer D. Mallon:** 153. **John F. Marriott:** 69. **Ells Marugg:** 54 (left), 105 (bottom, top left), 115 (top right), 123, 124, 141. **Jack McDowell:** 7, 14, 18, 21 (bottom right), 23 (left), 29 (left), 30 (right), 65, 66, 71, 77 (right), 78, 82 (right top, bottom), 84 (all), 116 (bottom), 122 (right), 155 (right), 156 (right). **Fred Nelson:** 133. **Dave Noland:** 61 (bottom right). **Norman A. Plate:** 9, 21 (left), 33 (left, bottom right), 34 (top left), 38, 42, 44 (left), 46, 48 (left), 79 (bottom), 85, 98 (bottom), 100, 101, 126 (left). **Pete Redpath:** 28, 53 (all), 115 (bottom right). **Redwood Empire Association:** 39 (all), 41 (left), 96. **John Reginato:** 140 (left). **John Register:** 33 (top right), 73 (top right). **Tom Riley:** 137. **John Robinson:** 140 (right). **Sea Ranch:** 79 (top). **Ted Streshinsky:** 91, 105 (top right), 109 (bottom right). **David Swanlund:** 81. **Mike Tilden:** 82 (left), 111 (bottom right), 116 (top). **University of California, Berkeley:** 47 (top left). **Darrow M. Watt:** 11 (left), 21 (top right), 111 (top right), 121 (left), 129, 134 (right), 136, 149 (bottom), 156 (left). **Peter O. Whiteley:** 41 (right), 56 (left). **Doug Wilson:** 77 (bottom left). **Baron Wolman:** 27, 30 (left). **George Woo:** 155 (top left). **Craig Zwicky:** 24 (right).